FUN *with* TOY TRAINS

Robert Schleicher

Published by

**krause
publications**

**700 E. State Street • Iola, WI 54990-0001
Telephone: 715/445-2214**

Please call or write for our free catalog.
Our toll-free number to place an order or obtain a free catalog is 800-258-0929
or please use our regular business telephone 715-445-2214
for editorial comment and further information.

Library of Congress Catalog Number: 99-61261
ISBN: 0-87341-701-1

Printed in the United States of America

K-Line Locomotives 188
Weaver Locomotives 189
Atlas Locomotives 191
Headlight and Fan Belt Replacement 191
Locomotive Troubleshooting 191
Painting and Lettering Locomotives 193

Chapter 14 Freight And Passenger Cars
Hauling the Freight...................................194
Freight Trains 194
Real Freight for Your Freight Cars 196
Passenger Trains 198
Mixed Trains...200
Era-Specific Freight Trains......................200
Era-Specific Passenger Trains................200
Painting and Lettering Freight Cars 201

Chapter 15 Operating A Model Railroad
Switching Moves 203
Track Planning for Operation 203
Picking Up a Car with Trailing-Point Moves 204

Spotting a Car with Trailing-Point Moves 205
Run-Around or Facing-Point Moves.......................207
Reversing Operations 212
Reversing with a Wye 212

Chapter 16 Moving Freight
Freight Train Makeup..214
Hauling Real Freight 215
The Waybill Freight Forwarding System 215
Waybills..217
Shipping and Receiving 219
Interchanges 220
Filling Out the Waybill 220
Operating with the Waybill System 220
Timetable Operations 220
The "Sequence" Timetable.....................................221
From Imaginary to Real...221

Glossary 222

Sources Of Supply.................................224

Chapter 1

Toy and Model Trains

Stand next to the tracks while a hundred-car freight train rockets by at 60 miles an hour and you'll understand what it must be like to be in the heart of a thunderstorm. There's a million tons of metal, a mass 2,000-times as heavy as your automobile, moving at the speed of your automobile. It's a rush—in every sense of the word—you are experiencing the most powerful machines you will likely ever see. And you can control a replica of all that power and energy when you operate a toy train.

You control both the speed of your version of a real railroad train and set the path that your train will follow. You can quickly establish its path by pushing sections of track together to make a simple oval or a tortuous labyrinth of steel-railed tracks. And you control the train's path through that network of steel rails by set-ting turnouts (switches)on the track to the left or right to pre-select the train's route. You're playing with a lot of power and it's thrilling when you set your imagination free to envision that toy train to be as powerful as the real one.

The Toy Train Hobby

I'll show you everything I've been able to discover about having the greatest fun with your toy trains with the minimum effort. The really large permanent layouts are illustrated but, frankly, you can have just as much fun with a layout on the floor of a den or spare bedroom. If you really want a permanent layout, you'll see how to build one. One of the pleasures of toy trains is arranging and rearranging the tracks and that is difficult to do with permanent scen-

Fig. 1-1. Lionel's "Phantom" pulls a string of Lionel corrugated-side streamlined cars through the portable scenery.

ery, so you'll see how to make portable scenery as well as scenery for a permanent tabletop layout. I've included the simplest methods of building a complete layout, with "portable" scenery that can be moved and reused (Figure 1-1), the easiest ways to operate two or more trains, and some proven methods of operating your toy trains like the real railroads. In all, there's everything you need to know to make toy trains your hobby, not just your collection.

There are dozens of books about toy trains and model railroads that can tell you more about building tables and scenery, books that have more track plans and more about wiring, books that have price guides to the collectible toy trains, even books that are reprints of the instruction sheets from the old Lionel and American Flyer accessories. You can find them all through the larger hobby shops. I would also suggest that you purchase catalogs from the toy train companies so you can see what products are currently available. There is only a small sample of the toy trains here, because the list of available products changes as often as twice a year. If you've read about any car or locomotive on a real railroad, the chances are you can buy it as a miniature. Similarly, most of the action accessories that were available in the forties and fifties are being reproduced, so you can buy just about anything you want if you are patient enough to wait for the reproduction.

You and Your Toy Trains

For many people, the concept of playing with a toy train is something they prefer to keep as a secret. If playing with toy trains bothers you, tell the world you are recreating a railroad in miniature. You and I know we're playing, but we can let the rest of the world think we're doing something even more 'important' than surfing the Internet. It all starts with a toy train set (Figures 1-2 and 1-3) that can be expanded into a double-track layout for two trains (Figure 1-4).

There's a history to these toy trains that dates back to the turn-of-the century. In a sense, just playing with trains on the floor is a recreation of that history. Your great, great, grandfather or grandmother may have done the same thing. Or, the history you are recreating may be your own recollections of playing with trains. Many adults, who have finally reached a stage in their careers where they have the money and the time, buy and operate toy trains that they wanted as kids but that their parents could not afford. Toy trains are one way of reliving the dreams of childhood.

Today's toy trains are far better than the originals of the forties and fifties. The newer toy trains are far more detailed than the models of the forties and fifties and, with inflation factored in, they are only a fraction as expensive as the originals. With the exception of some of Lionel's locomotives and cars, most of the toy trains of today are imported from Korea or China. The newer mod-

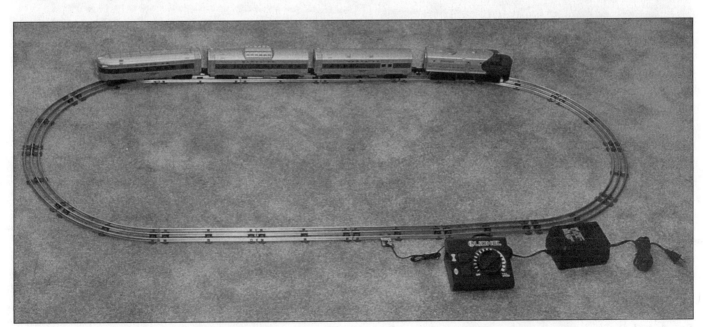

Fig. 1-2. Lionel's Santa Fe "Warbonnet" O-27 train set is one of the most popular starter sets.

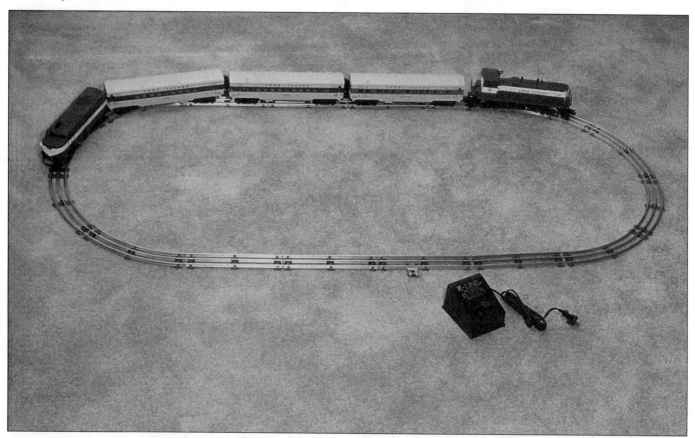

Fig. 1-3. K-Line's Long Island Railroad "Greenport Scoot" O-27 starter set includes a powered MP15 diesel and an unpowered FA1 diesel with three passenger cars.

Fig. 1-4. That simple oval can be expanded into this action-filled 4 x 6-1/2-foot layout.

els have far more detail in their moldings and more accurate paint and lettering schemes than any toy trains from the past. In addition, the top-of-the line models from Lionel, MTH and K-Line include digital sound effects for diesel engine sound, steam locomotives chuffs, whistles and bells. Lionel also offers a remote control system that allows two or more of their specially-equipped locomotives to operate on the same track under completely independent control.

Toy Trains and Model Railroads

The trains in this book fall into the category that the hobby refers to as "toys." These loco-motives, cars, tracks and accessories are designed to be rugged enough for a small child to handle without damaging them. These trains are heavy for their size, with large wheel flanges to grip the rails for fewer derailments, and have massive, easy-to-operate couplers. These large wheel flanges, large steel rails, and massive couplers make it easy to get the trains back on the tracks if they do derail.

This ruggedness requires a few compromises in the realism of the miniatures but, for most people, it's not noticeable. The charm of the oversize wheels, track and couplers make these trains somewhat of a caricature of the real thing, rather than a dead-accurate scale model.

The appeal of these O scale toy trains is that they are massive. When they operate, they really rumble and clatter much like a real train. It takes two hands to even lift some of the larger locomotives. Most toy train operators are more than willing to make some sacrifices in exact scale to run these massive models in relatively small spaces.

These toy trains are rugged enough so they can be operated on the floor. It is not necessary to build a table. The tracks that form your train layout can be taken apart and put back together thousands of times. Even if you choose to build a table for the trains, I would suggest you resist the temptation to attach the track to the table-top; leave it loose so you can readily change the layout and/or add more tracks.

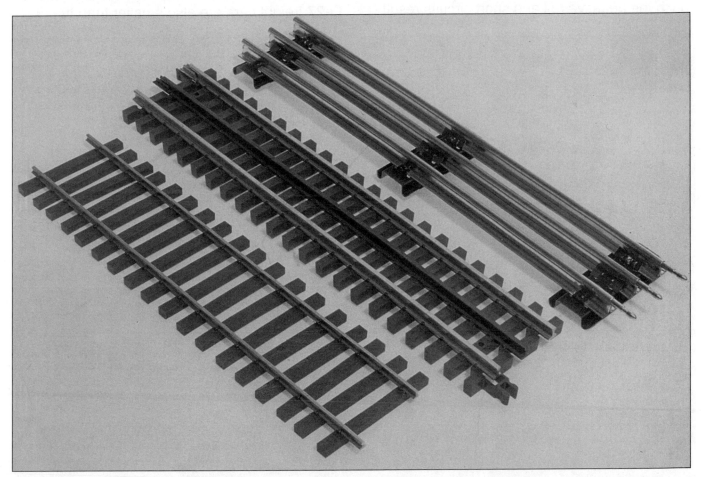

Fig. 1-5. Three-rail toy train track (top), Atlas's three-rail toy train track with blackened center rail and exact-scale O scale two rail track (bottom).

Toy Train Track

The track used for Lionel, MTH, K-Line, Weaver, Atlas, Williams, Industrial Rail, Marx, Third Rail, Crown Model Products, Red Caboose, InterMountain and similar brands of locomotives and rolling stock has three rails. Exact O scale track has just two rails and smaller ties, but you can buy Atlas, K-Line and GarGraves track with blackened third rail and additional ties that is more realistic than the traditional Lionel or K-Line toy train track (Figure 1-5). That third rail is certainly not realistic, although its presence can be disguised if you select a brand of track that has a blackened center rail. For many toy train operators, part of the charm of these models is that third rail and the massive metal ties that are common to most brands of toy train track. The three rails make it easier to build a complex layout because there is less chance of a short circuit when you lay-out tracks to form a reverse loop or wye to change the directions of the trains. With two rail track, reverse loops force the positive rail to touch the negative rail and short circuits result

unless complicated electrical gaps and electrical switches are installed. The third rail also makes the track more rugged than two rail track used by American Flyer toy trains and by all scale model railroads.

Scale and Hi-Rail Trains

The products being produced for this toy train hobby are becoming more and more realistic. Each of the major manufacturers now has both locomotives and freight cars that are exact-scale replicas of the prototype, with every dimension and every detail on the body or superstructure reduced to 1/48 the size of the real thing. The exceptions are passenger cars which are usually shortened about 16 scale feet (an actual 3-1/2-inches) to operate on the relatively tight-radius curves of toy train layouts. The O-27 cars are even shorter (Figure 1-6). This 1/48 proportion is called "O scale." Lionel and K-Line offer O-27 versions of the Alco FA1 diesel that is considerably smaller than an exact-scale FA1 from Weaver (Figure 1-7). The O-27 freight cars are also smaller than the O

Fig. 1-6. Lionel's O scale streamlined passenger car (top) and their O-27 version of the car.

Fig. 1-7. Weaver's exact-scale Alco FA1 diesel (top) and Lionel's O-27 version of the same locomotive.

Fig. 1-8. The three most common toy train sizes include exact O scale (top), O scale used in most medium-priced sets and the least-expensive O-27 size (bottom). All operate on the same track.

scale counterparts. This O-27 Lionel 2454 "Baby Ruth" 2454 box car from 1946 is smaller than the usual O-27 box cars like the K-Line car which, in turn is smaller than Lionel's O scale box car (Figure 1-8).

Scale models look most realistic on larger-radius curves that require more space for a permanent layout. For an O scale layout, 72-inches should be a minimum radius if you expect to operate full-length modern diesels or full-length passenger cars. If exact scale is important to you, you will need 7 x 14-feet of space for a simple oval and, preferably, at least 20 x 20-feet for a medium-size O scale layout. An S scale layout would require a minimum of 5 x 10-feet table or a 15 x 15-foot room. If you want to operate scale-size equipment and long passenger trains, consider using HO scale or even N scale models. HO scale models are 1/87 the size of the real thing, or about half the size of O scale models. N scale models are 1/160 the size of the prototype, or about a forth the size of O scale models. The majority of model railroaders choose one of these smaller scales because they can operate long locomotives and cars and long

trains in settings where the scenery dwarves the trains and do it in a relatively small space.

To be completely true-to-scale, the track should have just two rails and the rails and ties should be the same proportions as the prototype's. You can buy O scale two rail track by Peco or Roco from many hobby dealers. You can also purchase trucks with scale-size wheel flanges and Kadee couplers that are 1/48-scale replicas of the real thing rather than the massive couplers common to all toy trains.

There's a compromise that allows you to operate O scale or S scale locomotives and rolling stock on toy train track. Model railroaders refer to these models as "hi-rail" and it is simply the use of accurate scale locomotives and cars, but using oversize wheels and couplers so these models can operate on the tight curves of toy train track. The O scale models do not look quite as realistic traversing such tight curves, but it does allow you to use massive models in relatively small space. Not all model railroaders opt for hi-rail rather than O scale just to save space; some basement-size model railroads are built with three-rail GarGraves track and turnouts and both toy and scale locomotives and cars. These

Fig. 1-9. A toy train-size O scale box car (upper left), an exact-scale O scale box car (upper right), an American Flyer S scale box car (lower left) and a Lionel O-27 box car (lower right).

model railroaders prefer the reliability and easy-of-construction that hi-rail provides.

The toy train manufacturers have made hi-rail models since Lionel's introduction of their 4-6-4 New York Central Hudson locomotive and string of freight cars in the thirties. Today, every toy train company has a number of exact-scale locomotives and freight cars. In fact, nearly all of the higher-priced locomotives and cars are scale models, only the wheel flanges and couplers are toy-train-size. Most of the smaller-than-scale models are labeled O-27, but that is not always the case. There are a number of less-expensive toy train locomotives and cars that are labeled "O scale" that are closer to 1/64 scale than to 1/48 scale.

American Flyer S Scale Trains

American Flyer toy trains were almost as popular as Lionel in the fifties and sixties. American Flyer's trains are somewhat smaller than most of Lionel's and operate on two-rail track. Lionel now produces American Flyer and they usually offer a locomotive or two and some cars and accessories each season, based on the original American Flyer tooling. Other firms, like American Models and S Helper Service are making new locomotives and rolling stock with more detail than American Flyer but with wheels designed to run on American Flyer track. S Helper Service also has two-rail track with built-in ballast that can be used to operate American Flyer, S Helper Service or American Models equipment. K-line produces track that is a near-replica of the American Flyer toy train track but K-Line makes no turnouts and no locomotives or rolling stock in S scale.

Generally, the S scale models are more realistic than O scale toy trains, with finer details, smaller couplers and less space between the couplers and the ends of the cars and locomotives than Lionel, MTH or K-Line O scale products. Today, S scale trains are purchased and operated by just a small proportion of the toy train enthusiasts. O scale trains, made to operate on three rail track, are the choice of about 95 percent of the toy train enthusiasts.

Some toy train operators build layouts with both O scale three-rail and S scale two-rail on the same tabletop. It is not possible to operate S scale locomotives or cars on O scale three-rail track nor is it possible to operate S scale equipment on O scale track. With these toy trains, however, there is often not much difference in the size of S scale models and the size of the smaller O scale models, particularly the less expensive O-27 models. Bruce Pemberton's layout is shown in Chapter 3 and in the color section. He uses S scale track for two loops near the wall and O scale track for the foreground. He operates nearly all O-27 size Lionel, however, so both his S scale and O scale equipment is virtually the same size. The S scale American Flyer box car (Figure 1-9) is only slightly smaller than a Lionel O-27 box car (lower right), while the O scale Lionel box car (upper left) is the same length as an exact-scale O scale box car (upper right) on Bruce Pemberton's layout. The height of prototype box cars vary, so both the cars in the rear are close to exact scale sizes.

S scale does, however, have its appeal in offering often more realistic models, in a somewhat less bulky size than O scale, but larger than the proportions of HO scale model trains. Many of the people who select S scale do so because they want to build a permanent scale model railroad and they feel HO scale is too small and S scale becomes their choice. Ken Zieska's S scale model railroad is shown in both Chapter 3 and the color section. None of his equipment is American Flyer, however. He uses Scenery Unlimited-brand flexible scale track and American Models and S Helper Service ready-to-run models and kits from Pacific Rail Shops and others for his locomotives and rolling stock. The principles of layout construction and the special needs for electrical wiring to avoid short circuits with two-rail can be found in the *HO Scale Model Railroading Handbook*.

Scale Models or Toys?

Lionel, MTH and K-Line locomotives and cars are generally called "O scale." O scale models are 1/48 the size of the real thing, so a 48-foot long car would be just one-foot long as an O scale model. American Flyer models are S scale which is 1/64 scale. A 48-foot car in S scale would be 9-inches long. Lionel, MTH and K-Line produce some equipment that is, however, much smaller than true O scale. Lionel has a tradition of making smaller-size equipment for its lower-priced train sets. Lionel sometimes calls these products "O-27," which refers to the diameter of the circle of track that is included in the lower-priced Lionel train sets. Most of the O-27 models are closer to S scale in overall size but they operate on the three-rail O scale track.

Nearly all of these O scale trains make some major compromises in details to make the models more rugged and to allow them to operate through the very tight-radius curves common to toy train track. The couplers, for example, are about five-times larger than they would be if they were as accurate scale models as the locomotives or rolling stock. Also, the distance between the trucks and the bottom or ends of the cars and locomotives are increased to provide clearances for operations on toy train tracks. These out-of-scale proportions are most noticeable, of course, on the less expensive toy trains, especially O-27 models.

There is a trend in toy trains for the manufacturers to produce models that are more and more accurate replicas of the prototypes. Thus, the difference between toy trains and scale model railroading is blurring. The large wheels flanges, giant couplers and three-rail track are becoming the only differences. The more expensive Lionel, MTH and K-Line locomotives and rolling stock and the imported brass locomotives from Third Rail and Weaver are identical to their two-rail O scale counterparts except for the wheel flanges and couplers. There is also a growing number of O and S scale model plastic kits for both locomotives and rolling stock that are available with couplers and wheelsets to match the toy trains. The plastic rolling stock kits from Atlas, Weaver, Red Caboose, InterMountain and Crown Model Products and the locomotive kits from Red Caboose in O scale and the S scale plastic model kits from American Models, Centralia Car Shops and Pacific Rail Shops are all available with either scale wheel flanges and couplers or toy train wheel flanges and couplers. Remember, though, that some of these true-to-scale models require 72-inch or larger radius curves and turnouts so they cannot be operated in the smaller spaces of a typical toy train layout without modifications to the trucks and couplers.

Valuable Collector Items

All of the trains in this book fall into the category of "collectibles." By definition, these are

items that are produced for a relatively limited time, particularly with a specific paint and lettering scheme, so there is a limited number of them on the market and no chance of something identical being produced. Yes, there are reruns and replicas but they almost always differ in detail from the original production items. Some toy train enthusiasts combine collections of toy trains with collections of cast ceramic buildings like those marketed by Department 56 and others.

Some of these collector trains are, frankly, too valuable to play with. There are a variety of collector and price guide books available to help you identify which items you might have that are best displayed. The vast majority of these trains, however, are no more valuable as collector items than their replacement cost. You may have purchased a Lionel diesel in 1965 for $30 and, today, a nearly-identical diesel would sell for $130. Your 'collector' locomotive may be worth $125 but it's really no more valuable than the cost of a new replacement locomotive. Be wary, however, because that $125 locomotive could be worth $1250 if it's a rare one.

Today the prices of these new toy trains vary from as little as $300 for a train set to $3000 for a single locomotive. A Lionel GP7 diesel like that supplied in train sets may sell for as little as $130, but a Lionel GP9 with a nearly-identical body, but equipped with a more powerful motor, Magnetraction wheels and Lionel's Digital Train-Master Command and Rail Sounds may sell for $350 or more. The prices of some of the limited-production locomotives from Lionel, MTH, Weaver and Third Rail can exceed $1000.

Is it Really Lionel?

Lionel is one of the pioneer manufacturers toy trains. During the past decade or so, however, firms like K-Line and MTH have produced train sets, locomotives, cars, accessories and track that many people consider to be of a quality to match Lionel. These competing brands also produce limited runs, so they may be as "collectible" as current Lionel production. It will take another decade or so before the collector market will decide if, say, a Lionel locomotive made in 1996 is as valuable as a similar locomotive made in 1996 by K-Line or by MTH.

One of the charms of Lionel's products is that they are made from virtually the same production tooling as the original toys of the fifties or sixties. When Lionel does make a replacement for a worn-out manufacturing tool, they try to match the original in every detail. Conversely, the new diesels from MTH or K-Line, as well as Lionel's new production tooling, will have more realistic details than models based on what was state-of-the-art detailing in the forties or fifties.

Lionel, MTH, K-Line, Weaver, Atlas, Williams, Industrial Rail, Marx, Third Rail, Crown Model Products, Red Caboose, InterMountain and similar brands all offer products that operate on the same three-rail track and have universal couplers. All of these products can be purchased to operate using the standard 18-volt AC power packs. Some manufacturers, like Weaver, Red Caboose and Atlas, offer their locomotives for either 12 volt DC or 18 volt AC operation. Be sure to buy the type intended for AC operation if you intend to use them on the same layout with Lionel, MTH or K-Line locomotives. Some of the more powerful O scale locomotives may, however, require a larger-capacity power pack to match their larger motors.

Running a Railroad

The joy of toy trains is watching them run. And one of the major advantages of these toy trains is that they really do run. That may seem obvious until you've tried to run HO scale trains on the floor. HO trains require far more careful track alignment, more cleaning and more care than O scale toy trains. If you push the O scale steel track sections together tightly, you can count on the trains running for hundreds of hours with little or no maintenance. You'll find information on what little maintenance is required in chapters 6 and 13. You'll also see some examples of the variety of layouts you can build in chapters 4 and 5. There are some operating "games" in chapters 15 and 16 that you can use to duplicate

Fig. 1-10. Portable scenery can include mountains, rock cliffs, trees, bushes and even rushing rivers.

the back and forth operating patterns and actions of real trains or, you can watch them run around and around. There are some exciting operating accessories like gatemen, signals, and crossing gates that are set into action as the trains pass. You can also buy some of the automatic loading and unloading accessories to dump logs, coal or steel rails in and out of cars. The portable scenery techniques in Chapter 11 will allow you to have a realistic toy train layout on either the floor or on a tabletop (Figure 1-10). These trains are toys and, by definition, they are meant to be played with. Whatever else you may learn from these pages, understand that it's all supposed to be fun.

Chapter 2

Finding Space For Your Railroad

It may be a comfort to know that all of the real railroads had problems finding space for their rights of way, much as you do for your models. Fortunately, toy trains are designed to be portable. The track itself is usually made of steel to withstand thousands of uses in building and rebuilding toy train layouts. Since the track is so rugged, you have the option of building your layout on the floor. With other model railroads, it's best to build on a tabletop.

Portable or Permanent?

In this book you'll see examples of a half-dozen toy train layouts built on the floor. You'll also see some examples of extensive permanent layouts the size of a basement built on permanent tabletops. And, you'll see examples of the third option of a permanent tabletop with a movable train layout that can be built and rebuilt hundreds of times on the same tabletop (Figure 2-1). Again, these are options that are really most effective with O scale toy trains. The plastic track furnished with the newer HO scale train sets can be used on the floor but it is nowhere near as rugged as O scale steel track. The track with roadbed that is sold by MTH and the Atlas track are not quite as rugged as the steel rails and pins of Lionel, MTH, and GarGraves track,

Fig. 2-1. Portable scenery allows you to enjoy the realism of scenery with the advantages of a layout on the floor or on a store-away lightweight tabletop.

but all of those brands are still tough enough to use on the floor. If you are opting to build and rebuild on the floor, I'd suggest Lionel, K-Line or GarGraves O scale track. I'd even suggest that Lionel's and K-Line's O-27 track is best reserved for use on a tabletop, as are the MTH and Atlas track sections.

The primary reason why a permanent table is necessary with O scale or S scale toy trains is to elevate the trains so they are easier to see and to work on. The track and trains are, of course, less subject damage if they are not underfoot. It is also possible to create some truly spectacular scenic effects on a permanent layout as you can see from the examples in the color section. With the portable felt scenery system in Chapter 8, you can have dramatic scenery on the floor just as easily as on a tabletop. Dick Bruning combined the best of both worlds by building a permanent mountain in one corner of a 8 x 16-foot table and a small lake in the opposite corner. The space in between is left flat so the track can be changed. Dick's table is strong enough to walk on for access.

Room-Size Layouts on the Floor

If you can find the space to build a layout on the floor, you often have the opportunity for a far more extensive toy train layout than if you have to locate it on a tabletop. Sometimes, you can negotiate a "right-of-way" on the floor of one room in your home if the track is removed from the more heavily-trafficked areas of the room. Except of course for the times when you are actually operating the trains. The rugged steel rails of the toy train track make the process of removing and relaying the track relatively simple. If the tracks you are frequently moving are complex, you might want to mount them on a sheet of 1/8-inch plywood with a few wood screws so you can pickup the single piece of plywood rather than a dozen pieces of track.

With a floor-based railroad empire, you can reach the remotest corners of the layout by merely walking to them and bending over. With a tabletop layout, you must design the table so that no portion of the tracks will be more than about 2-1/2-feet from the edge of the table. That's about how far most adults can reach. That means that the table width is limited to a minimum of 5 feet so you cannot use the 72-inch diameter curved track sections because an oval or loop with these sections requires at last 6-1/2-feet of table width. The way around that one is to build huge tables that are strong enough to walk on. That's precisely what a lot of model railroaders including Dick Bruning, John DiCrisici and the builders of the layout at the Carnegie Science Center in Pittsburgh have done.

Fig. 2-2. The piers in the Lionel 110 Graduated Trestle Set can be attached to the track so you can have two-level layout on the floor.

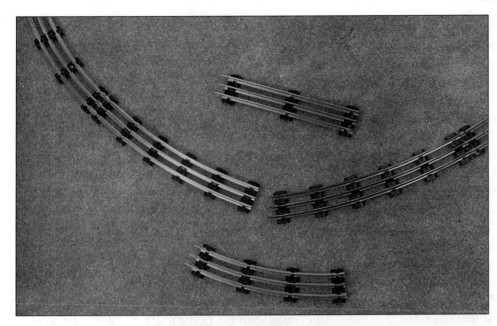

Fig. 2-3. The ends of this freelance track arrangement on a living room floor did not align.

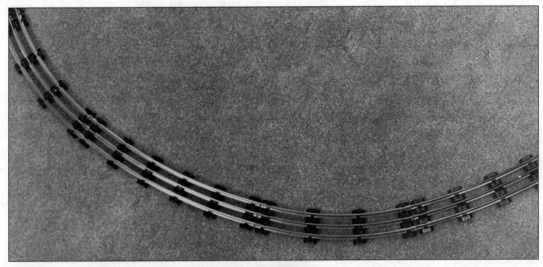

Fig. 2-4. The tracks in Figure 2-3 were aligned by removing two pieces of curved track and substituting two pieces with a slightly smaller diameter.

Fig. 2-5. The ends of a 42-inch diameter circle of track would not align with the 90-degree crossing unless two of the 42-inch curves were removed and replaced with two pieces of 72-inch diameter curved track and two straight track sections.

Railroading Beneath a Bed

If you do not have space for a large permanent tabletop toy train layout, consider building just a small layout like the 4 x 6-1/2-foot layouts in this book and operate trains on it all year long. These layouts are smaller than a queen-size bed so they can be built on a 4 x 6-1/2-foot board and stored beneath the bed. When you're ready to operate, pull out the board, set the layout on top of the bed, add the taller accessories and scenery, set up the locomotives and rolling stock and run trains. This scheme works best in a spare bedroom. Two of the layouts in Chapter 5 are designed to fit a 4 x 6-1/2-foot or smaller space.

The two-level layout from Chapter 5 (Figure 5-10) can be built as a temporary layout on the floor using Lionel's 110 Graduated Trestle Set to raise and lower the track on the upper level and a 318 Truss Bridge or the 2122 Extension Bridge (shown) across the tracks (Figure 2-2). Real or fake Christmas presents can be used to support the elevated loop. I made a "tunnel present" by cutting oval tunnel portals into the sides of corrugated cardboard box, then wrapping the outside of the box with Christmas paper. The box is handy for under-the-tree layouts because Christmas presents can be stacked on top of the box and over the track with no fear that trains will run into the presents. There's a tremendous amount of operation possible in just 4 x 6-1/2-feet including running up to three trains and hours of switching moves as described in Chapters 15 and 16.

The Freedom of Free-Form Layout Design

There's plenty of space, even a small room, for an extensive layout on the floor. The tracks can go behind and, sometimes, beneath the furniture to take advantage of nearly every square foot of space. With a room-size layout space you can actually lay track like the real railroads, running straights until an obstacle like the corner of the room appears to dictate the use of a curve. The curves can be combinations of 42, 54 and 72-inch radius curves to swing the track around the corners, to clear table legs or swinging doors.

The layouts in Chapter 4 are designed to fit specific spaces like a 4 x 6-1/2-foot board. For such small layouts, a track plan can be very helpful. If, however, you have the floor of at least part of a room, you can let the track dictate where you want the trains to run. It's much more like the way real railroads select their right-of-way than attempting to fit track into a given space. Just keep plugging in track until you either run out of track or run out of space.

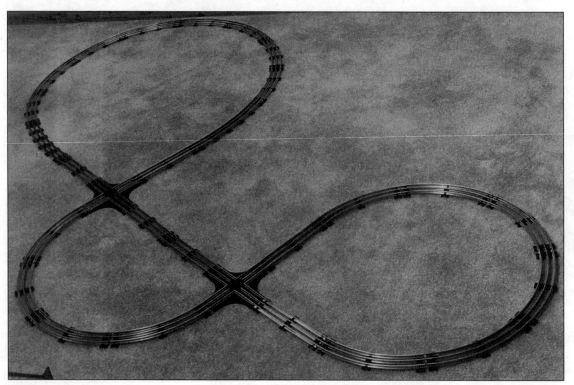

Fig. 2-7. The 42-inch diameter loop (top) is large enough to fit around a Christmas tree, with the other two loops meandering around the living room floor.

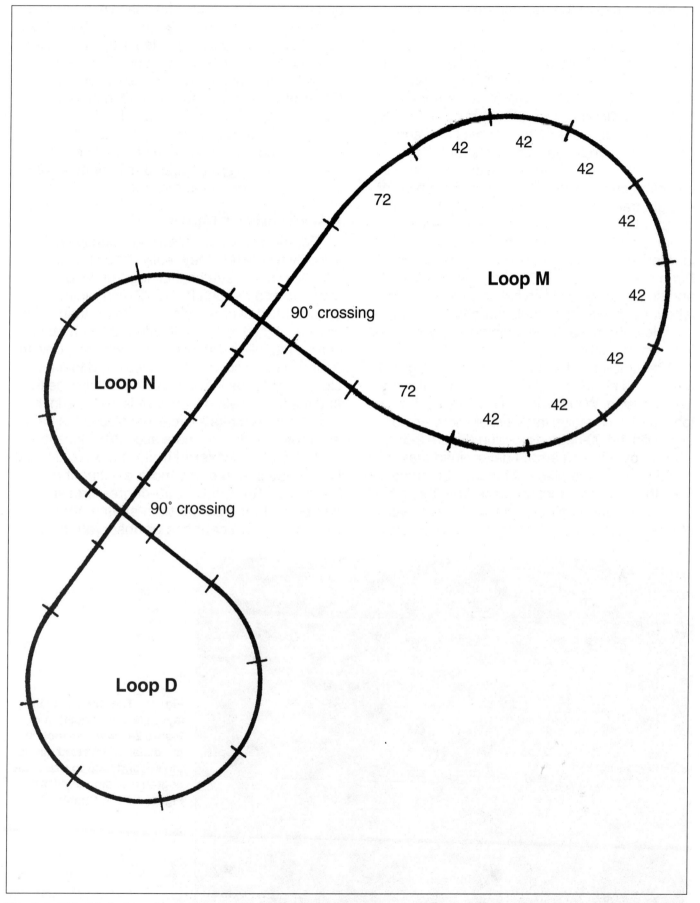

42
42
42
42
42
42
42
42
42
72
72

Loop M

90° crossing

Loop N

90° crossing

Loop D

Fig. 2-6. This triple-loop layout is a good starting point to develop an around-the-floor layout during the Christmas season.

If the ends of the track do not align, it is always possible to use combinations of curves and straights to correct the misalignment. Figures 2-3 and 2-4 are an example of one method of connecting seemingly-misaligned tracks. In this case, a circle of both 42-inch diameter and 54-inch diameter curves did not quite meet. By removing one of the 54-inch curves and adding a 42-inch curve and a standard straight, the tracks will connect. The lesson is to try various combinations of one or two pieces of curved or straight track, removing one or two pieces that do not align, until perfect track alignment is achieved. It's a technique that can only be learned with practice—and you do need two or three pieces of 31, 42, 54 and 72-inch curves and some full-length and half-length straights leftover to be used as replacements/fillers to complete the misaligned segments of your free-form on-the-floor layout.

The ampersand-shaped (&) layout in Figure 2-6 is a good place to start if you want free-flowing layout design. With this plan, I discovered that the loop of 42-inch radius track just did not want to align with the 90-degree crossing (Figure 2-5).

But, by trial and error, I determined that I could remove one piece of the 42-inch curve from the right and another piece from the left, then substitute a pair of 72-inch radius curves, plus a pair of standard straight track sections

and the crossing would fit as shown in Figure 2-7 and in the finished trackplan Figure 2-6. I've used this as the core for at least six Christmas season layouts in the living room. The tree itself fits inside the loop of 42-inch radius curves. Either of the loops made with 32-inch radius curves can, of course be assembled with 42-inch radius curves or even 54 or 72-inch radius curves or combinations of all three. I've tried them all. This plan requires a minimum 5-1/2 x 9-feet of floor or tabletop space.

A Christmas Empire

For many toy train operators, Christmas is the only time when they really get a chance to see their trains "stretch their legs' on long straights and through broad 72-inch radius curves. Most of us got started with toy train using an oval of track made with either 27-inch radius curves (supplied with the O-27 train sets) or with 31-inch radius curves. I've discovered that a circle this tight is usually much smaller than the tree and the train is almost not visible. The 42-inch radius curves make a circle that places the trains in a more visible and more accessible location.

I've also discovered that train operation at Christmas is somehow more exciting if at least one 45-degree or 90-degree crossing can be included so the train seems about to run into its own caboose or observation car.

Fig. 2-8. The Christmas time layout is a modification of Figure 2-6, with the loop in the distance inverted inside the second loop to use a 45-degree crossing similar to Figure 4-22 in Chapter 4.

Fig. 2-9. Another variation of Figure 2-6 with two additional pairs of turnouts used to create two passing sidings.

You can use a standard figure 8 layout or the three-loop ampersand layout plan (Figure 2-6) to construct a layout with one or two crossings. In truth, I've accidentally made-up trains that were too long for the loops so they really did crash into themselves. There's an obvious solution to this problem: make the train shorter. The alternative solution is to make the loops longer by adding straight track sections or by building the loops with larger-diameter curved track sections. These plans can be expanded with a passing siding so a third 90-degree crossing is required (Figures 2-9 and 2-10).

Fig. 2-10. The Christmas tree occupies the inside of the 42-inch diameter loop in the background.

Chapter 3

Toy Train Dream Layouts

Most of us dream of that basement-size permanent toy train layout complete with ceiling-high mountains and cascading rivers flowing to the level of the floor, while at least six 20-car trains boom and rumble through the terrain and in and out of the cities. We are willing to settle for a Christmas-time layout ranging around the living room floor or just a 4 x 6-1/2-foot beneath-the-bed empire. But we dream. And some of us have realized that dream.

Building Tabletops

If you are going to build a layout larger than 4 x 8-feet, you should build it strong enough to walk on. In essence, you are building a stage or a platform and you'll need the same construction techniques. The techniques to build something that sturdy are beyond the scope of this book, but the materials and know-how are available at any lumberyard. Just follow one of the patterns for adding an outside deck and adjust the dimensions to suit the size and height of the table you desire. This is the type of tabletop construction used by Dick Bruning and John DiCrisci for their layouts and by the builders of the Carnegie Science Center's huge 19 x 72-foot layout

If you can limit the width of the tabletop to 2-1/2-feet, by building the layout around the walls of the room or by providing access openings, you can use somewhat lighter construc-

Fig. 3-1. Three of the walls of Dick Bruning's layout room are reserved for his collection of Lionel equipment. His 8 x 16-foot layout is three ovals connected by pairs of turnouts to create crossovers. One of the loops rises about 8-inches above the tabletop to form the "mountain division", while the ends of the two lower loops tunnel beneath the mountain. There are more photos in the color section.

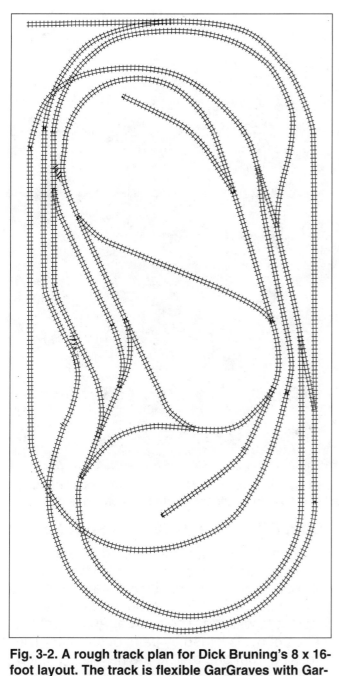

Fig. 3-2. A rough track plan for Dick Bruning's 8 x 16-foot layout. The track is flexible GarGraves with Gar-Graves turnouts. He used a long board as a trammel as a compass to draw the centerlines for the curves. (Dick Bruning artwork)

tion techniques. These layouts need only be a bit stronger than the 4 x 6-1/2-foot layout shown in Chapter 5. The techniques illustrated, step-by-step in my *HO Scale Model Railroading Handbook* for a 5 x 9-foot layout are similar to those used by Dick Bruning, Bruce Pemberton, Bob Yeakel, Ralph Johnson and Ken Zieska to build their layouts. Only Dick Bruning prepared a track plan for his layout, the other layouts were "designed" by laying track on the bench work or tabletop, and

the tracks were arranged and rearranged for best operation and appearance. Most of these layouts are also shown in the color section.

Dick Bruning's 8 x 16-Foot Layout

Dick Bruning has constructed a classic toy train layout on an 8 x 16-foot table (Figure 3-1). He used 1 x 4 lumber in an open-grid or egg-crate design with each square in the grid 24-inches on each side. This grid provides the strength to support a man walking on the table. The tabletop is spaced about 38-inches from the floor and the legs are braced to keep the entire structure from wobbling. The tabletop is 1/2-inch plywood covered with a layer of 5/8-inch thick Homosote. Homosote is a material much like cardboard used for some building insulation. It is soft enough to make it easy to attach the track with nails and it provides excellent sound-deadening qualities.

The majority of Dick's layout is constructed with track nailed and glued permanently in place. He uses mostly GarGraves track and turnouts with 1/4-inch cork sheet cut to fit beneath the ties. The turnouts are operated by remote control using NJ International switch machines activated by toggle switches on the control panel. He ballasts this track using a mixture of O scale ballast from a hobby shop and roofing gravel. The ballast is cemented in place with a mixture of 4-parts water to one-part Artists Matte Medium and a drop of dish washing detergent to act as a wetting agent. About half of the layout table is left flat and open so Dick can add track or install a city or an industrial area or a combination of all three.

The combination of permanent scenery provides the realism he desires and the open areas provide the versatility of changing the track and/or structures. The table's flat areas are covered with grass mat. The trackplan was developed right on the tabletop to include an inner oval with reverse loops for both directions, two outer ovals and a forth "mountain division" oval that climbs above the two outer ovals in the mountains (Figure 3-2).

The scenery on Dick Bruning's layout is made from Styrofoam insulation boards stacked together and glued, then carved to shape with a hacksaw blade. The surface is then covered with plaster cloth. Dick made his own castings for the

Fig. 3-3. John DiCrisci's 8-1/2 x 18-foot layout has a conventional plywood tabletop. It has two of the loops elevated to about 5-inches so those tracks can cross over the lower tracks. A 4 x 6-foot military layout rests on the floor.

rock cliffs and cuts in latex rubber molds like those sold by Mountains-In-Minutes and Woodland Scenics. The plaster castings were blended into the mountainside with more plaster. The surface is then painted with thin washes of beige, ochre and grays and Woodland Scenics ground foam sprinkled on the still-wet paint to simulate grasses and weeds. Most of the trees and bushes are from Noch and Life-Like.

The lake was cut through the Homosote and plywood with an electric saber saw. The piece that was removed was lowered about 3-inches below the level of the tabletop. Plaster cloth was then used to provide the sloping sides of the lake and river area. The bottom of the lake and river area was painted a dark blue/green to simulate the color of deep fresh water. Nearly two gallons of decoupage casting resin were then poured into the lake and river area. Only about 1/2-inch of the water area was poured at a time, allowing a few days for the material to cure before making the next pour. This method minimizes the chances for cracks.

John DiCrisci's 8-1/2 x 18-Foot Layout

John DiCrisci has constructed a traditional Lionel layout with the emphasis on track and lots of it. The tables are heavy 3/4-inch plywood framed with 2 x 4s. The layout is plenty strong enough to walk on. The track arrangement is a series of ovals joined by pairs of turnouts. The crossing from one oval to the next is insulated to allow up to five trains can operate at once on five different ovals interlaced through the layout (Figure 3-3). There is also a floor-level oval with Lionel's 175 Rocket Launcher, 470 Missile Launcher, a matching 44 Missile Launch locomotive, a variety of military cars and other military accessories.

John is a Lionel fan, so virtually all of his collection is Lionel equipment, including accessories and most structures. A few of the city buildings are collectible items sold by Hallmark in the late eighties, others are Plasticville kits. He has dozens of Lionel's original fifties-era accessories including the 282 Gantry Crane, 356 Station, 321 Trestle Bridge, 362 Barrel

Figures 3-4, 3-5 and 3-6 are a panorama of most of Bruce Pemberton's 20 x 20-foot layout. The fourth wall is also occupied by six parallel tracks, so the room is encircled with trains. A three-foot-wide hinged portion of the shelf allows access to the room without the need to duck under the layout.

Loader, 455 Oil Derrick, 464 Lumber Mill and others. His trains are all powered by Lionel including a ZW, and SW, a 1033, 1015 and 1032 transformers.

Bob Yeakel's 13 x 24-Foot Layout

Bob Yeakel, like many toy train operators, is mixing both two rail O scale and three-rail Lionel equipment on the same layout. His 13 x 24 foot layout has a series of removable panels in the center for access, so he can duck under the layout rather than walk over the top of it. There are three outer ovals of two rail O scale track and three inner ovals of GarGraves three-rail track, as well as dozens of turnouts to connect the two rail ovals to one another and the three rail ovals to one another, to provide industrial sidings, and to provide holding tracks and yards. Photos of his layout are included in the color section.

Generally, Lionel's less-expensive O-27 equipment, particularly the locomotives, are smaller than true O scale. By placing the Lionel equip-

ment on the inner ovals, the sense of perspective makes their smaller size, as compared to the full O scale equipment on the outer ovals, much less noticeable. Virtually all of the Lionel locomotives and rolling stock are original production items from the forties and fifties. The majority of the O scale locomotives and cars are built from kits.

Bruce Pemberton's 20 x 20 Foot Layout

Bruce Pemberton's layout can be classified as an "around-the-wall" or "shelf-style" layout because it really does occupy shelves around the walls of the room. He has one 6-foot wide peninsula that is occupied by the roundhouse and engine servicing facilities. Most of the layout, however, is on a 2-1/2-foot wide shelf so he can reach derailed locomotives or construct new track or scenery by simply reaching across the shelf with no need to crawl under the tables or walk over them. For now, his layout includes three loops or ovals of three-rail track around

Fig. 3-7. Ralph Johnson at the control panel for his 20 x 40-foot Lionel layout. The track is divided into electrically-insulated blocks so dozens of locomotives can be parked on the same track.

Fig. 3-8. Five of the six ovals that encircle Ralph Johnson's 20 x 40-foot layout room are on shelves near the walls. The sixth oval leads onto the peninsula for the yard and roundhouse in the center of the layout.

Fig. 3-9. Ralph Johnson uses a rare Lionel number 375 turntable, made in 1962 to 1964, as part of his roundhouse and engine servicing scene.

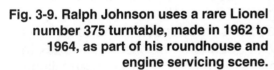

Fig. 3-10. Ken Zieska's 20 x 40-foot S scale layout meanders around the walls of his basement. The layout is built on a 2-1/2-foot wide shelf.

the inner edges and two loops of two-rail American Flyer track around the outer edges nearer the wall (Figures 3-4, 3-5 and 3-6). Eventually he plans on replacing the three-rail track with two-rail American Flyer track.

He prefers the relatively smaller size of Lionel's O-27 locomotives and freight cars. It is, perhaps, no coincidence, that he is also a fan of American Flyer equipment. The American Flyer models, although designed to run on narrower two-rail track, are very close to the size of Lionel's O-27 models. In fact, Bruce has rebuilt a number of old Lionel locomotives to operate on two rail by rewiring them and insulating the drivers. He sometimes fits Lionel O-27 superstructures or bodies to American Flyer mechanisms. He also moved the drivers and wheelsets inward so they will operate on American Flyer track. The conversion of Lionel O-27 freight cars and passenger cars to American Flyer three rail was much simpler, he replaced the Lionel trucks and couplers with American Flyer trucks and couplers. Yes, his work diminishes any collector value of the equipment, but he has purchased most of it very much used at swap meets so it had little collector value to start with. He keeps a few pristine pieces on display shelves and operates them occasionally along with his repainted and modified equipment.

Ralph Johnson's 20 x 40-Foot Layout

Ralph Johnson built a massive Lionel layout on a shelf around the walls of a 20 x 40-foot room. A 12-track double-ended yard with a turntable and roundhouse for engine storage occupies a six-foot wide shelf down the center of the room (Figure 3-7). The tabletop is about 54-inches high, so it is relatively easy to duck under the table to enter the room or to reach the access aisles on either side of the central yard. He has a two-foot high viewing platform across one end of the layout so visitors and small children can see the entire layout from one spot.

Five separate ovals roam around the four walls and out onto the central peninsula. Each of the ovals is connected to the next with a pair of turnouts so a single train can travel from one oval to the next to negotiate the entire layout (Figure 3-8). The track itself is GarGraves, with GarGraves and Lionel turnouts. He uses NJ International switch machines to activate the GarGraves turnouts by remote control. He has insulating pins and on-off switches so he can hold up to 50 locomotives while five trains are operating simultaneously.

The layout is wired much like a scale model railroad with dozens of "blocks" in the track to hold trains, remote control turnouts and illuminated buildings. An 8-foot long control panel

Fig. 3-11. An overall view of the Carnegie Science Center's 19 x 72-foot layout. Three mainline tracks circle the perimeter of the layout with additional ovals serving as mining or logging railroads.

near the central yard includes a schematic diagram of the entire layout with the on-off "block" switches located over their appropriate portion of the track on the diagram. The remote control levers for the turnouts are numbered to correspond to matching numbers on the control panel's schematic so he knows which lever to throw to actuate which turnout. Ralph prefers to operate complete trains, rather than perform yard switching movements to make up or break down trains. In any case, most of the "yard" tracks are occupied by locomotives waiting service on the next train. There's a roundhouse and turntable to turn individual locomotives (Figure 3-9). Like many collectors, he has almost as many locomotives as cars.

Ken Zieska's 20 x 40-Foot Layout

Ken Zieska's layout is an example of how toy trains can be developed into a realistic scale model railroad. All of the locomotives and rolling stock are scale models from American Models and S Helper Services, with relatively small wheel flanges and Kadee knuckle-style couplers, rather than the hook-style American Flyer

couplers (Figure 3-10). The track is two-rail from Scenery Unlimited with rails that are much smaller than the rails on American Flyer track and the ties are the correct size and proportions to match the prototype. The small rail is called code 100 which means that the rails are about 100-inch high. The larger wheel flanges on American Flyer equipment need rail that is .155-inch high. S Helper Services, American Models and GarGraves offer track with realistic ties and code 155 rail so you can have a layout this realistic and still combine both scale and American Flyer equipment.

This layout is an example of how you can use S scale or O scale toy trains, with accurate scale model locomotives and rolling stock and well-developed scenery to build a model railroad. The layout is built on open-grid style benchwork that is bolted to the walls of the basement on the far sides with legs on the aisle side. The open-grid construction allowed Ken more freedom to locate the tracks and roadbed on 1 x 4-inch wood risers elevated 6-inches above the open grid table. The elevation provides the space below the level of the

Fig. 3-12. This maintenance of way building and the three rows of miners houses, like all of the structures on the Carnegie Science Center's layout, are built from basswood with cast metal windows and doors.

tracks for highway underpasses and streams to flow beneath railroad bridges.

Carnegie Science Center's 19 x 72-Foot Layout

This massive toy train layout might be considered the ultimate in a "portable" toy train layout for the floor. In this case, the "floor" is really about 24-inches high and it serves as a platform for the trains (Figure 3-11). This huge layout is assembled each fall for the Christmas season and torn down during the summer months. The museum layout is really a three dimensional action history of a specific era in the hills near Pittsburgh, Pennsylvania. It is intended to bring the life style of the region, say in the twenties, to life as a three-dimensional action model.

The trains provide animation but some of the industries also have revolving wheels or simulated fires. The scenery includes a real water lake with boats that are replicas of the craft that worked the rivers of the region including barges, paddle wheel passenger boats and ferries. A variety of highway and railroad bridges are used on the layout. The toy trains are used to depict the appropriate part that railroads played in the history of the region.

The trains usually operate on three huge loops or ovals of track around the perimeter of the layout space with, perhaps, a small logging or mining train running around a smaller oval in the hills. The track is GarGraves with GarGraves turnouts. There are thousands of trees in both summer and fall shades so the seasons can be changed as the layout is reassembled each year.

All of the structures are mounted on boards that include surrounding landscapes. The museum keeps a "library" of these structures to draw on for each year's layout so not all of the structures appear on any one layout. One year, for example they might focus on the mining industry and include the various mine dioramas, mine shafts, mining towns, coal dealers, coal barges, coal wagons, coal-fueled power plants and steam locomotive coaling stations (Figure 3-12). Another year, they might focus on the farming industry, including farms, grain elevators, cattle pens, packing houses, milk depots, dairys, wholesale grocery warehouses, produce terminals, ice houses, cannerys and other related industries, as well as small towns and even a county fair (Figure 3-13). Another year they might include buildings and scenes to depict the various aspects of the oil industry, the brick industry, the logging industry, or a combination of all these industries. There are, of course, appropriate town centers with roads, stores, houses, churches, schools, libraries and offices.

Fig. 3-13. The Carnegie Science Center's layout is taken apart each spring and reassembled each winter. Most of the structures are mounted on boards like the grandstand for this fairgrounds' scene.

Chapter 4

Track Planning

When the real railroads build a new stretch of track, they prepare elaborate plans and surveys. You can do that with your toy train layout but, honestly, it's easier to just use track sections to see how the proposed layout will look and if it will fit the space you have available. There are plans on these pages and dozens of books with other plans if you want some guidance. Just how much guidance you will need will depend on how much track you want to squeeze into the space you have.

How Tight Can It Turn?

The one compromise that virtually everyone makes with their toy trains or model railroads is to use curves that are much tighter than those of the prototype railroads. These too-tight curves are one of the attributes of a model miniature railroad. The 72-inch diameter curved track sections offered by Lionel, MTH, K-Line, Atlas and GarGraves are about as large as is practical. It takes a table about 6-1/2-feet wide to accommodate an oval or reverse loop made with 72-inch diameter tracks. If you have the space for such curves, you'll see that all your toy trains look more realistic.

If you have less space, you have two choices: use the very tight curves that come with most toy train sets or use the smaller HO scale or N scale trains. The O-27 track forms a circle with a 27-inch diameter measured at the center of the track. I would suggest, however, that you use the O track

Fig. 4-1. The most common circles of O scale track include 31-inch, 42-inch, 54-inch and 72-inch diameter curves and turnouts (center) with 31-inch and 72-inch diameter curved routes.

Fig. 4-2. This complex two-level track arrangement is part of a portable layout.

which has a minimum 31-inch diameter circle. If you opt for N scale trains, rather than O, that 31-inch circle is very broad curve, indeed—it would "scale up" to a circle 112-inches in diameter for O scale. If realism is your only goal, you might want to consider some of the smaller scales like HO or N scale. For most toy train operators, however, the sheer mass and bulk of O scale or even S scale toy trains makes it worthwhile to make some compromises in the overall realism of the layout. The individual models are incredibly realistic, especially the more expensive products.

One of the advantages of toy trains is that they can operate on curves that are extremely tight. You can squeeze an O scale toy train layout into a space no larger than that needed for an HO scale layout, even though the O scale models are twice the size of the HO scale models. The most common O scale curved track sections, from Lionel and K-Line, include 31-inch, 42-inch, 54-inch and 72-inch diameter circles (Figure 4-1).

Lionel offers O scale turnouts with 31-inch or 72-inch curved routes and K-line offers turnouts with 42-inch diameter curved routes. If you are willing to use O-27 track, both Lionel and K-Line have turnouts with 27 and 42-inch diameter curved routes.

Virtually all of the toy train locomotives and cars will negotiate the 31-inch diameter curves, but some of them look pretty strange. If you are using large locomotives and cars, you might consider using turnouts with 42-inch curved routes or, whenever there is space, turnouts with 72-inch curved routes.

Danger! Curve Clearances

The 31-inch, 42-inch and 54-inch diameters for these curved track sections allow you to build concentric circles or ovals of track spaced just far enough apart so passing trains will not sideswipe one another. One of the side effects of these large scale cars and locomotives being able to negotiate tight curves is that the cars and locomotives produce large amounts of overhang. When two passenger trains pass each other on a curve, the car's ends overhang the outside of the rails and the center of the cars overhang the inside of the rails (Figure 4-3).

There is enough clearance between the 31, 42 and 54-inch curves to prevent the overhanging parts of one train from sideswiping the overhanging parts of the passing train. When you are building layouts, even using the plans in this book, be sure to use your longest cars or locomotives to check for clearance in all the curves. Some of these plans are so compact that you must shift the track as little as 1/4-inch to prevent trains from sideswiping each other. That same clearance must be checked, too, for any buildings or tunnels or cuts through hills on a finished layout.

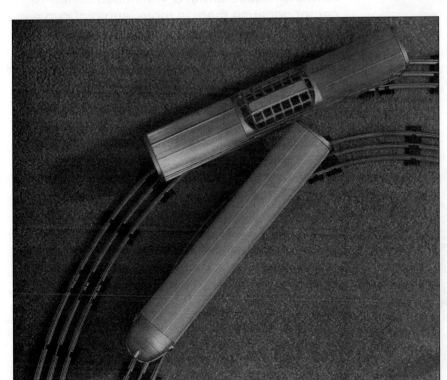

Fig. 4-3. The tight toy train curves produce considerable end and side overhang on passenger cars and large locomotives.

Understanding Track Plans

The track plans use single lines to identify the center of the track. All of the track plans in this book are designed to be built with Lionel's O-gauge track sections. Any unmarked curves are 31-inch diameter (45-degrees of a circle) and any unmarked straights are 10-inch standard track sections. The letters "RU" are used to identify uncoupling track sections. Half-length straight track sections are marked with the fraction 1/2. The 90-degree crossings are Lionel's 020 and the 45-degree crossings are Lionel's 020X. Most K-Line and some MTH track and turnouts are interchangeable with these Lionel sections. The turnouts used in the majority of the track plans in this chapter are Lionel's 031R and 031L that include a short piece of straight track (marked "S" on the plans and a short piece of curved track (marked "C" on the plans).

Most of these plans are also marked with letter codes for adding insulating pins (the circled letters A, B, C, D, E and F) with tiny dots or circles at the track joints indicating an insulating pin should be installed in place of the metal pin in the center rail. The extra Lockon connections for "block" wiring that must be installed so two or more trains can be operated are indicated with small rectangles across the track and the letters W, X, Y Z and ZZ. The wiring for two train operations and the need for the insulating pins and Lockons are explained in Chapter 8.

Lionel's O Turnouts

Lionel's 031R and 031L turnouts for 31-inch diameter O scale track are used on most of the plans in this book. These turnouts include a short piece of straight track and a short piece of curved track. Those short, removable pieces of track make it far easier to design and build track plans for confined spaces than when using the older Lionel O gauge turnouts, Lionel's O-27 turnouts, the MTH turnouts, or K-Line turnouts. You can substitute K-Line or MTH turnouts with 31-inch diameter curves if the plan shows these short sections attached to the 031R or 031L turnouts, including Figures 4-10 (if the three-track yard in the center is eliminated), 4-18, 4-22, 4-24, all of the plans in 4-27, 4-28, 4-16, and 4-29 (if the crossover pair of turnouts on the right of either of these last two plans is eliminated).

It is also possible to assemble some of these plans using Lionel's or K-Line's O-27 track sections, including Figures 4-18, 4-262, 4-24, all of the plans in 4-27 and 4-4-28 and 4-16 and 4-29 (if the crossover pair of turnouts on the bottom of either of these last two plans is eliminated). On these plans, you can substitute Lionel's 1024 R and 1024 L or 1122R and 1122L turnouts or K-Line's 0263, 0264, 0265 or 0265 turnouts if you are using O-27 track for the rest of the layout.

The Lionel 031R and 031L turnouts allow you to arrange a crossover with the parallel tracks spaced 4-1/4-inches center-to-center (Figure 4-4), while the older Lionel O scale turnouts, Lionel O-27 turnouts, K-Line and MTH turnouts require about 8-1/4-inches center-to-center because there is more length of curve in these turnouts. If you are using large locomotives and long passenger cars, the sudden transition from a right to a left hand curve through this crossover can cause derailments. The two

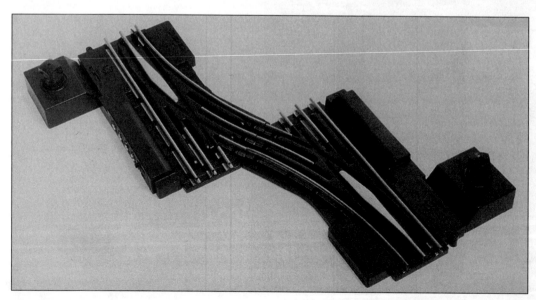

Fig. 4-4. If Lionel's 031L (left hand, shown) or two 031R turnouts are joined to form a crossover, the two parallel tracks will be spaced just 4-1/4-inches center-to-center.

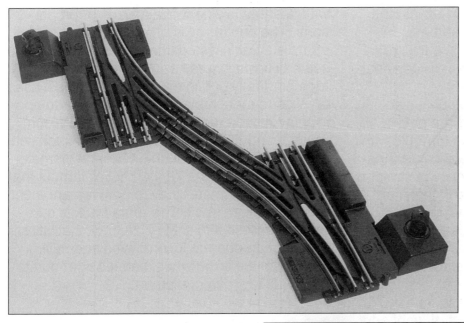

Fig. 4-5. The trains will travel more smoothly through the crossover if the two pieces of 2-inch straight track included with the Lionel 031L and 031R turnouts are used between the two turnouts.

Fig. 4-6. Two Lionel 031L and one Lionel 031R turnouts can be used to make a compact ladder for a yard like that in Figure 4-10.

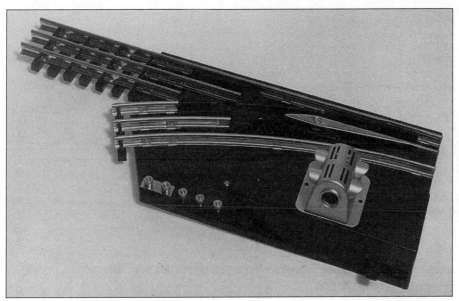

Fig. 4-7. K-Line offers an O scale turnout with a 42-inch diameter curved route. Note that the straight portion is 14-1/4-inches long.

short pieces of straight track included with the Lionel 031R and 031L turnouts can be combined to make 4-inch straight to ease this transition and the resulting track spacing will be about the same 8-1/4-inches (Figure 4-5).

The Lionel 031R and 031L turnouts also make it much easier to arrange three or four track yards with a "ladder" of three turnouts with the tracks about 5-inches center-to-center (Figure 4-6). Note where the short pieces of straight track (marked "S" on the plans) and the short pieces of curved track (marked "C" on the plans) are located to produce closely-spaced parallel tracks to connect one oval to another or to create a yard with four or more tracks.

The K-Line turnouts with 42-inch diameter curves (numbers 0373 manual, right and 0374 manual, left and 0375 remote-control, right and 0376 remote-control, left) are nearly as versatile, but they do require a bit more space because of the larger diameter (Figure 4-7).

The Atlas "21st Century Track System"

Atlas has developed its own three-rail track system that it calls the "21st Century Track System" (Figure 4-8 and Figures 6-2 and 6-10 in Chapter 6). It utilizes the smallest possible rail with ties that are near scale sizes or proportions. The center rail is blackened. The overall effect is a track system that is very similar to the scale O scale two rail track. The track snaps together firmly but, in my opinion, it is best used on a permanent tabletop layout, not for temporary layouts on the floor. Atlas offers 36-inch, 54-inch and 72-inch diameter curved track sections and 36-inch, 54-inch or 72-inch diameter turnouts as well as a 72-inch "wye" turnout that has 72-inch diameter curves both left and right with no straight track. The Atlas track is currently the closest to scale-size track that will still allow you to operate locomotives and rolling stock with the large wheel flanges common to nearly all toy train equipment.

A Layout That Grows

It is very difficult to fit an O scale toy train layout in an area as small as 4 x 6-1/2-feet. That's why I've prepared the variety of plans for that space. It's really about the minimum for a really enjoyable toy train layout. If you only have 3 x 6-feet, I would suggest you consider using N scale (1/160) toy trains which are about a fourth the size of O scale trains. However, 4 x 6-1/2-feet is enough space to provide a lot of action

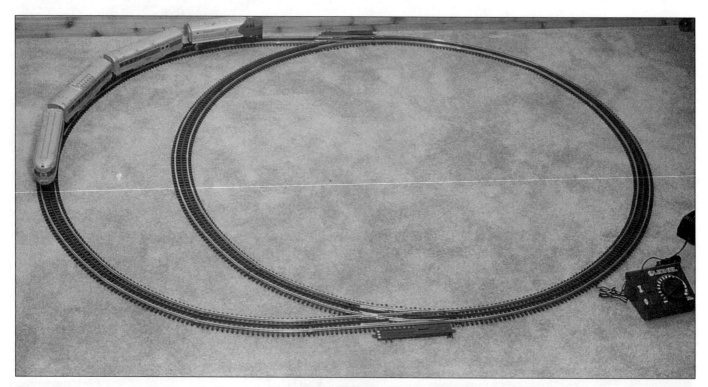

Fig. 4-8. The Atlas "21st Century Track System" is available with curved track sections and turnouts with either 54-inch diameter curves (shown) or 72-inch diameter curves.

with O scale toy trains, including operation of as many as three trains. Remember, you can expand any of these 4 x 6-1/2-foot layouts in either direction, including enough expansion to alter the layout for a tabletop to and around-the-wall shelf-style layout as shown in Figure 4-29.

Two-Trains and a Yard in 4 x 5-1/2-Feet

You can start your railroad empire with a simple oval like that furnished with most train sets. I would, however, recommend that you replace the O-27 track with the stronger and more massive O scale track if you are going to build your layout on the floor. If you add a pair of turnouts, two pieces of curved track and two pieces of straight track to the basic oval, you can have the 4 x 5-1/2-foot layout in Figure 4-9. The siding can be used as a place to switch cars as described in Chapter 16 or it can be used as a holding track to operate two trains as shown in Chapter 8.

These toy trains look more realistic on broader curves, so that the basic oval can be modified to include 42-inch diameter curved track sections on one side, while retaining the two tracks on the opposite side of the oval. One right hand and two left hand turnouts can be used to include a three-track freight yard so you can combine both two train operation and switching in this same space (Figures 4-10 and 4-11).

Two-Train Ovals in 4 x 5-1/2-Feet

An alternate method of expanding the basic oval is to simply place a second oval around the train set oval using 12 sections of 42-inch diameter curves and two more standard straight track sections. If you buy a second transformer and do not add any turnouts to connect the two tracks, you can run two trains, one on each track. If you decide to connect the two tracks with a pair of turnouts to make a crossover, you must add all of the fiber insulating pins and additional Lockons indicated in Chapter 8.

Two right hand Lionel O scale turnouts will allow you to make a double-track oval with a crossover. (Figure 4-12). Note that the two short pieces of straight track furnished with the two Lionel turnouts are located on the single track end of both turnouts. This was necessary to position the inner oval so it was far enough away from both ends of the outer oval so the longer passenger cars and larger locomotives did not sideswipe one another. This layout also requires just 4 x 5-1/2-feet of floor or table space.

With just one pair of turnouts, a train traveling clockwise on the over oval on the layout in Figure 4-12 can reach the inner oval easily. That train must, however, backup or reverse to get back onto the outer oval. To solve that problem, install two more Lionel O scale turnouts but these need to be left hand turnouts. There are several other modifications that must be made

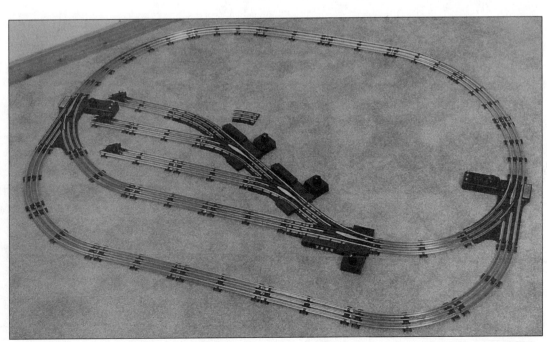

Fig. 4-11. The yard in Figure 4-10 utilizes two Lionel 031L turnouts and one 031R turnout. Two of the short curved track sections included with these turnouts are used to complete the third siding and one short curve is leftover.

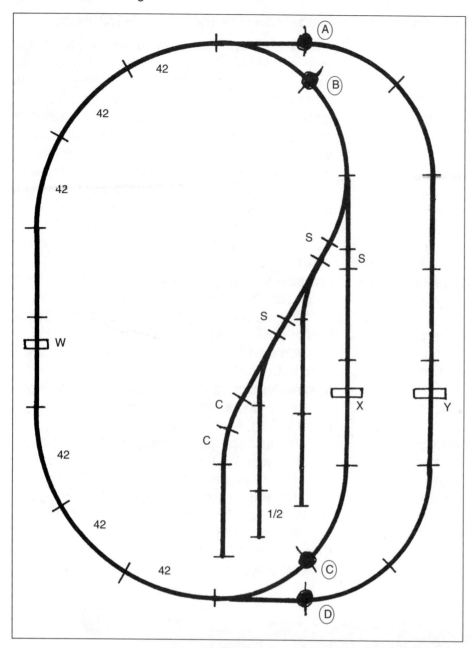

42
42
42
A
B
42
S
S
S
W
C
X
Y
C
42
C
42
1/2
42
C
D

Fig. 4-10. A track plan featuring an oval with a passing siding for two-train operation and a yard for switching cars. Note the locations of the 2-inch pieces of straight track "S" included with the Lionel 031L and 031R turnouts. The tiny rectangles denote the locations for Lockons for two-train operation and the dots indicate where to install fiber insulating pins as described in Chapter 8.

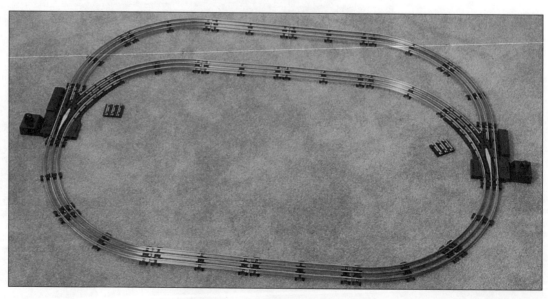

Fig. 4-9. Expand any train set oval into a layout with a passing siding by adding a pair of turnouts and four curved track sections.

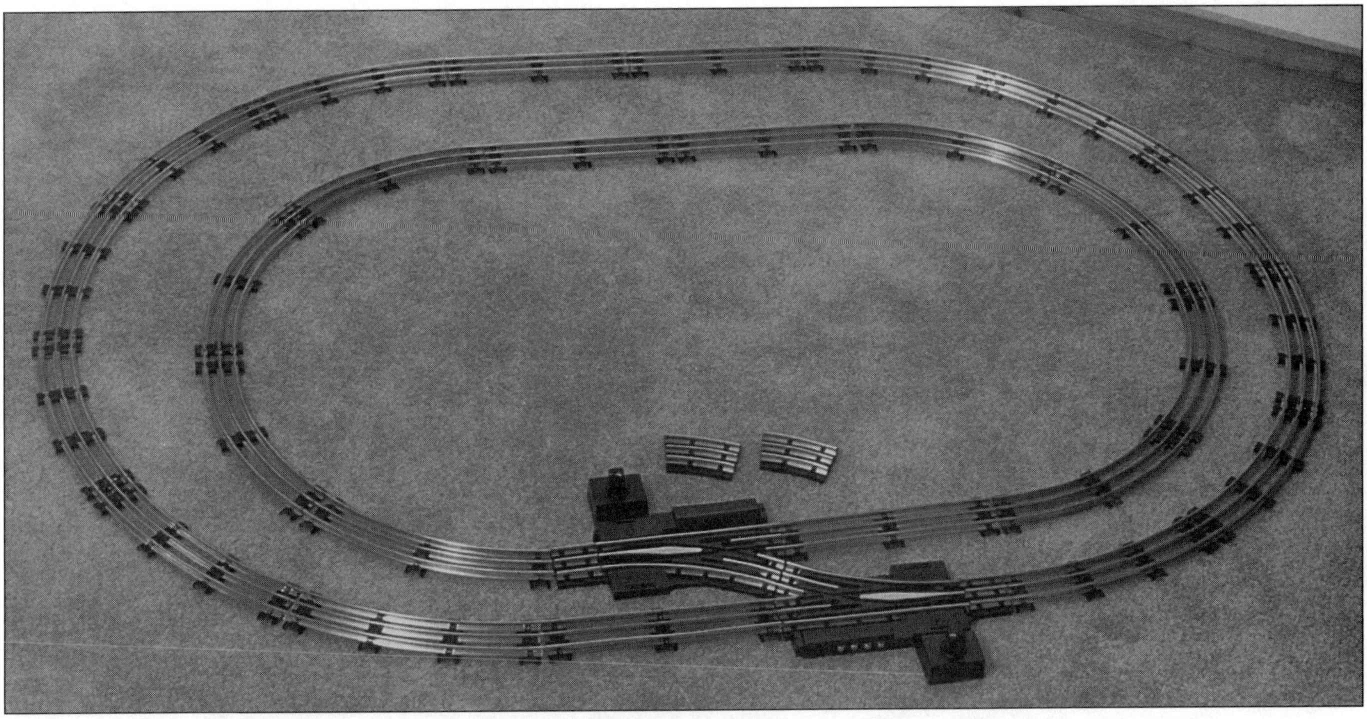

Fig. 4-12. A 31-inch diameter oval inside a 42-inch diameter oval connected with a crossover made from two Lionel 031R turnouts without the short curved track sections.

to the layout in Figure 4-12. Note that the short curved track sections furnished with these turnouts are installed on the curved routes of the two new turnouts (Figure 4-13). The short straight track sections furnished with these turnouts are not used on either of the turnouts on the inside oval. Also, a half-length straight track section is used on each side of the inner oval. These changes are necessary, again, to keep the inner oval centered inside the outer oval so longer passenger cars do not sideswipe each other on the curves. These curves are very tight, so you may need to move the tracks a quarter of an inch or so to get exactly the right clearance on both ends of the ovals. This layout also requires 4 x 5-1/2-feet.

Two Trains and a Reverse Loop in 4 x 6-1/2-Feet

The layout in Figure 4-14 is a development of the track plan in Figure 4-13. Two left hand turnouts are added to the inner oval to create two stub-ended sidings. The track arrangement leaves the center of the layout open for scenery or a town. This is the layout that was used for the switching moves in Chapter 15. The extra turnouts add about a foot to the layout's length, so it now requires 4 x 6-1/2-feet of space.

This layout (Figure 4-16) is one that was used to build one of the three "Project" layouts in Chapter 5. It is also used to demonstrate how to operate and reverse two trains in Chapter 8. The layout is a fourth development of the double-track oval layouts in Figures 4-12, 4-13 and 4-14. The tracks to make the two stub-ended sidings are removed and two standard curved tracks installed in their place to make the S-shaped reverse loop track across the center of the layout. If you want a stub-ended siding, add another left hand turnout (Figure 4-16). A second stub-ended siding could be added by replacing the one curved track section in the center with a right hand turnout. I like it as-is because there is space for a small town or a mountain or lake inside the left half of the inner oval.

A Double-Track Layout with a Turntable

A turntable is used by real railroads to turn locomotives and some passenger cars end-for-end. You can build your own using a lazy Susan that revolves on ball bearings from a hardware or kitchen supply store. Attach two lengths of standard straight track to the lazy Susan with double-sided foam poster-hanging tape. You may also need to elevate the end of the track leading to this turntable with a piece of wood or

Fig. 4-13. The second crossover can be made from two Lionel 031L turnouts but with both of the short curves in their proper plaooo between the two turnouts. The short track sections are not used on the two turnouts on the inner oval.

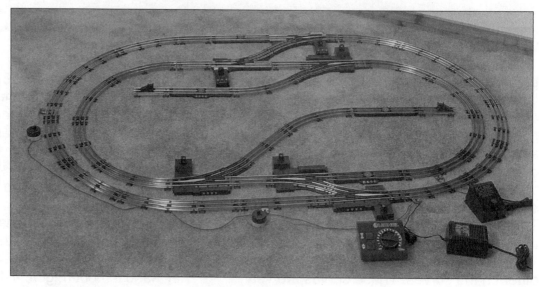

Fig. 4-14. Add a pair of Lionel 031R and 031L turnouts and the double-track oval can be expanded to include two stub-ended sidings for switching moves.

Fig. 4-15. The two turnouts on the inner oval can be connected with 31-inch curve track sections as shown in the plan in Figure 4-16 to create the S-shaped reverse loop cutoff across the center of the inner oval.

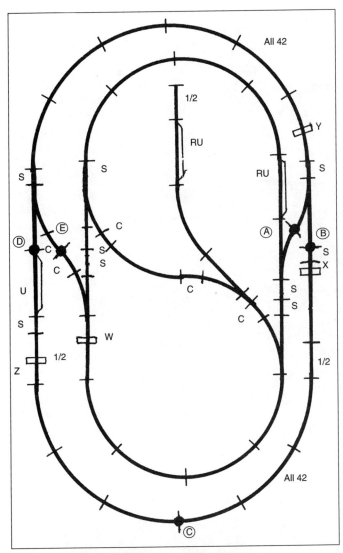

Fig. 4-16. This double-track oval plan includes a reverse loop and a stub-ended siding.

cardboard so it aligns with the track on the turntable (Figure 4-17). This layout also requires 4 x 6-1/2-feet of space.

Reversing Locomotives and Trains

There are three ways to arrange the track to reverse or turn locomotives, cars or complete trains. The easiest method of reversing complete trains is to use a reverse loop. Examples of reverse loops include the inner oval in Figure 4-16 and the layout in Figures 5-2 and 5-3 in Chapter 5. The problem with a single reverse loop is that you must back the train through the loop to re-reverse its direction.

The solution is to have two reverse loops. The plan in Figures 4-18 and 4-19 looks like a combination of a figure 8 and oval. Its real operating value, however, is that there are overlapping

reverse loops. This plan requires a 3 x 6-foot space. The plan in Figure 4-16 could be modified to include this overlapping reverse loop on the inner oval but another section of straight track would need to be added to each straight leg of the outer oval. The revised layout would then require about 4 x 7-1/2-feet of floor or table space.

The two reverse loops can also be stacked one above the other. The plan in Chapter 5 (Figure 5-10) is one reverse loop stacked 5-inches above a second reverse loop. The operations for running three trains on this stacked-reverse loop layout are shown in Chapter 8.

The second method of reversing trains is to use a track arrangement called a wye (Figures 4-20 and 4-21). The switching or train movements needed to use a reverse loop or wye to reverse a train are described in Chapter 15. Two of the legs of the wye in this plan are the layout itself, while the third leg is placed inside the layout. The length of that third leg determines the maximum length of train you can reverse with a wye. This plan requires just 3-1/2 x 5-1/2 feet. If you have another foot of length available, two straight track sections can be added to the oval and three more curves added to the stub ended siding on the wye. The longer siding length will allow you to turn a train with a locomotive and four short cars.

The third arrangement for reversing trains is a turntable (Figure 4-17), but the turntable is only long enough for a single locomotive or, perhaps, a very short locomotive and a single car. The turntable, like the wye, is often used to turn cars, like observation cars from passenger trains, as well as locomotives.

Upgrades and Downgrades

Most of these toy train locomotives are powerful enough to pull a four or five car freight train up a grade, so you can build layouts that allow one train to pass over another. Most of these trains will climb a grade as steep as 4-percent. (A 4 percent grade means the track rises 4 inches in 100-inches.) If you have the space, a 2 percent grade will allow you to operate longer trains without straining the locomotives. (A 2-percent grade elevates the track 2-inches in 100-inches.)

Figures 4-22 and 4-23 show an inverted figure 8-style layout with a 45-degree crossing. An almost identical plan can be used (Figure 4-24)

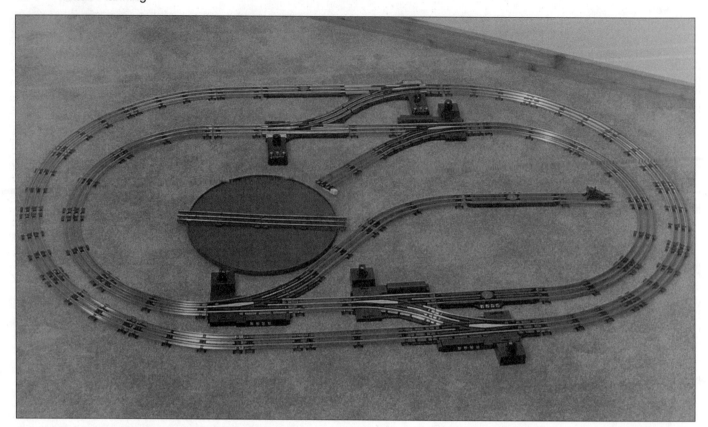

Fig. 4-17. A lazy Susan can be adapted to use as a turntable for an alternate method of reversing single locomotives or cars.

Fig. 4-19. This compact layout with overlapping reverse loops combines both oval and figure 8 operations.

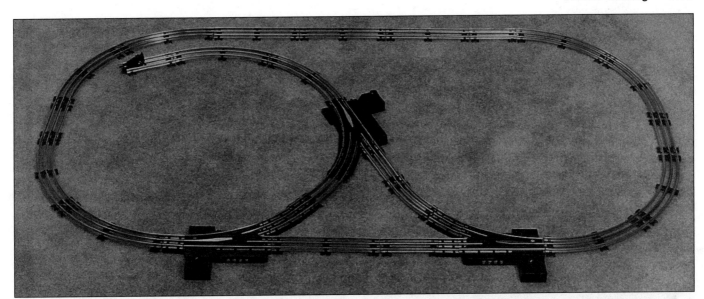

Fig. 4-21. This layout uses two Lionel 031R turnouts and one 031L turnout. The two short straight sections "S" are positioned on the single track end of the left hand turnout and no short straight is used with the right hand turnout in the center. Two half-length 31-inch diameter curved track sections are used in the curved routes of the wye.

to produce an over-and-under layout by replacing the 45-degree crossing with two pieces of standard straight track (Figure 4-25). To elevate one track above the other, use Lionel's 110 Graduated Trestle set, 920-5 Rock Piers, and the 2122 Extension Bridge (shown in Figure 4-26), 318 Truss Bridge, or a similar long bridge. The 110 Graduated Trestle set is designed to produce about a 4-percent grade.

The supports in the 110 Graduated Trestle set are designed so they can be attached to Lionel's metal ties with wood screws, so the piers are sturdy enough to be usable even for a layout built on the floor. You must be certain to check the track connections even more frequently to be sure they have not worked loose. The piers have holes for screws so they can be attached at their bases to a plywood tabletop which makes a far more sturdy installation. It is also possible to build upgrades for a tabletop layout using the Woodland Scenics Styrofoam "Incline" components as described in Chapter 9.

It requires 10 lengths of track to elevate the trains the 5-inches that are necessary to provide enough clearance for one train to pass over another. It takes another 10 lengths of track to get them back down again. The leftover piers in Figure 4-26 have been replaced with the 920-5 Rock Piers. This, then, is about the most compact layout you can build with this over-and-under feature.

The figure 8 layouts with 31-inch diameter curves just do not contain enough track sections to give the length of track needed to climb that 5-inches. The loop-to-loop layout in Chapters 5 (Figure 5-10) and 8 (Figure 8-21) requires only half of a set of 110 Graduated Trestle supports because a reverse loop at each end of the layout allows the trains to go back down the same track they used to climb up.

11 Track Plans

These 11 track plans (Figures 4-27 and 4-28) are classics for toy trains. All of these track plans can be built with K-Line or MTH turnouts as well as Lionel and all can be built with O-27 or O scale track. The dimensions are for O-27 track. If you build them with O scale track, add about 10-percent to the overall sizes indicated. You can use these plans as-is or, like all the other plans in this book, expand them to fit your available space. You can also add double-ended sidings to provide places to park trains and stub-ended sidings to serve action accessories and industries.

Study the routes the trains can travel carefully and you may be surprised. The oval with the figure 8 inside it is an overlapping pair of reverse loops, an expansion of the plan in Figure 4-18. The rectangular 92 x 82-inch plan, the P-shaped plan, the 122 x 62-inch plan and the 172 x 31-inch plan also include reverse loops. The 172 x 31-inch plan has a

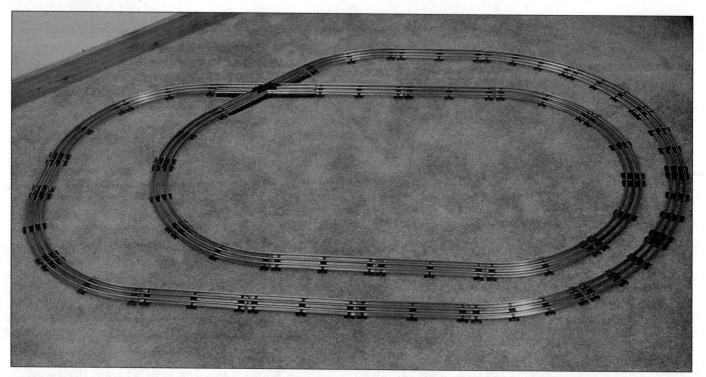

Fig. 4-23. If you want this layout to fit a slightly smaller space, one straight track section (four in all) can be removed from each of the straight portions of the two ovals.

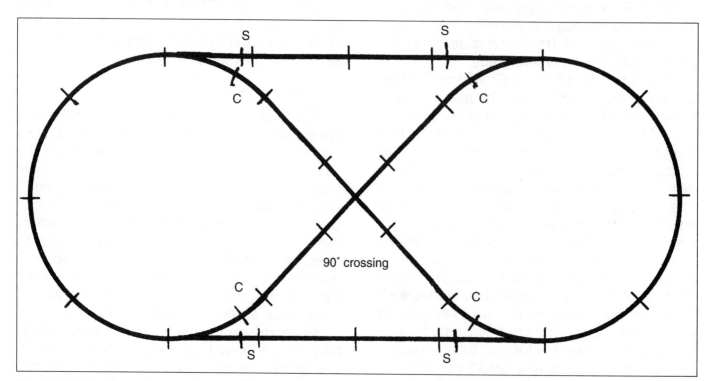

Fig. 4-18. This plan has overlapping reverse loops.

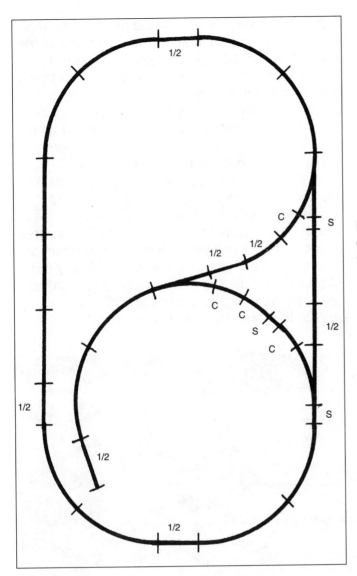

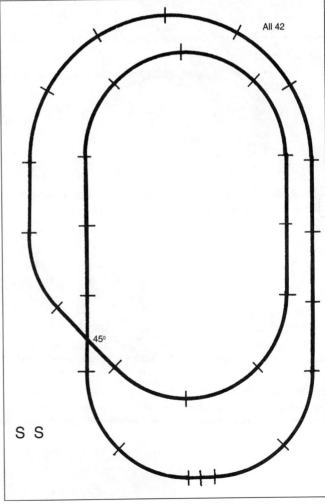

Fig. 4-20. This oval has a wye track arrangement that can be used to reverse a short train as described in Chapter 15.

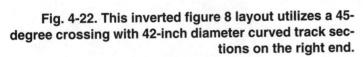

Fig. 4-22. This inverted figure 8 layout utilizes a 45-degree crossing with 42-inch diameter curved track sections on the right end.

three-track double-ended freight yard in the center with remote uncoupling ramps on each end of the three sidings.

Expandable Empires

When you look at the 4 x 6-1/2-foot layouts and others in this book, remember that they are infinitely expandable. Here is one example of a 4 x 6-1/2-foot layout (Figure 4-18) being expanded to a 9 x 11-1/2-foot layout (Figure 4-29) by simply adding five-foot sections (10-pieces) of straight track to the width and length of the original. You can expand nearly all the plans using a similar system of adding anything from a single half-straight (5-inches) to a dozen full-length straights (about 120-inches) on opposite sides of the oval.

By expanding these plans, you can often use them to run tracks around the floor nearer the walls of a room to keep the tracks out of the heavily-trafficked areas of the room. There is just one reverse loop that is best used for trains traveling counterclockwise around the layout. There is plenty of space for a second reverse loop in the layout in Figure 4-29 (that will allow trains traveling clockwise around the layout to be reversed) in the three inside corners

All of the permanent layouts in Chapter 3 are variations on this double-track plan but these layouts have up to six tracks in addition to sidings and yards. Most incorporate two reverse loops so trains can be turned in either direction. There are also crossovers between every pair of parallel tracks (as there are on this plan) to allow trains to travel around any of the ovals and/or to reach the reverse loops.

Fig. 4-25. The layout in Figure 4-22 can be converted to an over-and-under design by replacing the 45-degree crossing with two sections of straight track.

Fig. 4-26. Lionel's 110 Graduated Trestle Set is used to elevate the tracks. The leftover piers from the set were replaced with the 920-5 Rock Piers to support the bridge.

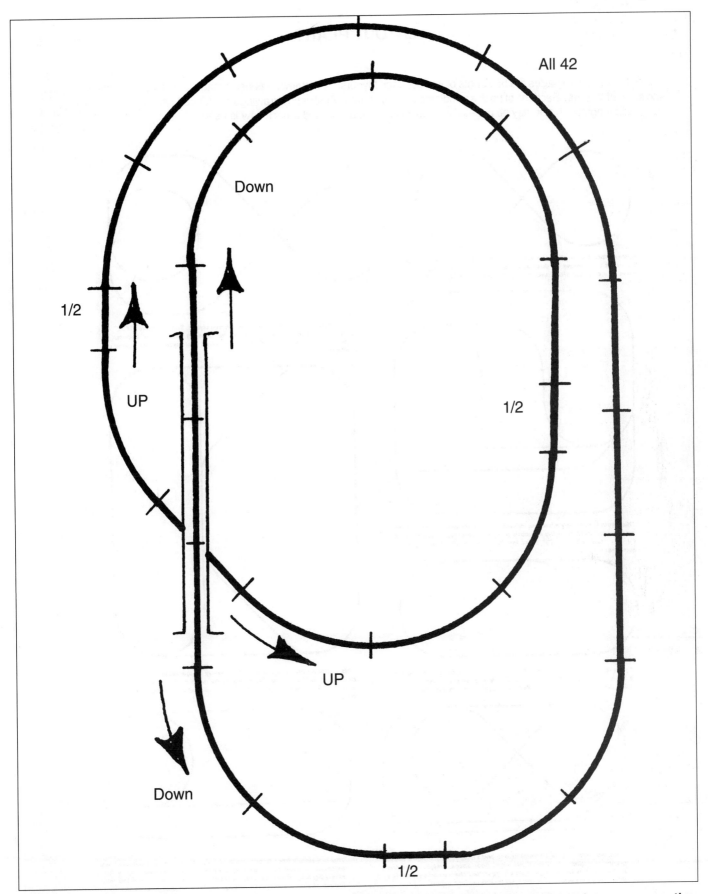

All 42

Down

1/2

UP

1/2

UP

Down

1/2

Fig. 4-24. A track plan for an inverted figure 8 layout with an elevated oval to allow one track to pass over the other on a bridge. The half-length straight track sections were used to move the bridge over the center of the lower straight track.

LAYOUT PLANS

On the following two pages are blueprints of various track layouts. An attempt has been made to include a variety of shapes and sizes of layouts. Sections of track are indicated by cross bars. Frequently drawings call for half-sections or pieces of track cut to odd lengths. Track may be cut easily when it is held in a vise and a hack saw is used.

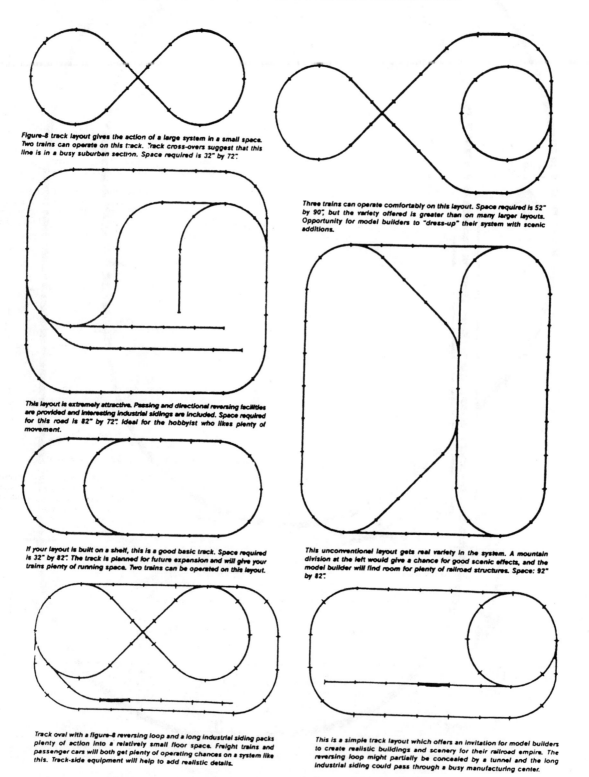

Figure-8 track layout gives the action of a large system in a small space. Two trains can operate on this track. Track cross-overs suggest that this line is in a busy suburban section. Space required is 32" by 72".

Three trains can operate comfortably on this layout. Space required is 52" by 90", but the variety offered is greater than on many larger layouts. Opportunity for model builders to "dress-up" their system with scenic additions.

This layout is extremely attractive. Passing and directional reversing facilities are provided and interesting industrial sidings are included. Space required for this road is 82" by 72". Ideal for the hobbyist who likes plenty of movement.

If your layout is built on a shelf, this is a good basic track. Space required is 32" by 82". The track is planned for future expansion and will give your trains plenty of running space. Two trains can be operated on this layout.

This unconventional layout gets real variety in the system. A mountain division at the left would give a chance for good scenic effects, and the model builder will find room for plenty of railroad structures. Space: 92" by 82".

Track oval with a figure-8 reversing loop and a long industrial siding packs plenty of action into a relatively small floor space. Freight trains and passenger cars will both get plenty of operating chances on a system like this. Track-side equipment will help to add realistic details.

This is a simple track layout which offers an invitation for model builders to create realistic buildings and scenery for their railroad empire. The reversing loop might partially be concealed by a tunnel and the long industrial siding could pass through a busy manufacturing center.

Fig. 4-27. Seven track plans designed for either O-27 or standard O scale track and turnouts. (Courtesy of K-Line)

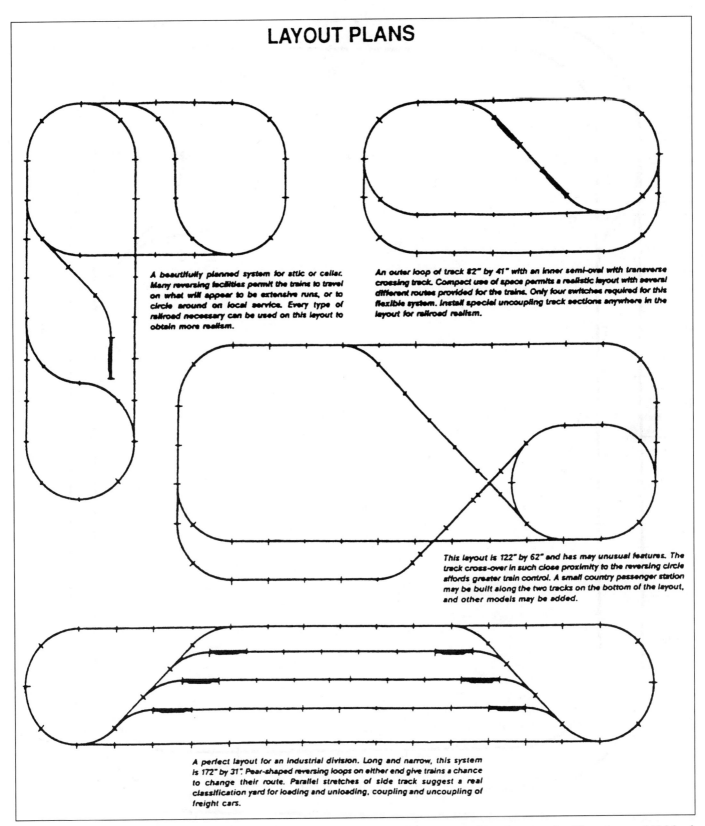

LAYOUT PLANS

A beautifully planned system for attic or cellar. Many reversing facilities permit the trains to travel on what will appear to be extensive runs, or to circle around on local service. Every type of railroad necessary can be used on this layout to obtain more realism.

An outer loop of track 82" by 41" with an inner semi-oval with transverse crossing track. Compact use of space permits a realistic layout with several different routes provided for the trains. Only four switches required for this flexible system. Install special uncoupling track sections anywhere in the layout for railroad realism.

This layout is 122" by 62" and has may unusual features. The track cross-over in such close proximity to the reversing circle affords greater train control. A small country passenger station may be built along the two tracks on the bottom of the layout, and other models may be added.

A perfect layout for an industrial division. Long and narrow, this system is 172" by 31". Pear-shaped reversing loops on either end give trains a chance to change their route. Parallel stretches of side track suggest a real classification yard for loading and unloading, coupling and uncoupling of freight cars.

Fig. 4-28. Four track plans designed for either O-27 or standard O scale track and turnouts. (Courtesy of K-Line)

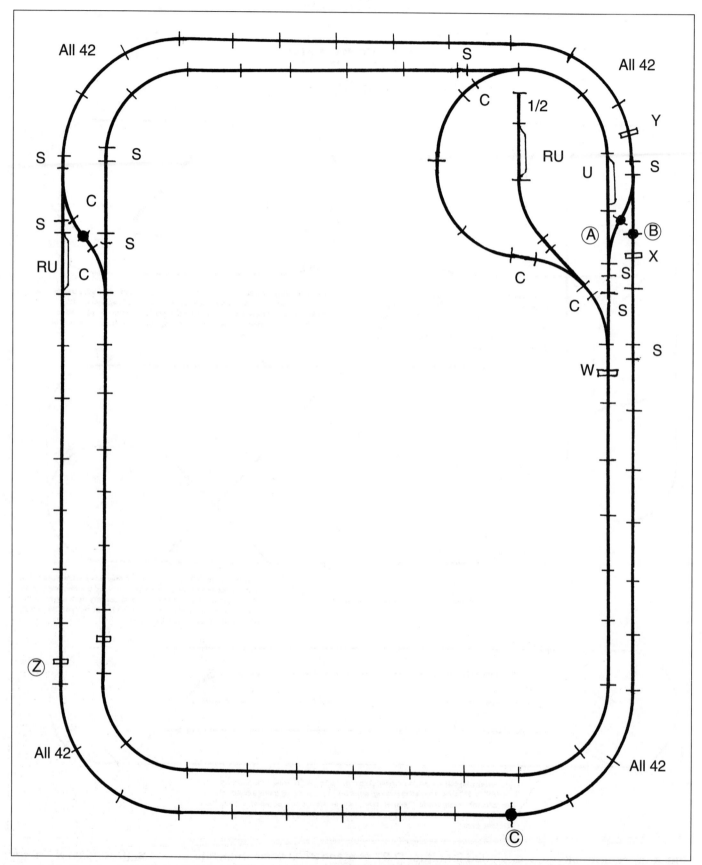

Fig. 4-29. The 4 x 6-1/2-foot double-track oval layout in Figure 4-16 can be expanded into this 9 x 11-1/2-foot around-the-wall layout by simply inserting additional pairs of straight track sections on opposite sides of the oval.

Chapter 5

Three Portable Layouts

Space is almost always a problem. Where do you find the space for a for toy train layout? If you can negotiate with your family to have floor use of an entire room, for at least part of the year, you may have all the space you want. If, however, you want a layout that you can operate almost any time, you may want to find a dedicated space.

Most of us can find 4 x 6-1/2-feet of space for a permanent or portable toy train layout. The 4 x 6-1/2-foot area is roughly the size of a queen-size bed. These 4 x 6-1/2-foot layouts can, then, be stored beneath a queen-size bed or temporarily placed on top of the bed. Or, you may even be able to convince your household to buy a Murphy bed so it could fold down over the layout built on the floor. We've built most of the layouts in this

book on the floor and one on a tabletop. You can choose to make any of these layouts on the bare floor, to build them on a bare piece of 1/2-inch plywood, or build them a piece of 1/8-inch plywood with some blue Styrofoam as described in Chapter 9. You can place this layout on the floor, hinge it from the wall, support it on sawhorses, on permanent legs, on folding legs or rest it on a bed while you are operating. All three of these layouts, as well as most of the layouts in Chapter 4, are small enough so they can be portable.

4 x 8-Foot Layouts

The 4 x 8-foot space has been common for model railroads for decades. This is, of course,

Fig. 5-1. Three trains can be operated on the loop-to-loop layout in Figure 5-10.

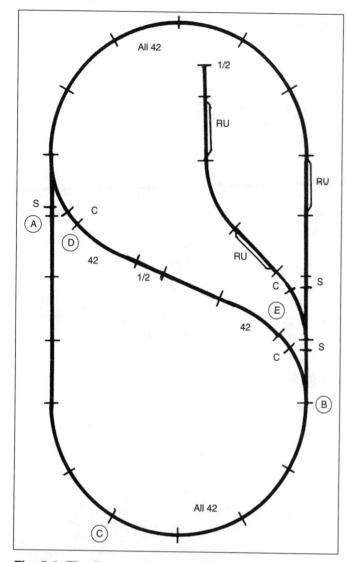

Fig. 5-2. The Reverse Loop Layout for a 4 x 7-foot space.

the size of standard sheet of plywood or particle board, so you can "build" a layout by simply attaching legs to the sheet of plywood. A 4 x 8-foot sheet of plywood is, however, extremely difficult to maneuver and to store. Most of the layouts in this book are designed for 4 x 6-1/2-feet of space or less. However, any of these layouts can be built on a 4 x 8-foot board by simply adding two standard straight track sections to the long, straight legs of every oval. If you want to build these layouts on a standard 5 x 9-foot ping-pong table, they can be extended to fill that space. The slightly longer straight sections will allow you to operate longer trains and provide more scenery.

4 x 6-1/2-Foot Layouts

A 4 x 6-1/2-foot layout will be a bit easier to handle when you do decide to store it. If you fol-

low the lightweight table construction methods in Chapter 9, the finished layout board will be light enough so one person can handle it if the tracks and structures are removed. Even if you decide on laying the track permanently and building plaster or Styrofoam scenery, the layout will be compact enough so two persons can carry it up or down stairs. It is far more difficult to try to maneuver a 4 x 8-foot layout, particularly one that might have mountains or other scenery a foot or so high, around corners and up or down stairs than to handle a 4 x 6-1/2-foot layout.

The reverse loop layout in Figure 5-2 actually requires 4 x 7-feet of space, but the layouts in Figures 5-5 and 5-10 require just 4 x 6-1/2-feet of space. The 4 x 5-foot and 4 x 6-foot layouts in Chapter 4 (Figures 4-10, 4-20, 4-22 and 4-24) can also be built on a 4 x 6-1/2-foot board. Each of these layouts, including those in this chapter, are designed to fit the absolute minimum amount of space shown, You can make any of these layouts longer or wider, but they cannot be made any more compact.

Realistic Layout Spaces

You will discover that you cannot reach more than about 2-1/2-feet across a tabletop. If you place the 6-1/2-foot or 8-foot or 9-foot side of a table against the wall, you will not be able to reach a large portion of the center, rear of the layout. If you place the layout in the corner, you will not be able to reach about half of it. To make every area of these layouts accessible, they should be placed with the short 4-foot end against the wall so the layout protrudes like a peninsula. You'll need a minimum 2-foot wide access aisle along one side of the layout and 2-1/2-feet is better. With that access aisle included, these layouts require 6-1/2 x 6-1/2-feet of floor space. It is possible, of course, to mount the legs on casters so you can roll the layout out when you want to operate it or for emergency access. It also possible to build the layout strong enough so you can walk on it to reach those trains that always seem to stall or derail just out of your reach.

A Reverse Loop Layout in 4 x 7-Feet

It is possible to build a toy train layout with an oval and a reverse loop cutoff in a space as small as 3 x 5 feet if you use standard O scale

Fig. 5-3. Start building the portable scenery by laying a piece of 5 x 8-foot green felt on the floor or the tabletop. Add the track, then stuff a pile of newspapers under the felt to make a mountain.

Fig. 5-4. The riverbed, bushes and trees are added as described in Chapter 10.

31-inch diameter curves and just the inner oval from the plan in Figure 5-5. Your trains will look much more realistic, however, if you use 42-inch diameter curves, rather than the 31-inch diameter curves. The track plan in Figure 5-2 utilizes these 42-inch curves. The right and left turnouts, however, are standard O scale turnouts with 31-inch diameter curved routes. The stub-ended siding also has a 31-inch curved track section. You can use Lionel, K-Line or MTH track and turnouts for this layout or you can substitute O-27 track and turnouts from Lionel or K-Line.

If you want to use K-Line's O scale turnouts or Lionel's O-27 turnouts with 42-inch diameter curves, this layout will require 7-1/2-feet of space because the straight route through the 42-inch diameter turnouts is about 4-1/4-inches longer than the straight route through turnouts with 31-inch diameter curved routes. The extra length is also needed so the S-shaped 42-inch curves will join. If you also want to use 42-inch diameter turnouts for the stub-ended siding, you will need to cut a piece of straight track to 5-3/4-inches to fit the turnout into this location. You will need three more pieces of 42-inch diameter curved track.

This layout is designed to provide a minimum amount of track and a maximum amount of scenery for the space (Figures 5-3 and 5-4). There is room for downtown buildings and houses on the "industrial" end of the layout.

It would be possible to operate two trains on this layout by electrically-isolating the S-shaped reverse cutoff track through the layouts center with fiber insulating pins in the center rails at the locations of circled letters D and E (Figure 5-2) as described in Chapter 8 for the passing siding on the layout in Figure 8-3. You will also need to divide the oval itself into three "Blocks" by installing three additional fiber insulating track pins at circled letters A, B and C (Figure 5-2). You will, however, only be able to operate very short two or three car trains that will fit in the length of that reverse cutoff track across the center of the layout.

The three remote-control uncoupling tracks will allow you to perform the switching moves described in Chapter 15, including how to use automatic couplers. The uncoupling tracks also provide places to unload action cars like log-dump cars, coal-dump cars, milk cars or box cars. I chose to build a mountain inside one of

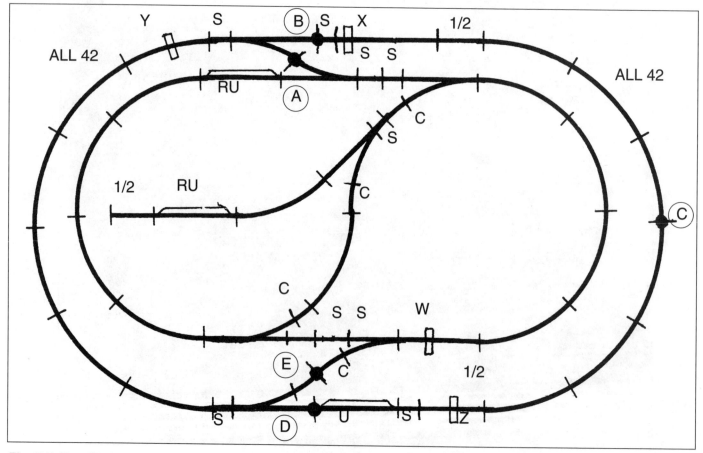

Fig. 5-5. Two-Train Action in a 4 x 6-1/2-foot space.

Fig. 5-6. I opted to use two stub-ended sidings for the "Two-Train Action" layout, rather than reverse loop, to leave more room for scenery.

Fig. 5-7. From floor level, you can see that the mountain breaks-up the scene and helps promote the illusion of "distance" needed for the switching movements described in Chapter 15.

Fig. 5-8. The Lionel log loader and magnetic crane provide action accessories in addition to the operation of two trains explained in Chapter 8 and the switching moves described in Chapter 15.

Fig. 5-9. The "Two-Train Action" layout can become a winter scene by using white felt rather than green felt. The milk unloading platform has been replaced with a coal mine from Chapter 11 to change the industrial theme of the layout.

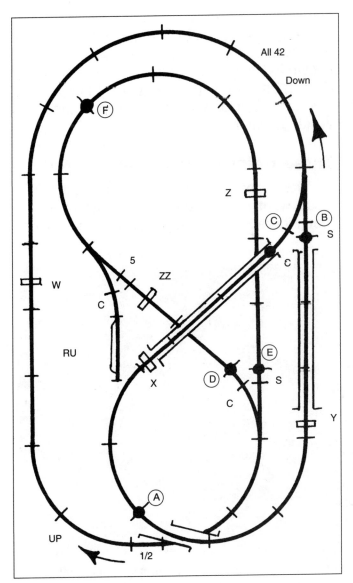

Fig. 5-10. "This Three Trains on Two Levels" layout fits a 4 x 6-1/2-foot space.

the loops and to use the long straight section for a bridge to span a river. The industrial buildings include a Lionel 824K Freight Platform, a Lionel 832K Lumber Shed with a modified Lionel 834K Barrel Shed for an office, and a die-cast gasoline truck that is filled directly from tank cars so the tank truck is the industry.

That single stub-ended siding can, then, be used to "unload" log cars, lumber cars, box cars and tank cars. The passenger station is a Walthers 3307 "Fairfield Station" shortened as described in Chapter 11. The station provides an excuse to operate passenger trains. The Lionel 138 Water Tower will give you a reason to stop steam locomotives so they can take on more water. There's room for a Lionel 164 Log Loader, like that in Figure 5-7, in place of the

passenger station or it could be replaced with a Lionel 32931 Electric Coaling Station or a Lionel (ex-American Flyer) 22997 Oil Drum Loader. You could also install a Lionel milk car unloading ramp, a Lionel 464 Animated Sawmill or even Lionel's extensive 22918 Locomotive Backshop, in place of the freight station.

Two-Train Action in 4 x 6-1/2-feet

The layout in Figure 5-5 is developed in Chapter 4. You can start with a train set oval, add the outer oval and a pair of turnouts for a crossover, then add another pair for a second crossover and a third pair to create either a reverse loop (Figure 5-5) or a pair of industrial sidings (Figure 5-6). If you add a seventh left hand turnout, you can also have the industrial siding shown in Figure 5-5. You could even add an eighth, left hand, turnout to provide a second industrial siding inside the inner oval. The outer oval utilizes 42-inch diameter curves, so you might want to keep your longer cars and locomotives in action on that track.

The train movements necessary to operate two trains on this layout are shown in Chapter 8. That chapter also includes the sequence needed to reverse two trains so you can operate one train on the outer oval and one train on the inner oval and reverse the directions or change their positions without ever touching the trains. The stub-ended sidings also provide places to perform switching moves as described in Chapter 15. This is, in fact, the layout that is used to illustrate those two-train movements and switching movements.

I modified the layout slightly by using just a remote control uncoupling ramp and a half-length straight track section on one industrial siding (Figure 5-7). This was a place to position a Lionel milk car unloading platform, but you could also use it for a bin to accept dumped coal or logs. The shorter siding leaves room for a mountain inside one end of the oval (Figure 5-8). I also utilized part of the outer oval as an industrial track by positioning a Lionel 282 Triple Action Magnetic Crane over the track with a dump bin within reach of the magnet. The two crossovers allow trains on the outer oval to cut through the inner oval to bypass the crane when it might be in use loading a gondola.

The structures are simple to leave as much room for the action accessories and scenery as possible. The station near the log loader is a Walthers 3307 "Fairfield Station" shortened as described in Chapter 11 and the station for the outer loop is an Atlas 6902 Station Platform.

Summer and Winter Scenes

Any of the layouts in this book can be assembled on a scenery base of green or white felt as described in Chapter 10. The white felt provides a more striking contrast to the track and buildings than the green felt that is used for summer scenes (Figure 5-9). This layout has somewhat different structures, including a Lionel 824 K Freight Platform modified to a coal mine with balsa wood legs and braces as shown in Chapter 11, and a second 824K Freight Platform serving as a freight depot beside the log loader. There's also a Lionel 138 Water Tower in one corner.

Three Trains on Two Levels

This is about the most complex layout you would want to consider building in just 4 x 6-1/2-feet (Figure 5-10). I've assembled this layout on

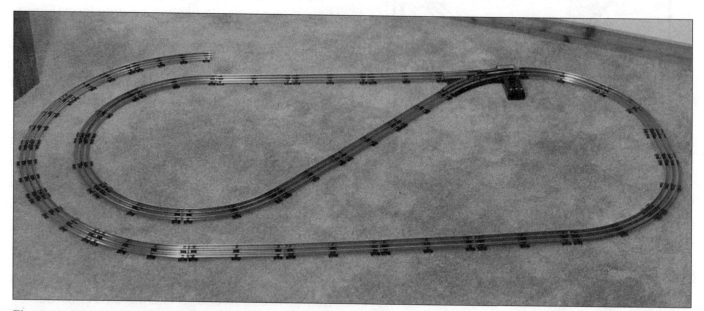

Fig. 5-11. The track construction begins with the lower level reverse loop and the mainline oval that will later lead upgrade.

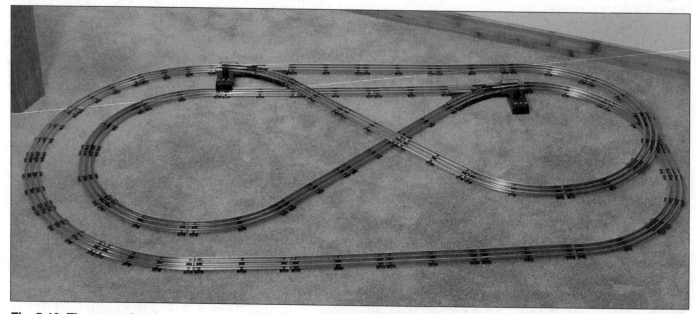

Fig. 5-12. The upper level reverse loop is added to complete the basic track work.

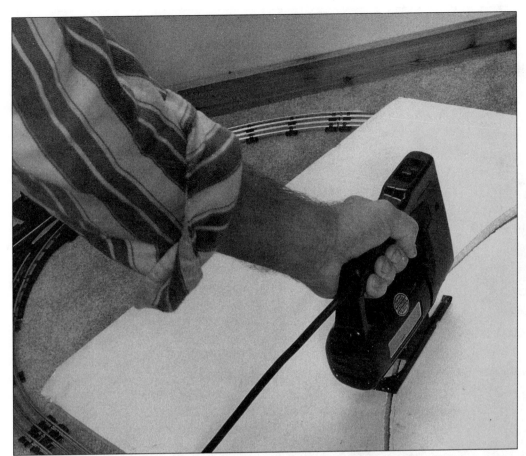

Fig. 5-13. Use an electric saber saw with a fine-tooth blade to cut the lightweight Foamcore board that will support the upper level reverse loop and town.

Fig. 5-14. Two truss bridges were used to carry the legs of the upper level reverse loop over the lower level tracks so the upper level board is a minimal size.

Fig. 5-15. The tabletop for the "Three Trains on Two Levels" layout was built using the lightweight construction techniques in Chapter 9 with Woodland Scenics "Inclines" and "Risers" to support the outer oval's upgrade. The hills, trees, bushes and river construction for this layout are illustrated in Chapter 10.

the lightweight Styrofoam tabletop described in Chapter 9 and utilized Woodland Scenics "Incline" Styrofoam to elevate the tracks above the table-top. An alternate method of elevating the tracks using Lionel's 110 Graduated Trestle Set for this same layout is shown in Chapter 2 (Figure 2-2).

The layout assembly begins with the lower level reverse loops and the mainline oval (Figure 5-11). The upper level reverse loop is then added (Figure 5-12) to complete the mainline trackwork. There's room for a stub-ended industrial siding inside both reverse loops but I opted to include only one on the lower level.

It will be necessary to cut a supporting plat-form for the upper level loop even if you are going to build this layout with temporary scenery on the floor. The lightweight 1/4-inch thick Foamcore board is available at larger art supply stores. This material warps very little and is very lightweight so it's a good choice for a portable layout. Mark the places to cut the board with a pencil and use

an electric saber saw with a very fine-tooth blade to cut the Foamcore (Figure 5-13). You can sub-stitute 1/4-inch plywood if you prefer.

I chose to expose as much of the lower level reverse loop as possible, so only a small size Foamcore board was necessary. I used small cardboard boxes to support the upper level with Lionel's 920-5 Rock Piers to support the forties-era Lionel 317 stamped-metal Trestle and left-over piers from the 110 Graduated Trestle Set to support the Lionel 2122 Extension Bridge.

Lionel no longer offers either of these bridges but the 318 Truss Bridge is the same length. The Graduated Trestle set was used when building the layout on the floor. When the layout was rebuilt on a lightweight 4 x 6-1/2-foot tabletop (as described in Chapter 9), I used the Woodland Scenics "Inclines" to elevate the track from the tabletop to the upper level as shown in Chapter 9.

The 4 x 6-1/2-foot double-loop layout is finished with portable scenery including flexible rock walls as described in Chapter 10. I used only a minimum number of buildings on the layout to leave room for the bridges, the stream and the mountain. The action accessories include Lionel's 138 Water Tower and a Lionel operating milk car. The town on the upper level consists of a Walthers 3307 "Fairfield Station" shortened as described in Chapter 11, a Lionel 832K Lumber Shed and the water tower, with a few die cast metal vehicles and people to add life. The town on the lower loop consists of just an Atlas 6902 Station Platform and the Lionel milk car unloading platform.

This layout is designed to be operated loop-to-loop with trains circulating between the town on the upper level and the town on the lower level. Three trains can be operated on this layout if the track is divided into electrically-isolated "Blocks" at the circled letters A, B, C, D, E and F and with Lockons at W, X, Y, Z and ZZ and wired as described in Chapter 8. Chapter 8 also describes the operating sequence to operate three trains, with one running on the mainline while the other two are held in one of the two blocks on the upper reverse loop and the two blocks on the lower reverse loop.

Notes On Portable Layouts

Chapter 6

Track

The O and O-27 toy trains are designed to operate on track with three rails. The third rail in the center of the track is used to allow the electrical current to return to the transformer, after it is fed to the trains through either of the outer two rails. This system avoids the short circuits that can occur when the track is arranged into a reverse loop or a wye. S scale toy trains, like HO and N scale model railroads, use two-rail track.

If the third center rail seems too toy-like, you can buy K-Line and MTH track with a blackened center rail that makes it much less obvious. For most, the third rail is part of the character of toy trains, along with oversize wheel flanges and giant couplers.

Standard O Scale Toy Train Track

Both Lionel and K-Line have two complete series of track sections for "O-27" and another compete set of track sections for "O" (Figure 6-1). Since the train sets are usually furnished

with O-27 track, you probably have some. The O track has slightly larger rails and ties and is far more rugged than O-27. I sold all my O-27 track and purchased O track because I prefer to play with my trains—whoops, operate my model railroad—on the floor, and the O track seems to hold together more firmly so it provides fewer problems with derailments caused by the track sections working apart or by twisting at the joints. Any of these toy trains will operate just as well on O-27 as on O track. Some of the larger and most expensive locomotives, will, however, derail on the tight curves of standard O-27 switches (turnouts). These locomotives will also derail on the standard O turnouts, which have a diameter through the curve of 31 inches. Some larger locomotives and longer cars require a minimum 42-inch diameter turnout and some even a 72-inch diameter turnout. The turnouts with a 42-inch diameter curved route are available from both Lionel and K-Line in O-27 and K-Line has 42-inch diameter turnouts in O. Lionel

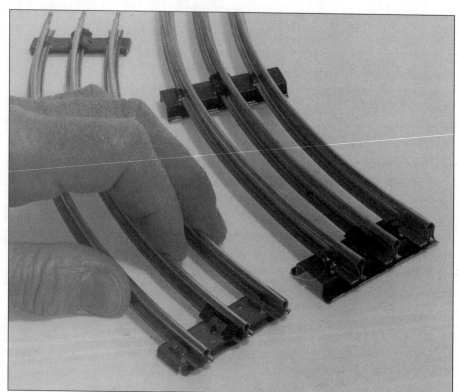

Fig. 6-1.The O-27 track (left) is lighter with smaller rails and ties than the O scale track.

Figure 6-2. The O scale trains will operate on any of these brands of track (top to bottom): GarGraves. K-Line Super "K", Atlas, MTH Real Trax and Lionel O scale track.

also offers turnouts with a 72-inch diameter curved route in O.

All of the track plans in this book use the O scale turnouts with 31-inch diameter curves through the curved route. You can substitute O-27 turnouts if you replace the 31-inch diameter curves with the 27-inch diameter curves. Some of the plans combine 31-inch and 42-inch diameter curves, but the turnouts are all 31-inch diameter. Also, some of the track plans are designed to be built with Lionel's O scale 031R and 031L turnouts that have a separate short piece of curved track and a short (about 2-inches long) piece of straight track. These turnouts make it easier to build compact layouts because parallel tracks can be placed closer together.

GarGraves has also been producing track for Lionel and other three-rail toy trains since the forties. The GarGraves track, like the K-Line "Super K" track, Atlas track and MTH Real Trax track (with built-in ballast) have ties spaced proportionally closer-together than most toy train track (Figure 6-2). The ties, and the rails are still many-times larger than accurate scale models but the effect is realistic enough. These brands also offer their track with the third rail blackened

so it not as obvious as conventional toy train three-rail track.

The MTH Real Trax that has built-in plastic ballast with smaller ties and a blackened center rail. The Real Trax is offered in standard O scale 31-inch curves, straights, turnouts and 90-degree crossings as well as 72-inch diameter curves and 72-inch diameter turnouts. The joints at the end of Real Trax do not seem to me to be as strong as the steel rail and steel pins of standard Lionel or K-Line track, but the Real Trax will certainly work well on any tabletop layout.

Atlas offers O scale toy train track with plastic ties and a blackened center rail that they call the "21st Century Track© System". The plastic ties are nearly scale size and the center rail is blackened, but there is no simulated ballast. Atlas offers adapters to connect their track to Lionel or K-Line track but not all the Atlas track sections match the size of Lionel's, K-Line's or MTH's track.

GarGraves track has a choice of plastic or wooden ties and is available in flexible track sections so you can form your own curves. The sectional track is offered in 31, 42, 54, 63, 72, 89, 89, 96, 106 and 138-inch diameter curves. It is also offered with wooden ties and the track with wooden ties is available with turnouts with 42-inch or 100-inch diameter curved routes. You must, however, provide your own means of remote control for the GarGraves turnouts. NJ International and others make devices to actuate the moving switch points of these turnouts. These are called switch machines and they are small electronic solenoids to be actuated by toggle switches mounted on a control panel. The GarGraves turnouts do not, then, lend themselves to use on portable toy train layout. They are best used on tabletops where you attach both the turnout and the switch machine to the table with screws.

Assembling Track Sections

The O scale toy train track is rugged steel but it takes some muscle to push the track sections together. I'd recommend wearing old leather gloves or gardening gloves if you are assembling more than a dozen pieces of track. New track sections often have small burrs inside the open ends of the steel rails that can make it difficult to press two sections together. If you have difficulty, try using just one track pin from a second track sections to open up the end of the rail (Figure 6-3). If the rail end has accidentally been smashed, you can enlarge it

by wiggling the tip of an awl or ice pick into the open end (Figure 6-4).

After many repeated assembly and disassembly operations, the ends of the rail can be enlarged so the track joints are not tight. Use a pair of pliers to squeeze the inside of each rail (Figure 6-5), then the outside of each rail (Figure 6-6) tightly around the track pins. I would recommend you tighten each rail, on both sections of track and on every section on the layout. It's the type of preventative maintenance that can help to eliminate mysterious stalled trains and derailments.

The operations of the trains can cause track joints to work loose even after they are tightened with this process, so it's a good idea to look closely at each and every track joint every week or so, especially if the layout is being operated on the floor.

Lionel makes Track Clips (O27-C for O-27 track and C-1 for O scale track) that can be used to hold most of the track sections together. The clips snap onto the ends of the ties of one track section and clip over the bottom of the tie on the adjacent track section (Figure 6-7). If you are mounting the track on a plywood tabletop, you can use a number 2 x 3/4-inch round-head or fillister-head screws. Atlas has them (number 6094) in packages of 48 if you cannot locate them in a hardware

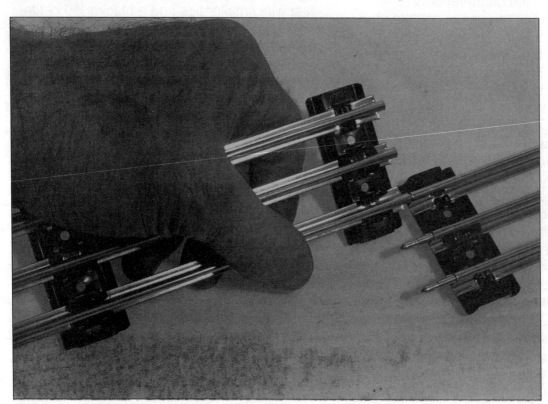

Fig. 6-3. Use a the track pin in a second section of track to clean the inside of the rails on new track sections.

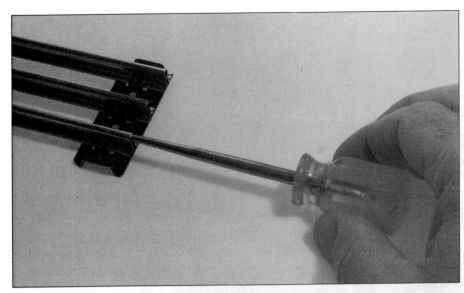

Fig. 6-4. Use an awl or an ice pick to expand the inside of the rails if they have been squeezed too tightly.

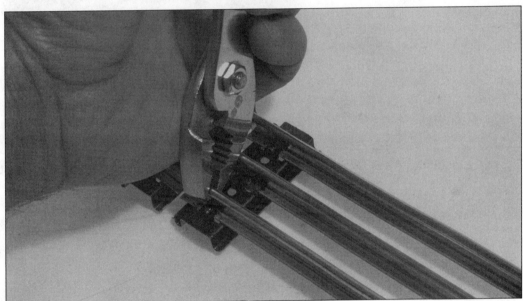

Fig. 6-5. To be sure each joint between track sections is tight, use pliers to squeeze inside the rails.

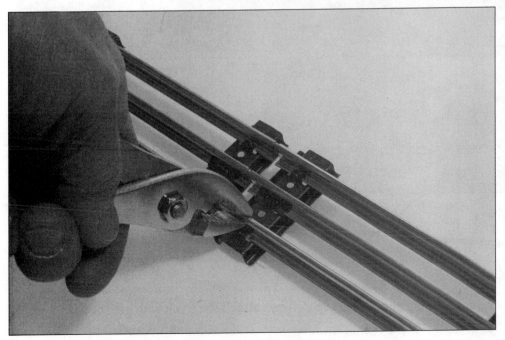

Fig. 6-6. Also squeeze the outside of each rail at each track joint to be sure the joints are tight.

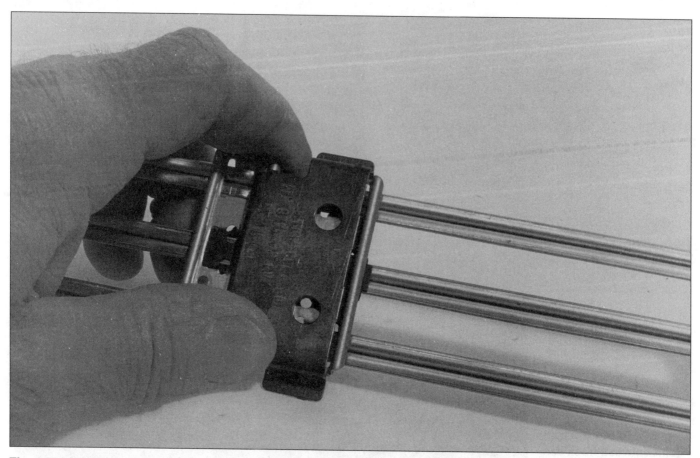

Fig. 6-7. Lionel has Track Clips for both O and O-27 track to clamp the track sections together.

Fig. 6-8. If you are mounting the layout on a plywood table top you can attach the track with an Atlas 6094 wood screw inserted through one of the holes in the tie.

store. Use an ice pick or awl to start the hole for the screw, then install the screw with a screwdriver. You'll only need one screw every three or four track sections (Figure 6-8).

Interchanging O and O-27 Track

The standard curve for O-27 track has a 27-inch diameter, as compared to the 31-inch diameter of O track. Also, the standard O-27 straight track section is just 8-3/4-inches long while the O scale straight track is 10-inches long. The O-27 turnouts and crossings are also proportionally shorter than their O scale counterparts. If you alternate between O and O-27 track on the same layout, you may have difficulty getting the track sections to align correctly and fit together snugly. If you are going to use both sizes of track, try to use complete circles or ovals of a single size.

The O-27 track is fine if you are willing to attach it to a permanent plywood tabletop with screws. I feel, however, that it just not tough enough for repeated use and reuse in building and rebuilding layouts on the floor. You can mate O-27 track to O track by squeezing the O scale track tighter around the O-27 track pins and by using an awl or an ice pick to slightly enlarge the openings in the O-27 track's rails so they will accept the O scale track pins.

Interchanging Different Brands of Track

Most of the three-rail track made by Lionel and K-Line is interchangeable in both size and the interface at the ends. GarGraves track will also interface or join Lionel or MTH track, but the track section sizes may differ. MTH's Rite Trax has the same sizes of sections as Lionel and K-Line but the interface or joining ends are different. The three rail track made by MTH and Atlas, however, has built-in ballast and a different system of joining the ends of the track sections. Both MTH and Atlas offer adapters to mate their track to Lionel's or K-Line's.

Switches and Turnouts

The word "turnout" is used, here, to describe that piece of track that allows the trains to travel over one of two diverging routes. It is usually called a "switch" in toy train catalogs, but the word switch is also used to describe on-off levers that turn the power on and off in a room or on a portion of a toy train layout. In this book, I'll try to use the word turnout whenever I'm describing a piece of track and switch when describing an electric devise.

Turnouts are available with either manual operation at the turnout or remote control operation. The track itself is virtually identical for the two types, but the manual turnouts have a slid-

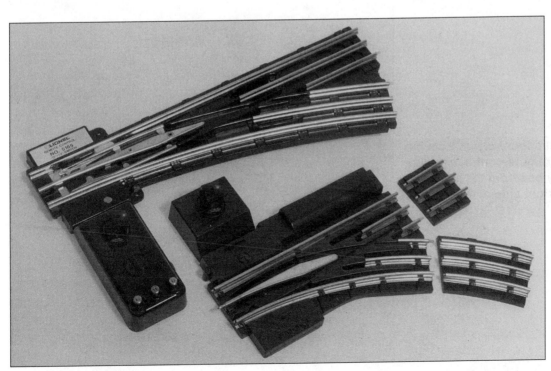

Figure 6-9. Lionel's 0-72 turnout (left) with a 72-inch diameter curved route and the 031R turnout with a 31-inch diameter curved route and its separate short straight and short curved track sections.

ing lever that you must push to move the turn-out points to change the train's path through the turnout. Remote control turnouts are actuated electronically using a lever that can be mounted on a control panel or on the edge of the layout. The remote control adds a bit to the feeling of "magic" because the turnouts' points move without your being near them and the train automatically takes a different path. The O scale Lionel turnouts are available with either 31-inch diam-eter curved routes or 72-inch diameter curved routes, both with only remote control operation (Figure 6-9). K-Line offers O scale turnouts in both manual and remote control with 42-inch diameter curved routes. Atlas offers turnouts with 56-inch (Figure 6-10) and 72-inch diameter curved routes but adapter pins are needed to connect this track with Lionel or K-Line track.

The control boxes on Lionel's O-27 and O scale turnouts and on the MTH turnouts can be

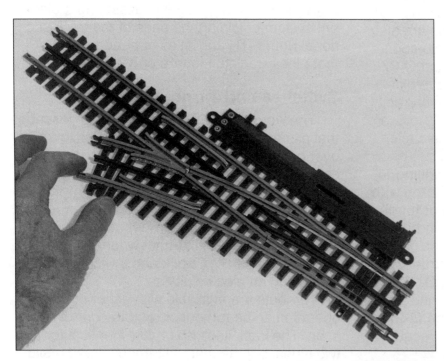

Fig. 6-10. A turnout with a 54-inch radius curved route from the Atlas "21st Century Track System."

Fig. 6-11. Remove the four screws from the bottom of the Lionel remote-control turnouts to move the control box from the left to the right side of the turnout.

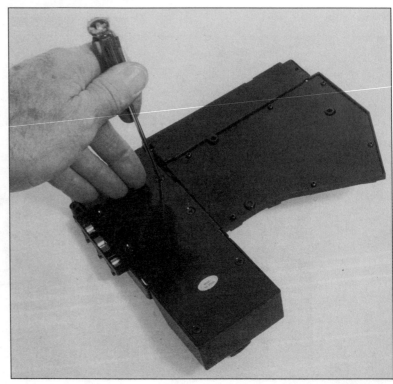

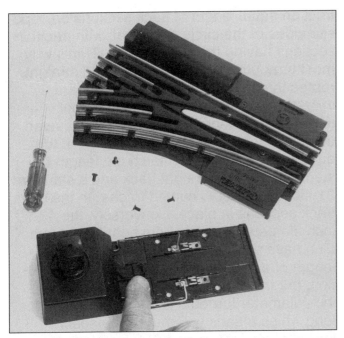

Fig. 6-12. Be sure this oval loop engages the moving pin beneath the turnout when you replace the control box on the Lionel remote-control turnouts.

moved from the right to the left side of the turnout to allow the turnouts to be located closer to adjacent tracks or to move them from the outside edge of he layout to the inside. To remove the mechanism from the Lionel turnouts, remove the four mounting screws (Figure 6-11). When the turnout mechanism is reassembled, be certain the small peg that actuates the moving switch points engages the oval loop in the mechanism (Figure 6-12). Try working the manual mecha-

nism as you assemble the turnout control to be sure the points are operating correctly.

If you are using GarGraves track and turnouts, you must provide your own system of remote control operation. NJ International and others make electronic "switch machines" that use a solenoid to move a lever to push or pull the moving points of the turnout. These switch machines can be mounted beside the turnout. You will also need a momentary-contact SPDT toggle switch from an electronics hobby store or you can use the Atlas 56 Switch Control Box to control up to four turnouts. These types of turnouts and their switch machines are designed for use on permanent layouts like Ralph Johnson's tabletop empire (Figure 6-13).

The Geometry of Toy Train Track

The standard O-27 and O scale curves are 27-inch and 31-inch diameter. It takes just four of these small curves to make a complete circle, so each curve makes up 90-degrees of a full circle. Half-length curves are available and these curves are 45-degrees of a full circle (it would take 8 half-length curves to make a full circle). That same geometry is used with the O scale 54-inch diameter and 72-inch diameter curved track sections from both Lionel and K-Line. These larger-diameter curved track sections are 22-1/2-degrees of a circle so it takes 16 sections of 54-inch or 72-inch diameter curved track sections to make a full circle. The

Fig. 6-13. Ralph Johnson uses NJ International switch machines (the round devices beside each turnout) to provide remote-control operation for his GarGraves turnouts.

42-inch diameter curves from Lionel and K-Line are based on 30-degree segments of a circle.

A rule: if you start a curve with 30-degree track sections always complete that curve through 90-degrees or 180-degrees before switching to curved track sections using 45-degree sections of a curve. If you mix 45-degree and 30-degree curves, you'll almost always end up with misaligned jogs in the curve that can derail trains because, instead of 90-degree or 180-degree curves, you'll produce something odd like 75-degrees (a 30-degree plus a 45-degree curve) that's not quite 90-degrees and there's no way to get a 15-degree curve (to add to that odd 75-degree curve you just made to bring it around to a full 90-degrees) without cutting a section of track. If you are building more-or-less permanent layout and you need that odd 15-degree curve (or whatever length piece of track), go ahead and use a vise and a hacksaw and cut the track to fit.

To maintain the geometry and, hence, the alignment of the track, you must add or sub-tract an equal length of track sections on opposite sides of the circle of or oval. with track sections having the same length. That's why most turnouts have both curved and straight routes that match the length of standard curved or straight track sections. Lionel includes short lengths of straight and curved track with their O scale 031R and 031L turnouts so the turnout will match the length of standard 10-inch straight track and a standard 31-inch diameter O curved track with the extra track sections in place. Conversely, the 42-inch diameter turnouts from both Lionel and K-Line have a curved path that matches the length of a standard 42-inch curve track section, but the straight route through these 42-inch diameter turnouts is about 14 3/8-inches long which means you must cut a special length of straight track 4 3/-8-inch long to add to a standard straight track section when you replace that section of track on the opposite side of the oval.

There are some suggestions in Chapter 2 on how to correct misaligned track for a large

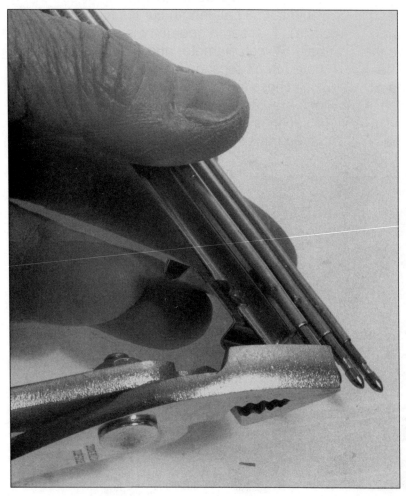

Fig. 6-14. Grip the track pins with pliers and pivot the pliers against the bottom of the rail to work the track pins free.

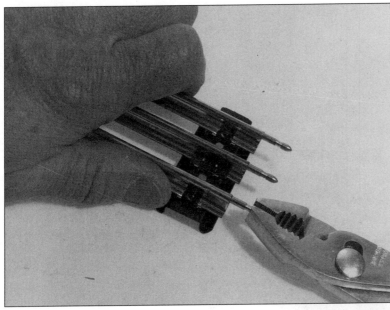

Fig. 6-15. Use pliers to grip the track pin as you push it firmly into the end of the rail.

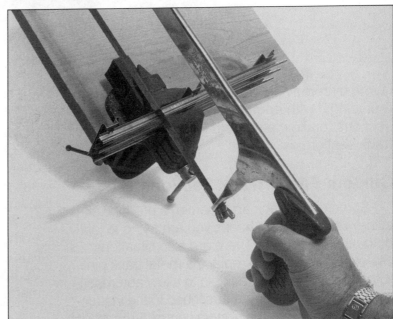

Fig. 6-16. To make custom-fitted track sections, grip the track in a vise while you gently saw through the rails with a hacksaw.

Fig. 6-17. Use a file to smooth any burrs left from sawing the rails.

Fig. 6-18. Lionel's 261N track bumper(foreground) and out-of-production 1025 track bumper.

layout by removing one size of curved track and replacing it with another and/or with straight sections to allow a smooth joint between every track section.

Custom-Fitted Track Sections

Some of the track arrangements produce situations where the two tracks you are trying to join both have track pins. There are also situations where you will want to replace a metal track pin with a fiber insulated track pin to allow automatic operation of turnouts (as described in the instructions furnished with the remote control turnouts) or to allow operation of two trains as described in Chapter 8. Use pliers to remove track pins. Grip the track pin and use the bottom of the rail as a fulcrum or pivot point to pull the pin out (Figure 6-14). Wiggle it lose about 1/16-inch at a time. To replace a track pin, use pliers to push it straight into the track section (Figure 6-15). Be sure to tighten the rail (Figures 6-5 and 6-6) whenever you have removed or replaced a track pin.

For some layouts, it may be necessary to cut special length of track. Lionel, K-Line and MTH offer half-length straight track sections and half-length curves, but they are not always the exact length needed. To cut the track, hold it in a vise while you saw gently through the rails with a hacksaw (Figure 6-16). Use a medium-

cut file to smooth the cut ends and an awl or ice pick to remove any burrs from inside the rails (Figure 6-17).

One place where you might want to use a custom-fitted track section would be on a stub-ended siding. Sometimes, these sidings end inside a curve and with just a few more inches of track, you could squeeze another car onto the siding. Lionel offers inexpensive 261N Track Bumpers (Figure 6-18) and 261 Illuminated Bumpers or you may find some of the older cast metal 1025 Illuminated Bumpers at a swap meet.

American Flyer Track Plans

American Flyer S scale trains operate on two-rail track but the rails are spaced closer together than with Lionel, MTH, K-Line and the other O scale toy train tracks. Lionel owns and produces American Flyer locomotives, cars and accessories, but they have not produced track. The only genuine American Flyer track has not be produced for about 40 years. K-Line has straight and 54-inch diameter curved track sections (Figure 6-19) that are virtually identical to the original American Flyer track, but K-Line has not produced S scale turnouts. You can find original American Flyer turnouts at some swap meets.

American Flyer's track system is based on 30-degree segments of a circle for 38, 48 and

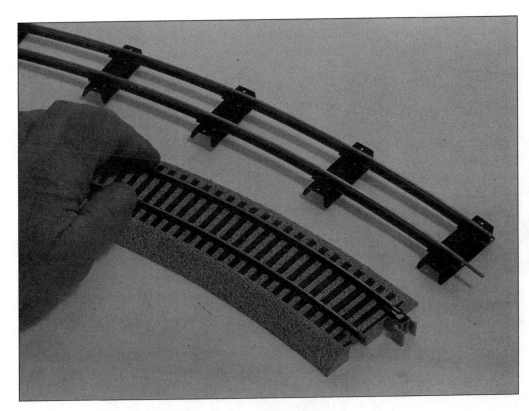

Fig. 6-19. S Helper Services track with built-in ballast is designed for use with American Flyer S scale trains. The K-Line track (top) is similar to original American Flyer track.

58-inch diameter curves. The straight track sections are 10-inches and 15-inches. S Helper Services produces the S-Trax System with correct-scale ties and built-in plastic roadbed that effectively simulates loose ballast. The track sections match the geometry of American Flyer's track and the length of the track sections. S Helper Service also has S-Trax turnouts to match the geometry of American Flyer turnouts. The turnouts allow track spacing of 5-inches center-to-center for passing sidings and the diameter of the curved tracks allow you to maintain that spacing through the curves. American Models also has sectional track and turnouts in S scale.

Lionel's and K-Line's O scale 42-inch diameter curves are based on the 30-degree geometry so plans that use O scale 42-inch diameter curves can often be used for layouts made with American Flyer or S Helper Service track sections. S scale track plans are available from S Helper Service.

Ballast, Another Name for Grit

Real railroads use crushed rock or stone to anchor the wooden ties. There are several brands of O scale ballast including Life-Like, Woodland Scenics and Rick Johnson, that can be used if you want to simulate that effect on your toy train layout. Frankly, I do not recommend using ballast unless you are building a permanent tabletop model railroad with the track glued firmly in place. Ballast really is another name for grit when it is reduced to the size of O scale trains. That grit can easily find its way into the gears or motor to create extensive damage. If you can cement the loose ballast firmly in place, you can minimize the problem. The techniques for applying ballast are described in Chapter 10.

There are a couple of alternatives to loose ballast. First, consider if it is the ballast you want or just more ties. K-Line, Atlas, and Gar Graves offer track with more and smaller ties that more closely match the real thing. The extra ties are often enough to capture the effect you desire. Another alternative is to paint the layout beneath the track with a dark grey to simulate the color of ballast, avoiding the loose texture. The MTH Rite Trax has built-in ballast.

Track Maintenance

Dirt, dust and lint are the primary causes of trouble with track. Dirty track can make locomotives run erratically or stall completely. It's wise to cover the layout between operating sessions. Use a large sheet of clear plastic or an old bed sheet. Dust the cars, locomotives and the track every week or so with a soft one-inch wide paint brush.

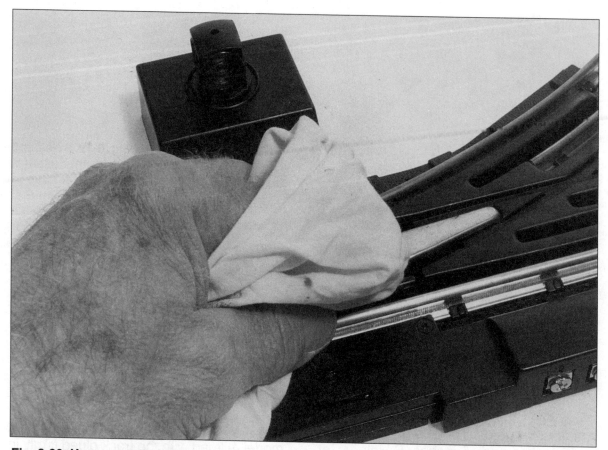

Fig. 6-20. Use a rag, dipped in track cleaning fluid, to clean the rails and turnouts.

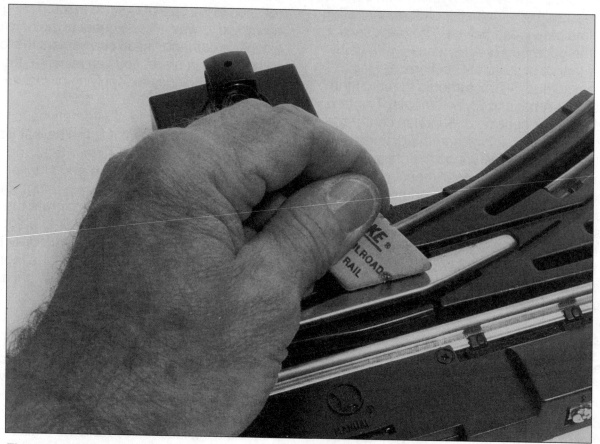

Fig. 6-21. Use a track cleaning eraser to scrub the tops of the rails clean.

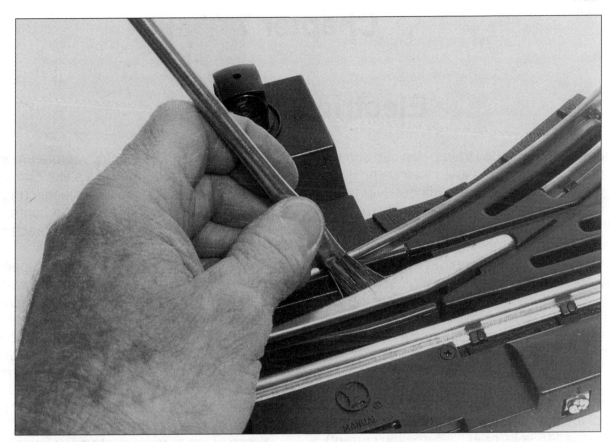

Fig. 6-22. Sweep dust and debris from the turnouts and crossings with a stiff-bristle brush.

Use a lint-free rag, wetted slightly with Lionel, Atlas or Life-Like Track Cleaning Fluid, to clean the track after every tenth operating session (Figure 6-20). If the track is particularly dirty, use one of the track cleaning erasers like Life-Like's or a Bright Boy to scrub the rails clean. Pay particular attention to the center contact areas of the turnouts (Figure 6-21). Do not ever clean track with sandpaper or steel wool. The sandpaper will make permanent scratches that will attract dirt more quickly. The small fibers from steel wool can be attracted by the motor magnets inside the locomotives to cause short circuits that can ruin the motor.

Use the paint brush to clean the switches thoroughly, especially the areas where the moving switch points pivot (Figure 6-22). Apply a single drop of oil to the pivot about once a year and carefully wipe away any excess. Too much oil or grease can create trouble because it attracts dust and lint. The toy train turnouts are assembled with small screws. You can remove those screws to inspect the mechanism to be certain it is functioning correctly.

Track Troubleshooting

Most of the faults blamed on track are the fault of the locomotives or rolling stock. Derailments are most often caused by the train hitting a trackside object. In some cases, however, the track will work loose from the rocking action of the train. If the rails do not grip the track pins tightly enough, use common pliers to squeeze one side of the rail, then the opposite side, to snug the vertical portions of the rail against the track pin as illustrated earlier in this chapter. To check for track misalignment, lay your head on the track so you can look down the tops of the rails. Any sudden bumps or dips will be visible and can be corrected.

Sometimes, the track itself can cause a short circuit if the black fiber insulation pads have been damaged by bending the track on disassembly. It is rare, but if all the troubleshooting checks listed in Chapter 7 on short circuits and Chapter 13 on locomotives fails to solve the problem, it might be a piece of track with a broken black fiber insulator.

Chapter 7

Electrical Wiring

There's a magic to toy trains. You can control their speed, direction, and even their path through complicated trackage without ever touching the train. It's done by electricity running from the power pack through the rails, to the motor inside the locomotive. Some of the more expensive power packs even have hand-held remote-control units so you can walk around the room beside your train while you operate the speed controls, and in some cases, even control the whistle, horn, bell, and other sounds or operate turnouts to change the train's route.

How Electric Toy Trains Operate

Most toy train sets include a power pack that reduces the 115 volts of AC (alternating current) to a harmless 18-volts. The electric power reaches the locomotives through the two outer rails, and is returned through the center or third rail or visa-versa. The electric motors are sometimes mounted inside the trucks like Lionel's and K-Line's lower-priced FA1 diesels (Figure 7-1). The power pack allows you to control how much electricity or power is able to reach the locomotive to control its speed.

These power packs also include a speed control knob or throttle that controls the speed of the train and a direction control button. With most toy trains, the reversing sequence requires that the reverse button be pushed once to stop the train, then pushed again to reverse its direction. The sequence is repeated to change the train's direction back to forward. Toy trains are fitted with an electronic devise called an "E unit" that is activated by the direction control button.

Some of the more expensive toy trains and most scale model HO, N, S and O scale trains have motors that operate with 12 volts of direct current. These models require a different type of

Fig. 7-1. The Lionel O-27 Alco FA1 diesel (bottom) and the K-Line O-27 version of the same locomotive both have the motors mounted inside the trucks.

power pack that will both reduce the 115 volts of AC current to 12 volts and rectify that current from AC to DC. With these power packs, a simple reverse switch is used to change direction. It is still a good idea, however, to stop the train by reducing the speed to zero before changing direction to avoid unnecessary wear on the gears and motor.

Some manufacturers, like Atlas, Weaver and S Helper Service, offer their locomotives wired in your choice of 12 volts DC or 18 volts AC. Be sure to buy the type of locomotive to match the power pack you are using with that locomotive.

Selecting a Power Pack

The power pack that is furnished with the train set is just large enough to handle the requirements of the locomotive that came with that train set. The more expensive locomotives usually require more power than the train set power packs can provide, so you will probably have to purchase a more powerful power pack to control that more expensive locomotive. Some of the power packs also include a button to activate the horn or whistle if the locomotive is equipped with such a sound-generating devise (Figure 7-2).

The amount of electrical current the locomotives' motors require is measured in watts. Typically, a single motor will require about 60 watts, while two motors or a large single motor will require over 100 watts. In addition, light bulbs require 3 or 4 watts each and a whistle or smoke generating electronic devise may require 25 watts. If you are planning on running two locomotives at the same time, using one power pack, you will have to add the power requirements of both locomotives together. Some of the transformers have enough power for two trains, others, like Lionel's new ZW, allow you to add as many transformers as you feel are necessary to provide the power for your trains (Figure 7-3). MRC's Dual Power 027 provides 270 watts and Lionel's PH-1 PowerHouse transformer generates 135 watts, their PowerHouse 190 generates 190 watts and you can use two or more of them if you need the power. The Z-4000 transformer from MTH has 400 watts of power and controls for two trains.

You will also need additional power for action accessories. A motorized log-loader, for instance, can draw as much as 25 watts. It's best to connect all the action accessories directly to a

Fig. 7-2. One of the transformer sets used in Lionel train sets includes a separate box with the speed, reversing and horn controls that plugs into the transformer. The transformer and speed control are in one box in the K-Line train set transformer.

Fig. 7-3. The new version of
the Lionel ZW transformer
has speed, directional and
sound control for two locomotives. (Photo courtesy
Lionel LLC)

Fig. 7-4. The
Lionel Lockon is
nearly identical
to those used by
K-Line. It simply
clips to the
edges of the
rails, but it fits
best on straight
track sections.

separate power pack, including items like crossing gates, automatic gatemen and sound-generating accessories as well as action accessories like log loaders, coal loaders, magnetic cranes, locomotive back shop and lumber mills. Power packs are labeled with the amount of adjustable or variable AC current they will deliver.

Wiring Your Layout

Use stranded number 16 gauge wire for most toy train layouts. This wire is large enough so there should be minimal current loss even over 15-foot runs of wire. Connect the power pack to the track using the Lockons supplied with most train sets and available separately. Install a Lockon and wire to the power pack for about every 40-feet of track, so you are not relying entirely upon the rails and the rail-connecting pins to carry the current to the remoter parts of the layout (Figure 7-4). Use wire large enough to carry the necessary current. For large locomotives and distances of over 5 feet, I'd suggest 14 or 16 gauge insulated wire. For shorter distances, you can use the 20 gauge wire like that supplied with most train sets.

Use diagonal cutters to cut the wire to length. Use the diagonal cutters, too, to strip the insulation from the wire (Figure 7-5). Remove about 3/8-inch of the insulation. Squeeze the wire gently in the jaws of the diagonal cutters so you break

through the insulation but not the wire. Rotate the wire 90-degrees and take another gentle bite with the cutters. You should then be able to pull the insulation away from the wire by gently scraping the wire through the diagonal cutters. If you are going to install the wire on a screw-type or nut-type terminal, wrap the bare end of the wire around a screwdriver handle (Figure 7-6). Place the wire around the terminal with the open end in a clockwise direction so tightening the screw or the nut or screw pulls the wire on around the terminal (Figure 7-7).

You may also want to purchase some on-off toggle switches to provide places to park trains while you operate other trains as described in Chapter 8. Some of the action accessories also require push-buttons to activate, for example, a log-loader or a diesel horn. And you may want to use remote-control turnouts which have their own actuating boxes or levers.

Remote Control Turnouts

Remote control turnouts are usually powered from the track. Some of the turnouts, like Lionel's O scale turnouts, have a separate wire connection so you can provide power for the turnouts from your "accessory" power pack. By providing outside power, you eliminate the chance that the train will slow down every time you use a remote control turnout (Figure 7-8).

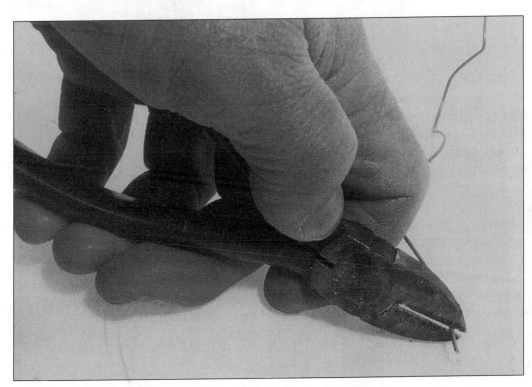

Fig. 7-5. Use diagonal cutters to strip the insulation from wires.

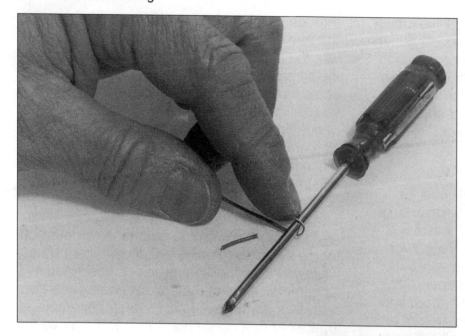

Fig. 7-6. Wrap the bare end of the wire around a screwdriver blade to form a loop.

Fig. 7-7. Wrap the wire loop around the terminal post in a counterclockwise direction so the nut or screw tightens the wire around the terminal.

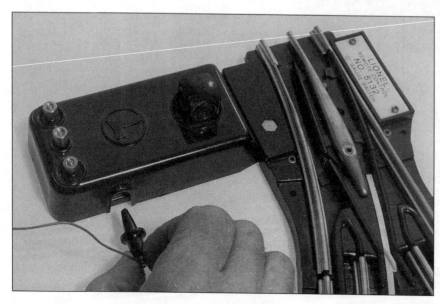

Fig. 7-8. The Lionel remote-control turn-outs, including the older versions, have a socket or a terminal so that the electrical current to actuate the turnout can be routed directly from the transformer rather than from the track.

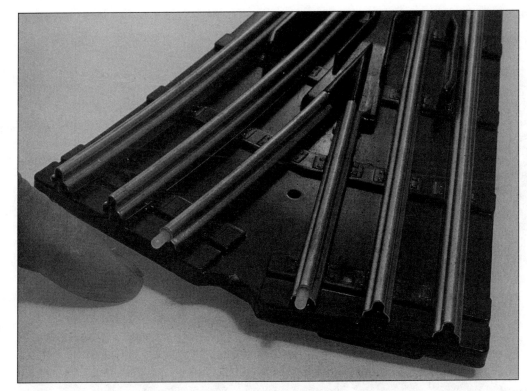

Fig. 7-9. The Lionel remote-control turnouts have a non-derailing feature that can be activated by installing fiber insulating pins on the inside rails of the two diverging tracks.

Lionel's remote control turnouts offer a non-derailing feature. If you install two fiber or plastic insulated track-connecting pins, one each on the inside of the two diverging tracks, trains entering the turnout through either of those diverging routes will automatically trigger a mechanism that moves the turnout's points to match the train's route (Figure 7-9). Also, most of these turnouts can be wired so the trains entering from the single-track side of the turnout automatically throw the points in a predetermined direction. Wiring diagrams are included with the turnouts to show you how to activate this feature.

Control Tower Panels

You can locate the controls for the turnouts and the on-off toggle switches for the train-holding tracks near those tracks or you can group all the controls at a central control pane (Figure 7-10). Real railroads use both systems. The on-off switches are available at larger hardware stores and there are mounting holes in the ceramic base so they can be attached to the face of he layout or to a control panel. The switches are larger enough, however, that they simply rest on the layout table or on the floor if you are building a portable layout.

If you have a fairly complex layout, you may even want to make a board with a schematic of

Fig. 7-10. The Lionel remote-control turnouts include these levers (from the forties, left; and the current style) to be mounted on the edge of the layout table or on a control panel.

the track plan applied to the face of the board with 1/8-inch wide white drafting tape. The on-off switches that turn power on and off for the holding tracks or Blocks (described in Chapter 8) can be attached directly to the schematic control panel board. The turnout control levers can also be mounted directly to this control panel at the appropriate locations for each turnout (Figure 7-11).

Fig. 7-11. Ralph Johnson operates his layout from this control panel with a schematic diagram of the tracks and a bank of Lionel turnout-control levers.

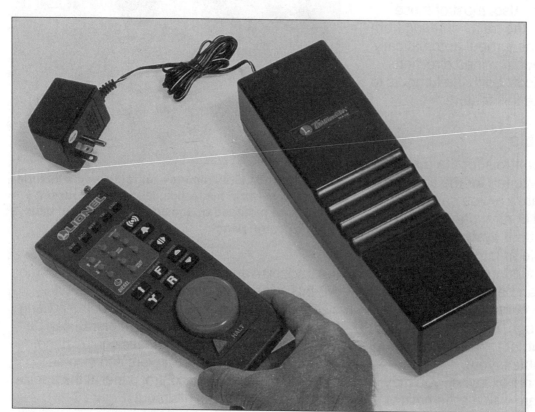

Fig. 7-12. The Lionel TrainMaster system with a CAB-1 hand-held remote control.

Walk-Around Control

Walk-around control allows you to get closer to the trains so you can literally walk along beside them. It's far more exciting to be close to the trains than to just sit beside the throttle controls of a power pack. Lionel provides walk-around control with the CAB-1 Remote throttle in their TrainMaster™ system (Figure 7-12). You can use the CAB-1 Remote control unit with the Lionel Power Master Distribution Center (and a source of AC power like a Lionel PowerHouse transformer) to provide walk-around control for conventional toy train locomotives (as well as locomotives equipped with Lionel's TrainMaster Command Control—Figure 7-13). This system provides walk-around control with no wire connections between the CAB-1 control and the power source. You can even add the Lionel SC-1 Switch and Accessory controller to actuate turnouts or action accessories from the buttons on the CAB-1 keypad. The CAB-1 can also provide adjustable starting and stopping momentum, horn, bell, whistle and sound-actuation. Note that this system only allows one locomotive to be operated at a time, however, unless the second locomotive is on a separate track system with a second power pack as described in Chapter 8.

The MRC Dual Power 027 is a 270-watt transformer with two walk-around controls on the electrical cables (Figure 7-14). This power pack is just a box with two sockets on the side to accept the plugs from two of MRC's Dual Power walk-around 027 hand-held controllers. These controllers have a knob to control the speed and a key pad to actuate reversing, horn and other locomotive sounds. There are two sockets and 270 watts of AC power, so two of the tethered hand-held walk-around throttle scan be used at once.

A more expensive alternative is to use Lionel's TrainMaster Command Control locomotives and walk-around CAB1 system or the model railroad DC Command Control systems with radio control throttles like Digitrax. Both systems are described in Chapter 8.

Real Railroad Sound

Some of the more expensive Lionel, MTH, K-Line, Williams and Third Rail locomotives are

Fig. 7-13. The Lionel TrainMaster locomotives with Command Control have electronic circuits that allow the operation of up to 99 locomotives on the same track.

Fig. 7-14. The MRC Dual Power 027 transformer produces 270 watts of power and includes two walk-around train controllers on tethered cables. The cables are long enough so the transformer can be placed on the floor, rather than on the layout.

equipped with sound effects that digitally reproduce diesel locomotive growl, steam locomotive chuffs, bells, whistles and horns. These sounds can be activated by remote control and their volume raised or lowered. Sound units that can be fitted to diesel locomotives or in steam locomotive tenders are also available from QSI Industries and Dallee Electronics. QSI offers its own control box to with three controls for sound, bell and horn (or whistle). QSI also has a conversion system so MTH, Williams and Third Rail locomotives can be have the sound systems activated by Lionel's Train Master CAB-1 remote control walk-around unit.

The simplest way to fit sound effects to "quiet" locomotives is to purchase a sound-equipped car. Lionel offers a Railsounds-equipped box car with either steam or diesel sounds. MTH offers Proto-Sound units that can be installed in almost any car. You can couple these sound-equipped cars behind the locomotive and activate the sounds anywhere on the track. The proximity to the locomotive is usually enough to make the sounds seem to emanate from the locomotive rather than the car.

An alternate source of sound is to purchase one of the accessories like Lionel's Diesel Horn Shed or Steam Whistle Sound Shed. These

Fig. 7-15. Many of the O-27 toy train cars and locomotives have a dummy (non-operating) coupler (right) that will couple with the operating knuckle couplers (left).

accessories contain a sound unit that is activated by a remote control button. In the real world, locomotives usually only blow their horns or toot their whistles at highway crossings or when entering yards so awakening the sound from a specific site is realistic.

Remote-Control Uncoupling

Most toy train locomotives and cars are equipped with at least one operating knuckle coupler. They may be a dummy or non-operating knuckle coupler on the opposite end of the car or locomotive but it will allow the operating couplers to couple and uncouple. If you have cars with these dummy couplers, try to keep them turned so they are always connected to a car or locomotive with an operating coupler (Figure 7-15). Virtually all the popular brands of toy train locomotives and cars have couplers that will couple with all the other brands. Some of the couplers have small levers beside the coupler that can be used to open the knuckle automatically. You can use the eraser end of a pencil to reach between the cars to actuate these couplers. These couplers will also uncouple automatically.

The toy train couplers usually have a small round steel disc about the size of a dime hanging parallel to the track below the coupler (Figure 7-16). When this disc is positioned above

the center of the remote uncoupling tracks, the electromagnet in the track is energized by a remote-control button to attract the disc to pull it downward and open the coupler's knuckle to allow the coupler to uncouple.

These magnets are located in the center of the uncoupling tracks made by Lionel, K-Line and MTH (Figure 7-17). Some of the O scale Lionel cars and locomotives have couplers that are actuated by an electromagnet wrapped

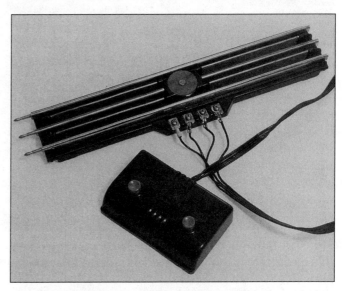

Fig. 7-17. Lionel's O scale remote uncoupling ramp has an electromagnet in the center for the disc-style couplers and accessories and fourth and fifth rails for electronically-actuated couplers and accessories.

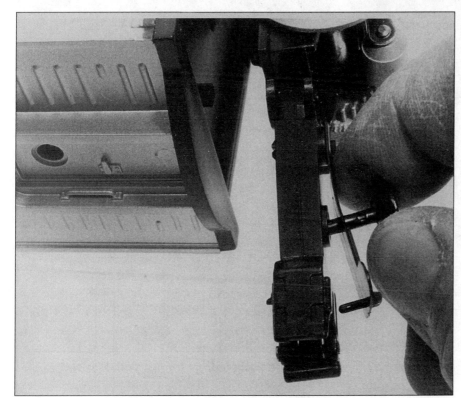

Fig. 7-16. This spring-mounted metal disc opens the coupler knuckle when the disc is pulled downward by the eletromagnet in the remote uncoupling ramp.

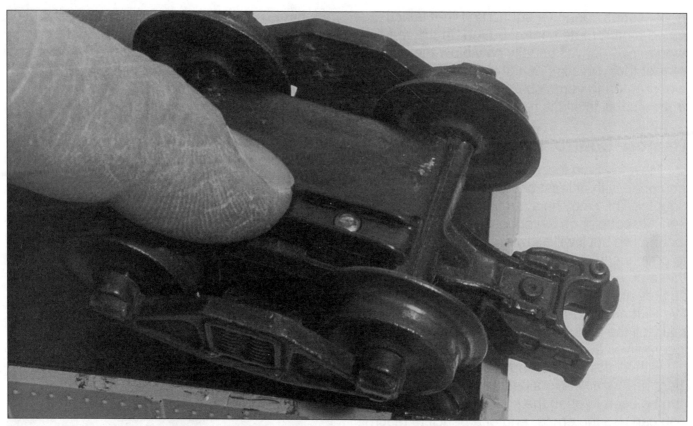

Fig. 7-18. Some of the Lionel O scale cars and locomotives have electromagnetic couplers that are activated when this electrical pickup shoe receives current from the fourth or fifth rails of the remote uncoupling track section.

Fig. 7-19. The Lionel Electro Couplers can be opened anywhere on the track using Lionel's TrainMaster Command Control system.

around the shank of the coupler inside the truck. These couplers use the forth and fifth rails of the remote uncoupling ramp to pickup electric current to open the coupler knuckle (Figure 7-18).

Remember, the magnet is only active while you are pressing down on the button. It is best, however, to only press the button for brief period or the magnet coil wires can overheat to cause a short circuit. Usually, the short circuit is corrected when the magnets cool but excessive use can burn-out the wire's insulation and require a replacement track section. The train can sometimes be uncoupled without stopping as it passes over the magnet if the train is moving very slowly while you synchronize depressing the button with the passing of the couplers you wish to uncouple.

It is difficult to position these uncoupling ramps in every place on the layout where you might want them, because they are positioned in the center of the section of track. It takes that extra five-inches (a half a track section) of track length and there often is just not enough room on the layout for the extra length. If you lack space, simply uncouple the cars by hand. Fortunately, the couplers will couple automatically if the knuckles are left in the open position so you can couple two cars or a car and locomotive together anywhere on the track.

Lionel's Electro Coupler System

The Electro Couplers fitted to the Lionel Digital TrainMaster Command locomotives are activated by their own magnets that are part of the coupler, and those magnets are energized by the remote-control CAB-1 controller. Therefore, so these locomotives will uncouple anywhere (Figure 7-19). Lionel also offers a few TrainMaster cars, like their aquarium car, each season that are equipped with the Electro Coupler system.

These cars can also be uncoupled anywhere on the track with Lionel's TrainMaster Command system. If you buy enough of these cars to make every other car in a train a Train-Master car, you could uncouple any car from the train anywhere. The system is not, however, available for other individual freight or passenger cars, so you can only uncouple between a TrainMaster locomotive or a TrainMaster car and an adjacent car. Lionel also offers replacement trucks with Electro Couplers that can be adapted to fit freight cars.

Troubleshooting Short Circuits

When a short circuit occurs, the circuit breaker in the power pack automatically interrupts the power to turn off the power pack. Short circuits are almost always caused by derailed cars or locomotives. It only takes a slight derailment to cause a short, so you need to look carefully at every locomotive and car wheel. If the problem is not a derailment, the cause of the short circuit may be that something has fallen across the track, perhaps near a turnout or behind a building or some scenery where it is not visible. Check every inch of the track for any foreign metallic objects.

Sometimes a locomotive will fail to run but there is no visible short circuit. The first thing to check is the reversing mechanism. Remember, most of these toy trains will not reverse direction until you turn the power off, then on again to provide power but no movement, then on a second time to reverse direction.

Sometimes, a slight derailment can interrupt the flow of current enough to put the locomotive in that "stall" condition where the lights are on but no movement takes place. Try turning the power on and off several times to see if that gets things going. If not, try another locomotive to see if the fault lies in the locomotive, or the power pack. If this still does not solve the problem, perform the troubleshooting checks listed in Chapter 6 on track and Chapter 13 on locomotives.

Chapter 8

Running Two Trains

Most of us just cannot resist the temptation to buy another locomotive and enough cars to make up a second complete train. Some toy train operators have dozens of locomotives and dozens of trains. It is very difficult, however, to operate more than one train on a layout at a time. Most power packs are not powerful enough to operate both locomotives at once. And, if either locomotive stalls, it will be a different operating sequence from the first locomotive so it may be sitting or reversing while the first locomotive is going forward.

How to Operate Two Trains with One Transformer

There are two ways to operate two trains on a toy train layout: The first method allows you to operate one train while you park the second train. Arrange the tracks and turnouts so there is a place to park the second train so you can turn-off the power to that track while you operate the first train.

To operate two trains on the same layout, you really must arrange the track and turnouts so there are two portions of the layout that can be turned-off. That way you can park a train on either section. The simple oval with a passing siding is one example (Figure 8-2). You can isolate the track electrically by replacing only the center steel track pins with a plastic or fiber pin at each end of the section of track (Figure 8-4) where you want to park the train.

Replace that center pin with a Lionel 011-11 Fiber Pin for O gauge track or a 1013-18 Fiber Pin for O-27 track. If you are using the "non-derailing" feature of the Lionel remote control turnouts described in Chapter 7, you will also want a second fiber insulating pin on the inner rails of the turnout. The locations of those insulated pins are shown with white circles in the photographs and black dots marked A, B, C and D on Figure 8-3.

These pins divide the track on this layout into three electrically-isolated sections. Model railroaders call these electrically-isolated sections of track "blocks," so you now have Block X, Block Y and Block Z.

Buy two more Lockons and some 14 or 16 gauge insulated electrical wire. Install one Lockon to each of the electrically-isolated sections (marked X, Y and Z on Figure 8-3). The Lockons are shown near the center of the layout, but they can be grouped in one corner as shown in Figure 8-6. Connect a single wire to the tab on the Lockon to the center rail on all three Lockons. Attach the other end of the wire from Lockon Y to one of the terminal screws on the on-off toggle switch (Figure 8-5). The toggle switches can be purchased at a hardware store or you can use the Atlas number 205 Connector switch.

Attach a second wire to the second terminal screw on the on-off switch and connect that wire to the third Lockon X. Connect the wire from Lockon Z to a second on-off switch. The wire from that on-off switch can also go directly to Lockon X or, to save wire, you can simply connect the wire from Block Z's on-off switch to the wire leading from Block Y's on-off switch to Lockon W.

The wires are "jumping" the current from the center rail from the mainline Block W to the sidings Block X and Block Y, with on-off switches in the circuit so you can turn the power off to Block X or Block Y. Finally, connect the two wires from the transformer to Lockon W. The completed wiring is shown in Figure 8-6.

If you turn both the on-off switch to Block Y and the on-off switch to Block X to "off" a train will still run on the remaining portion of the oval (Block W) because of the original first Lockon W and its two-wire connection to the layout. Park a train on each of these two electrically-isolated sections of track (Blocks X and Y). When you turn on the on-off switch to the first train's track Block X, that train will run around the oval while the first train is parked in Block Y.

Return the first train to its siding in Block X, and turn that on-off switch to "off," then turn the on-off switch to the second section of track in Block Y "on" and the second train will run. You

Fig. 8-1. Three trains can be operated on the two-level layout in Figure 8-22.

Fig. 8-2. The two parallel tracks are electrically isolated from the rest of the layout with fiber insulating pins at the locations marked with the white dots.

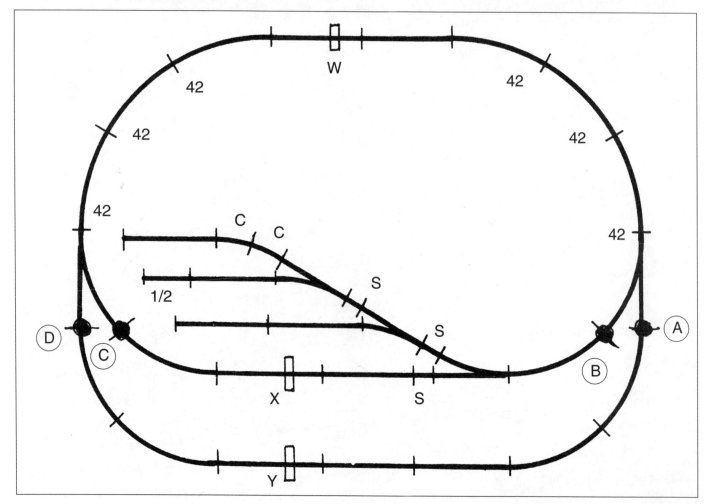

Fig. 8-3. Install fiber insulating pins in the center rail at A, B, C and D and Lockons at X, Y and Z for two-train operation.

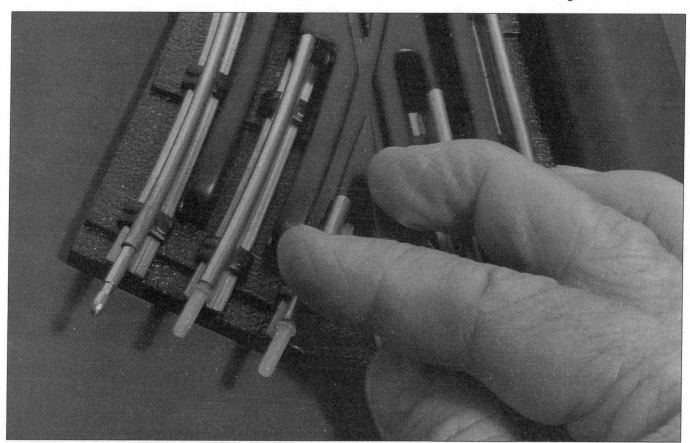

Fig. 8-4. The fiber insulating pin in the center rail electrically isolates that rail from the rest of the layout. A second fiber pin is needed at the other end of the electrically-isolated section of track.

Fig. 8-5. On-off toggle switches like this are intended for use outdoors but their bulk makes them easy to use for a toy train layout.

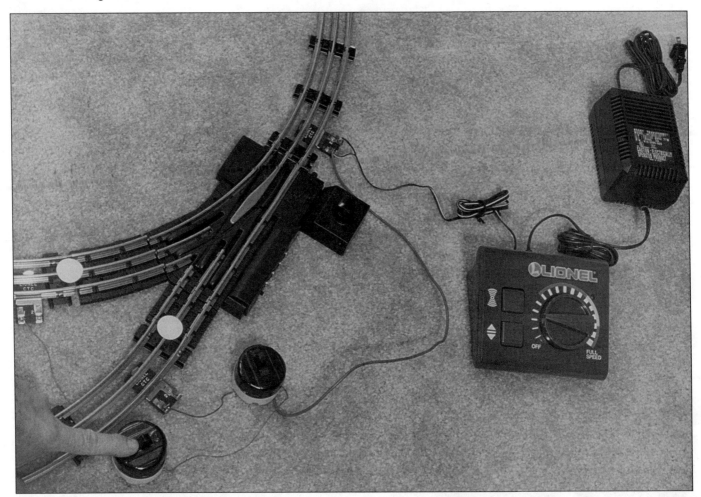

Fig. 8-6. Connect two on-off toggle switches to the Lockons at Y and Z in Figure 8-3, then to the Lockon W to complete the wiring for this layout.

may, of course, need to move the points or lever on the turnouts to allow the train to operate through the correct paths through the turnouts.

You can make the operation of this layout automatic by running the two trains in opposite directions and using Lionel's remote-controlled turnouts. You can connect the wires to the turnouts, as shown in the instructions furnished with the turnouts, so they will be actuated automatically by the trains themselves.

Transformers for Two or More Trains

For the second method of operating two trains, you will need to build a layout that has two separate loops of track, one for each train. Buy a second transformer to operate the second locomotive at the same time you are operating the first locomotive with the first transformer. Also, it is wise to arrange the track sections so you have two completely independent loops or ovals of track that are not con-

nected by turnouts or any other type of track. In essence, you must arrange the track sections so you have two toy train layouts, one inside the other. Each of these layouts will be controlled by its own transformer, connected to Lockons T and V in Figure 8-7.

The track can be arranged with additional pairs of turnouts so each of these inner and outer ovals can have one or more places (sidings) where a second (or third) train can be parked while the first train operates. You could, for example, build a larger and separate oval of track around the perimeter of the layout in Figure 8-3 so two trains could operate on the inner oval (one at a time) and a third could operate independently on the outer oval.

MRC makes a single transformer, the Dual Power 027 (the 027 stands for 270 watts of power, not O-27 scale) with sockets for two hand-held throttles (speed controls) on tethered electrical cables. The Dual Power O-27 has enough power to operate two separate locomo-

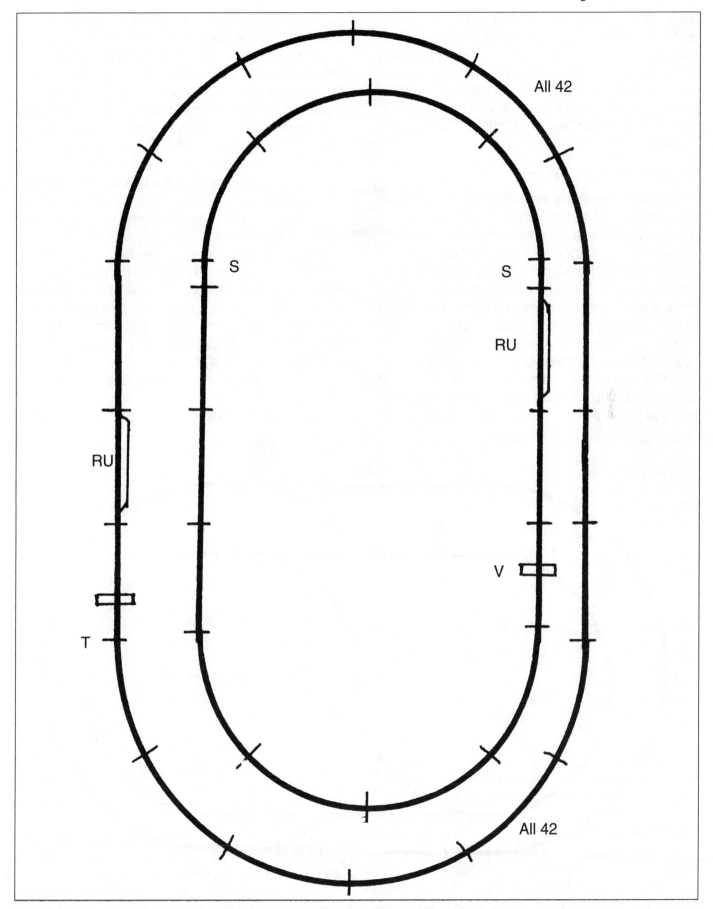

Fig. 8-7. The easiest way to operate two trains is to have two separate ovals of track with two transformers. The track plan in Figure 8-8 was developed from this basic layout.

tives. The new Lionel ZW(with two Lionel Pow-erHouse 190 transformers) and Z-4000 transformer from MTH (with 400 watts of power) are other larger power packs with two speed controls and enough power for two of the largest toy train locomotives. The Lionel and MRC transformers are shown in Chapter 7 (Figures 7-3 and 7-14).

Wiring for Two Trains

If you connect the inner and outer oval with turnouts, the electrical current from one transformer will be able to reach the other transformer to cause short circuits. To electrically isolate one oval of track from the other oval, simply remove the center steel track pin from the track joint between the two turnouts that join the inner and outer ovals. This insulated pin will stop the electricity from either transformer from reaching from the inner oval to the outer oval. To allow one train to travel from one transformer to the next, you will also need a place to park that train while you maneuver the first train. To

do that, the layout will need to be divided into additional electrically-isolated areas.

You will need more fiber insulating pins, more Lockons and more on-off toggle switches. The track plans in Chapters 4 and 5 that are designed for operation of two or more trains are marked with letter codes for adding insulating pins (the circled letters A, B, C, D, and E) with tiny dots or circles at the track joints indicating an insulating pin should be installed in place of the metal pin in the center rail. Those insulating pins electrically-isolate the layout in Figure 8-8 into four sections or "blocks"; Block W, Block X, Block Y and Block Z. Also, the extra Lockon wire connections for "block" wiring must be installed as indicated on the track plans (so two or more trains can be operated) are indicated with small rectangles across the track and the letters W, X, Y and Z. Use 14 or 16-gauge insulated wires to connect the Lockons and on-off toggle switches as described earlier. For this track plan it is easiest to use a single transformer (call it transformer 1) to connect to the

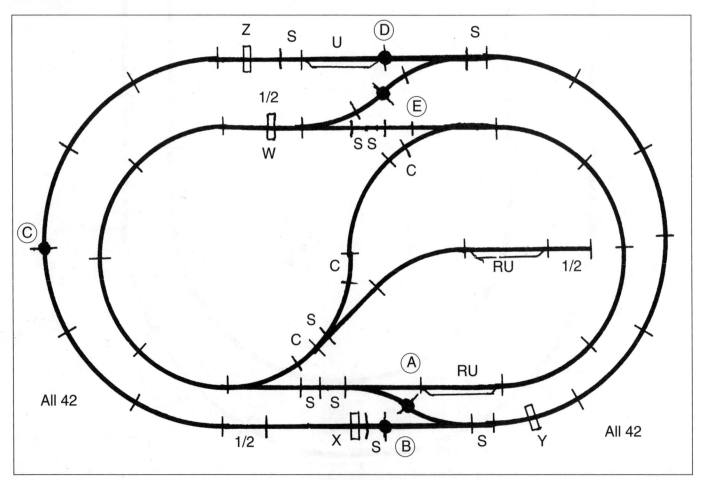

Fig. 8-8. Install fiber insulating pins at the circled letters A, B, C, D and E and Lockons at W, X, Y, Z and ZZ to prepare this layout for two-train operation.

Lionel's 4-4-0 steam locomotive and matching passenger cars are replicas of 1865 era prototype trains. You can buy passenger trains with simulated steel cars from the thirties, streamlined cars from the forties and fifties or modern hi-level Amtrak cars.

A Christmas time layout can be assembled on the floor with white felt to simulate snow. Wrap an empty cardboard box with Christmas paper and cut tunnels into the sides to support the presents above the trains.

This double-track layout occupies just 4 x 6-1/2-feet of floor space. You could tuck it under a queen-size bed. The plan is described in Chapter 5 (Figure 5-5). The movements to operate two trains are described in Chapter 8.

Simulate snow with white felt to add portable scenery to the double-track 4 x 6-1/2-foot layout. This layout has a coal mine theme with a Burlington Northern train of Rio Grande hoppers and a Pennsylvania Railroad coal train in action.

Three trains are at work on the loop-to-loop layout from Chapter 5. The Pennsylvania Railroad F3A diesel and the blue and white Long Island Railroad MP15 diesel are K-Line locomotives. The green Burlington Northern GP7 on the bridge is a Lionel locomotive.

Two trains can be operated with several wiring systems and a choice of one or two transformers. Lionel's TrainMaster Command Control or DCC command control systems as described in Chapter 8.

You can combine several brands of toy train equipment on a single layout. The track, the green Burlington Northern caboose and the log loader are Lionel products and the GP38-2 diesel and Rio Grande hoppers are K-Line. The "Fairfield" station is a modified Walthers kit.

This double-track 4 x 6-1/2-foot two-oval layout can be assembled on the floor or on a tabletop with either green felt scenery for summer scenes or white felt scenery to recreate wintertime effects.

This 4 x 6-1/2-foot two-oval layout can be wired to allow up to two trains to be operated. The techniques for building the lightweight tabletop are in Chapter 9, the scenery is described in Chapter 10, and the track plan is in Chapter 5 (Figure 5).

Dick Bruning has completed what many toy train operators would consider the ultimate layout. The three most popular brands of toy trains are shown in operation, including MTH (Mike's Train House) New York Central "Empire State Express" 4-6-4 streamlined silver and black steam locomotive, and a beige K-Line 0-27 work train. All these trains are highly collectible.

The K-Line Santa Fe "Warbonnet" three-car 0-27 passenger train streaks around the inner oval of this 4 x 6-1/2-foot layout, while a K-Line GP38-2 heads a train of Lionel freight cars around the outer oval.

The lake below the bridge is plastic, the bushes are lichen and the trees are Life-Like, Heiki, and Noch ready-built products. The techniques for "portable" scenery you can use on layouts built on the floor or layouts built on tabletops are described in Chapter 10. The BNSF GP38-2 diesel and the silver box car are K-Line products. The green box car, corrugated streamlined passenger car, the tank car, the 1860 passenger car in the background and the water tower are Lionel products.

This 4 x 6-1/2-foot "Three-Trains On Two Levels" layout is described in Chapter 5. The operating patterns for the three trains are explained in Chapter 8. The layout is assembled on the lightweight Styrofoam tabletop described in Chapter 9 and utilizes Woodland Scenics "Incline" Styrofoam to elevate the tracks above the tabletop. The scenery is portable so it can be removed and reused again and again.

Some of the more-collectible toy trains are painted for "private owners" that never operated a real car or locomotive in those colors. Dick Bruning's "food train" was produced by K-Line.

The river and lake on Dick Bruning's 8-1/2 x 18-foot layout were created by cutting a hole the size of the shore in the plywood tabletop. The riverbanks are plaster-soaked gauze, painted and textured with ground foam. The water is a dozen 1/4-inch layers of decoupage clear resin, each poured, then allowed to cure before pouring the next layer.

An F3A, F3B and F3A set of Lionel Santa Fe diesels rumble through a cut on Dick Bruning's layout. The mountain was carved from a two-foot high stack of two-inch thick layers of Styrofoam insulation board, covered with plaster-soaked gauze, then painted and textured with ground foam. The rock textures were cast in latex rubber molds using plaster, then painted with thinned-down acrylic colors.

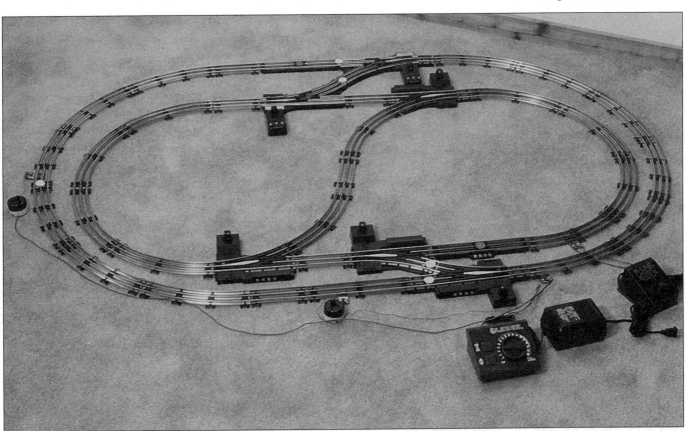

Fig. 8-9. Two on-off toggle switches and two power packs are needed to use this layout for the independent control of two trains.

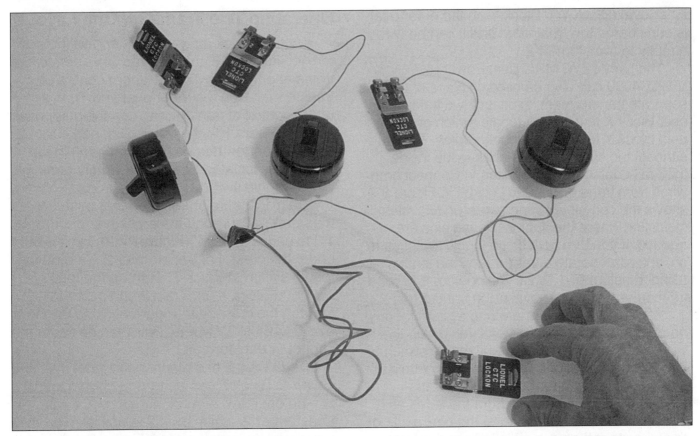

Fig. 8-10. The on-off toggle switches for a layout of two or three (shown) blocks can be wired together to connect to single Lockon (lower right) for power.

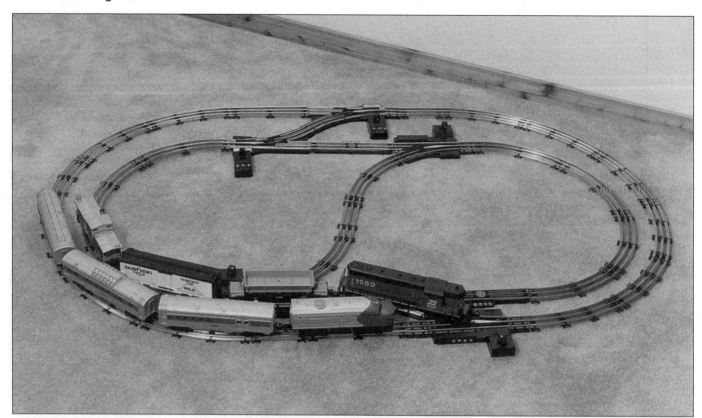

Fig. 8-11. The two trains begin the operating sequence traveling clockwise around the two ovals. The freight train (Train 1) moves to the outer oval through the lower crossover.

inner oval (Block W). Block Y on the outer oval is considered the "mainline" and it can be wired directly to transformer 2.

The Lionel ZW, MRC Dual Power 027 or MTHZ-4000 can also be used, in place of two separate transformers, to control two trains. Connect Block X to its on-off toggle switch and connect Block Y to its on-off toggle switch. Then connect the two toggle switches to the inside third rail-contact clip on Lockon Y. Connect both wires from transformer 2 to Lockon Y. Figure 8-9 shows the completed wiring, with white circles indicating where the fiber insulating pins are needed. If you turn both of the toggle switches to on, you can operate a train around the inner oval using transformer 1, while you operate a second train around the outer oval using transformer 2.

You can use this same wiring system for any number of blocks. It is easier if you group the wires from more than two on-off toggle switches into a common junction (Figure 8-10), with a single wire leading to the Lockon or transformer. Strip the insulation from the wires as shown in Chapter 7, then twist the bare ends of the wires together in a pigtail. Wrap the bare wires tightly with plastic electrical tape.

Operating Two Trains on One Layout

With the track arrangement and wiring system in Figures 8-8 and 8-9, you can operate two trains at once, with Train 1 under control of transformer 1 on the inner oval and Train 2 under control of transformer 2 on the outer oval. To move Train 1 to the outer oval, park Train 2 (the passenger train on the outer oval) in the electrically-isolated Block X by simply turning-off the toggle switch to that block.

Train 1 (the freight on the inner oval) can then proceed through the crossover (Figure 8-11) to park in Block Z (Figure 8-12), but it is then under the control of transformer 2. Turn off the toggle switch to Block Z. Turn on the toggle switch to Block X, so Train 2 can proceed through the crossover (Figure 8-13) to the inner oval and Block W where it will then be under the control of transformer 1.

Once Train 2 has reached the inner oval, the power to Block Z can be turned on and train 1 can be operated around the outer oval with transformer 2, while Train 2 is operated on the inner oval by transformer 1(Figure 8-14). It's a bit complicated, so you can see why it's simpler

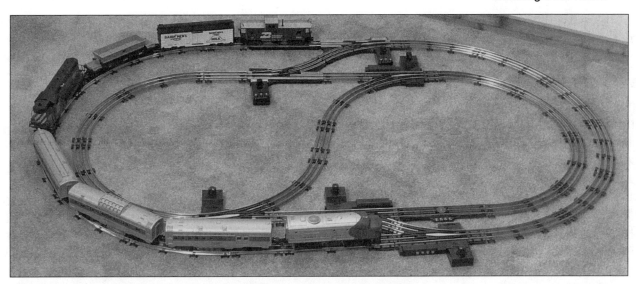

Fig. 8-12. The freight proceeds around the oval to stop in Block Z.

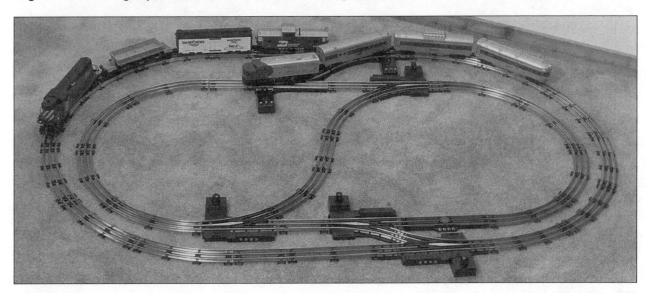

Fig. 8-13. The passenger train (Train 2) proceeds around the oval to enter the inner oval through the upper crossover.

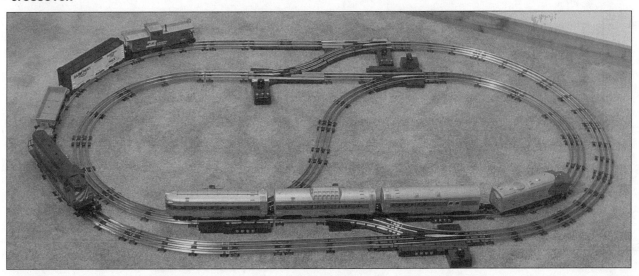

Fig. 8-14. The two trains have now swapped positions so the freight train (Train 1) is running around the inner oval and the passenger train (Train 2) is running around the inner oval.

to just have two separate layouts and leave Train 1 on layout 1 and Train 2 on layout 2.

Reversing Two Trains

It is also possible, to reverse the direction of each train as it takes its turn traveling counter-clockwise around the inner oval (Figure 8-14). Once the trains are both traveling clockwise around this lay out, they must be backed-up through the reverse loop to change their direc-tion back to clockwise.

To reverse Train 2 (the passenger train), set the turnouts so it can travel through the reverse loop (Figure 8-15). It can make as many laps

around the inner oval running, now, in clockwise direction as you wish.

When it is time to reverse the direction of Train 1 (the freight rain), park Train 1 in Block Z and turn off the power to that block. Set the turnouts so Train 2 can reach the outer oval where it will be under the control of transformer 2 (Figure 8-16). Run Train 1 around to Block X (Figure 8-17) and turn off Block X.

Turn on Block Z and back Train 1 into Block Y until it clears the switch points at the cross-over turnout (Figure 8-18). Move the turnout points so Train 1 can now proceed forward and onto the inner oval (Figure 8-19) where it will be under control of transformer 1. Train 1 is now

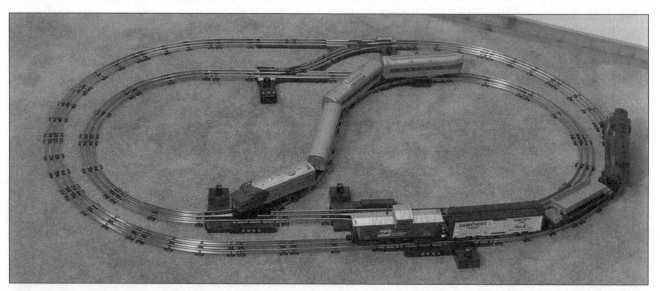

Fig. 8-15. The passenger train (Train 2) reverses its direction by traveling through the S-curve of the reversing loop.

Fig. 8-16. When it is time for the passenger train (Train 2) to leave the inner oval, it uses the upper crossover.

Fig. 8-17. The passenger train (Train 2) proceeds around the oval to stop in Block X.

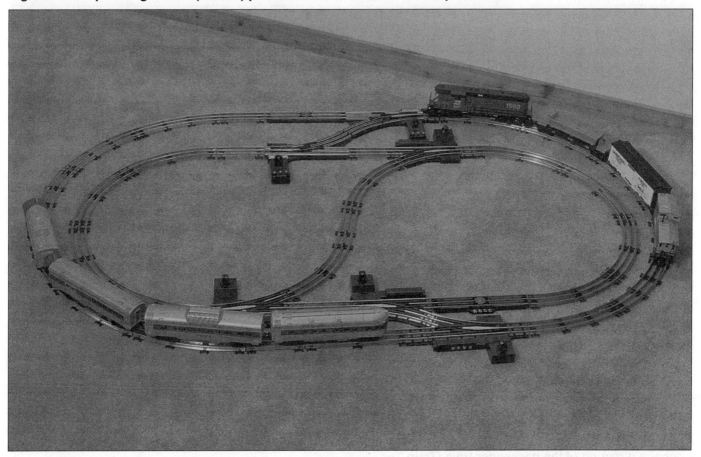

Fig. 8-18. The freight train (Train 1) backs up until lit clears the crossover turnouts.

Fig. 8-19. The freight train (Train 1) proceeds forward through the upper crossover to the inner oval.

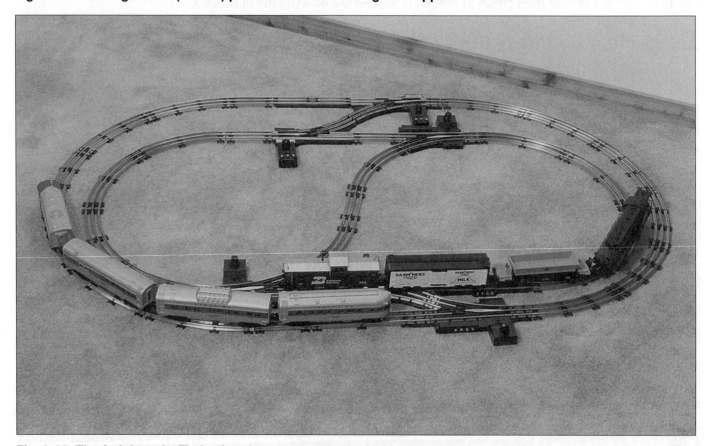

Fig. 8-20. The freight train (Train 1) makes as many laps of he inner oval as you wish. It is now traveling in the opposite direction of the passenger train (Train 2).

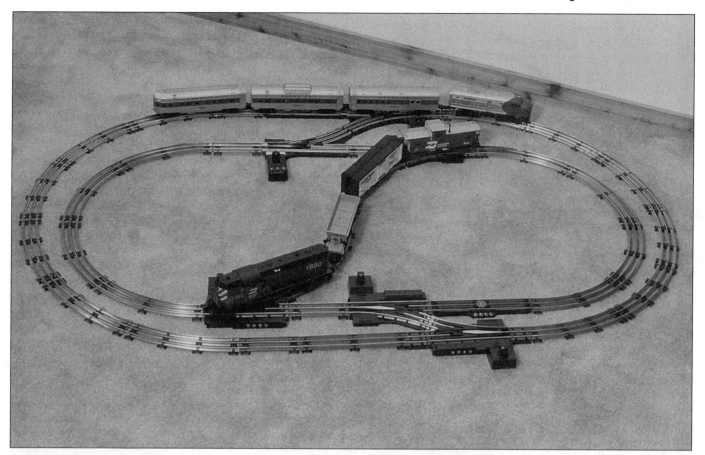

Fig. 8-21. When it is time to reverse the freight train's direction, route it through the S-shaped reverse loop track to emerge on the inner oval, traveling in the same clockwise direction as the passenger train.

circulating in a counterclockwise direction around the inner oval under control of transformer 1 and Train 1 is circulating in a clockwise direction around the inner oval under control of transformer 2 (Figure 8-23).

To reverse Train 2, set the turnouts for the reverse loop and run Train 2 through the reverse loop (Figure 8-21). Both Train 1 and Train 2 are now traveling around the layout in a clockwise direction (where they started, much earlier in this chapter, but now both are running in the opposite direction).

Loop-To-Loop Operations for Three Trains

The loop-to-loop track layout shown in Chapter 5 can be used to hold up to two trains while a third train traverses the mainline between the two loops. The mainline is connected directly to the transformer through Lockon W as shown in Figure 8-22. Install on-off toggle switches between the Lockon at X and the transformer and between the Lockon at Y and the transformer on the upper level reverse loop. Also install on-off toggle switches between the Lockon at Z and transformer and between and the Lockon at ZZ and the transformer on the lower level reverse loop.

Up to three trains can now be "parked," one each at X, Y, and Z (Figure 8-22). The transformer is connected directly to the mainline at W. Start the train parked at X by turning the power on to the train using the appropriate on-off toggle switch. When this train arrives at ZZ, turnoff the power to ZZ and the train at Z can head for the now empty "block" X. Next, Train Y can travel over the mainline "W" to be parked at "block" X.

The sequence can be repeated or you can vary it depending on which direction each train heads into the reversing loop. Notice that you can really only operate one train at a time. If, however, you decide to use all Lionel locomotives equipped with TrainMaster Command Control or if you have a dealer install Digitrax decoders and use the Digitrax DCC system, you can actually operate any or all of these trains at once so they will be following each

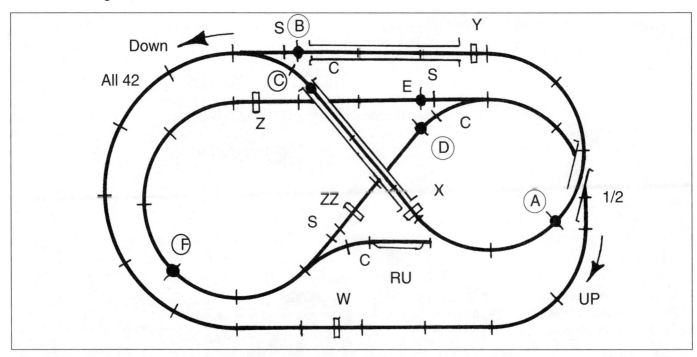

Fig. 8-22. To prepare the loop-to-loop layout for operating three trains, install fiber insulating pins in the center rail at circled letters A, B, C, D, E and F, and Lockons at W, X, Y, Z and ZZ.

Fig. 8-23. Connect two on-off toggle switches to Blocks X and Y on the upper reverse loop and Blocks Z and ZZ on the lower reverse loop and connect the power pack to the Lockon at W.

other around the reverse loops and down the mainline, with all three trains operating at once.

Lionel's Command Control for Two-Train Operation

There are two other ways to operate two trains on the same track: Buy Lionel's Digital TrainMaster™ Command Control system (Figure 8-24) and two locomotives (Figure 8-25) to go with it or buy a DCC system like that sold by Digitrax with decoders and have a dealer install the decoders in your locomotives. The Lionel system is essentially ready-to-run but it is more expensive; just purchase Lionel's Digital Train-Master™ Command control system with the hand-held CAB-1 throttles and buy a second (or third or forth) Lionel locomotive fitted with their Digital TrainMaster Command control.

With this system, you can operate up to 99 trains under completely independent control on the same track anywhere, pulled by Lionel loco-motives equipped with Digital TrainMaster Command Control. Command control is becoming a popular option with HO scale model railroaders but, so far, only Lionel offers it for O scale toy trains. The system will operate with other Lionel locomotives or with other brands, for that "first" train as long as the second locomotive is equipped with Lionel's Digital Train-Master Command Control.

The Lionel Digital TrainMaster Command Control system is similar to the DCC systems used for HO scale in that it sends a constant higher-voltage electrical current through the rails. Separate digital commands are carried through the rails to a decoder in the locomotive to "tell" the motor so slow down, speed up or reverse. The system can also be used to activate Lionel's Railsounds and the ElectroCoupler on the Lionel TrainMaster locomotives.

The Lionel TrainMaster Command system begins with a Lionel locomotive equipped with the system, you must then add the Lionel Train-

Fig. 8-24. The Lionel TrainMaster Command Control System uses the CAB-1 hand-held remote control (bottom), the Command Base (center) and the PowerHouse transformer (top).

Master Command Base and the matching CAB-1 remote control throttle. You will also need a source of 135 or more watts of AC power from a toy train transformer or Lionel's own Power-House 190 transformer with 190 watts.

If you add the Lionel SC-1 Switch and Accessory Controller to the transformer, you can use the TrainMaster Command control system to operate turnouts and action accessories, as well as locomotives, from the hand-held CAB-1 remote control throttle.

DCC for Two-Train Control

The Digital Command Control (DCC) systems are popular with HO and N scale model railroaders. These systems provide a steady 18 to 20-volt current through the rails, with digital electronic "commands" to slow, stop, or reverse carried as electronic signals through the rails to a decoder in each locomotive. Digitrax is one of a half-dozen firms that produce Digital Command

Control (DCC) systems for model railroads.

So far, they are the only firm to offer systems for these larger toy trains like Lionel, MTH, K-Line and others. You can purchase HO and N scale locomotives with decoders already installed and many of these models have a socket that allows plug-in installation of the decoder. The O scale toy train locomotives from Lionel, MTH, K-Line, Weaver, and others are not wired for plug-in installation of DCC decoders, so you must be willing to cut and solder wires. Many of the dealers that sell the DCC systems can perform the installations, however, Digitrax offers a radio control hand-held throttle as well as a tethered walk-around control.

These systems are not, however, compatible with Lionel's TrainMaster™ system. They can be used to operate some sound systems, turnouts, uncoupling tracks and accessories, but, so far, only Lionel's system will operate the special TrainMaster couplers.

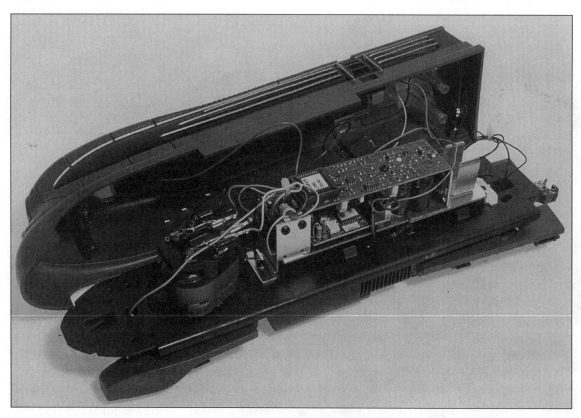

Fig. 8-25. The Lionel TrainMaster Command Control electronics are available only in specific locomotives like this "Phantom." You can operate up to 99 Lionel locomotives equipped with this system on the same track.

Chapter 9

Tables For Toy Trains

When you look at the various toy train layouts in this book you'll see portable layouts simply resting on a 4 x 6-1/2-foot piece of plywood as well as 20 x 72-foot empires on very sturdy tables. The larger ones are built much like the deck of an outdoor patio or deck, with 2 x 4 and 1 x 4-foot framework and 1/2-inch or thicker plywood tabletops. Technically, all of them are tables, but some are more difficult and costly to build and more permanent than others.

Why Build a Train Table?

The advantages of a tabletop layout are that the trains are closer to your eyes so you don't have to bend over so far, nor crawl along on the floor, and, if you really do want permanent scenery and ballasted track, the tabletop layout is necessary to provide a solid support. Before you decide to make a tabletop layout, understand that you will lose much of the freedom of design you have by operating on the floor. You will be confined by the edges of the table, rather than the walls of the room.

The train table cannot be any wider than 2-1/2-feet if you expect to reach across. That works just fine for shelf-style layouts like Ralph Johnson's O scale layout and Bruce Pemberton's O-27 and American Flyer layout (Figure 9-1) in Chapter 3. These layouts have what are essentially shelves that run around the walls of

Fig. 9-1. A permanent layout table provides the space for major recreations of real railroading like this turntable and engine servicing area on Bruce Pemberton's O-27 and American Flyer layout.

Fig. 9-2. Use 1 x 2 lumber to brace a sheet of 1/4-inch plywood to build a portable 4 x 6-1/2-foot train table.

the layout room with a peninsula protruding into the center of the room. Most of the tracks are within 2-1/2-feet of the edge, but some are five-feet away. The peninsula portions of both of these layouts have tables that are built strong enough so they can support the weight of an adult. This allows the builder to climb up on the layout and walk across it to reach any problem or to make changes. If you walk in your stocking feet, the toy tracks are strong enough to support you without any damage to the track. You may, however, have to move some of the buildings and scenery to reach back into the layout.

Portable Tabletop Layouts

There are four track plans for 4 x 6-1/2-foot layouts in Chapter 4. The size is no accident, it's something you can slide beneath a queen-size bed. Or, you may be able to place the layout on top of the bed. In either case, you need a board of some kind to support the layout. A sim-

ple 1/4-inch plywood panel is adequate but it will be a bit wobbly and can warp if not braced.

There are two vastly different ways of bracing that tabletop: The conventional method is to attach a framework of 1 x 2 or larger boards, placed on edge, beneath the edges of the plywood (Figure 9-2). Use number 8 x 1-1/2-inch screws reinforced with carpenter's glue to attach the framework (Figure 9-3).

Styrofoam Layout Construction

The second method of bracing a plywood tabletop provides "bracing" made from one or two 2-inch thick layers of Styrofoam blue insulation board cemented to the top of the plywood. There are other brands, but the material you want is extruded polyfoam, not the expanded type like the white Styrofoam board sometimes known as "bead board." The white expanded-polystyrene stuff is too soft for this application, although it can certainly be used to carve scenery (as shown in Chapter 10) if

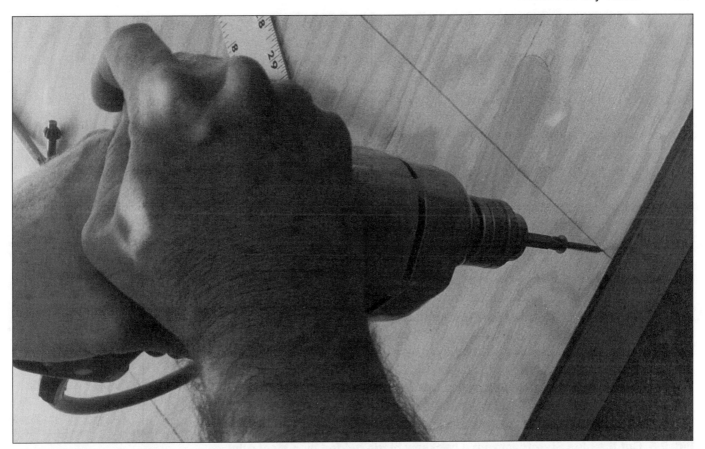

Fig. 9-3. Use wood screws or drywall screws to assemble the 1 x 2 bracing and the plywood tabletop.

Fig. 9-4. If you use blue extruded Styrofoam for the scenery base and tabletop, a single sheet fof 1/4 or even 1/8-inch plywood is thick enough and it is lightweight.

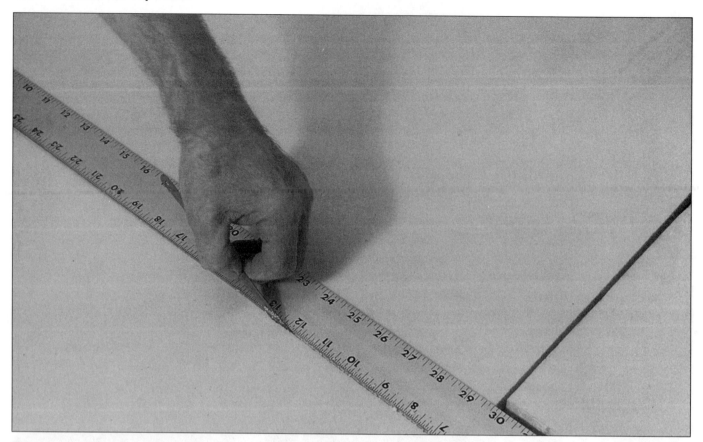

Fig. 9-5. Cut the blue Styrofoam with a hacksaw blade guided by a steel ruler.

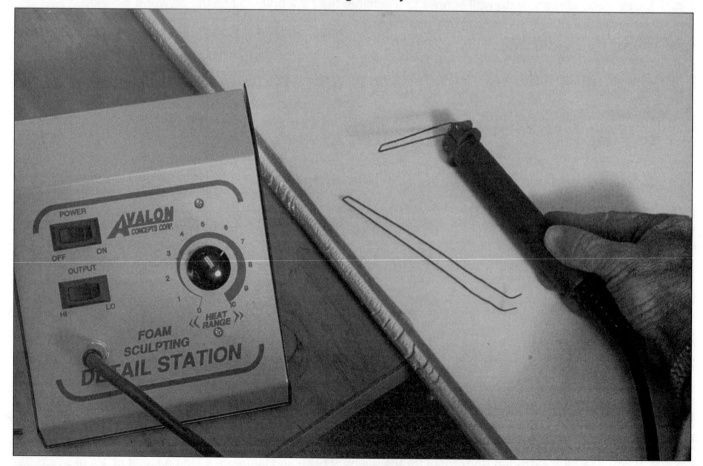

Fig. 9-6. Bend two wire "blades" for the Avalon Concepts "Detail Wand" hot wire-cutter handle.

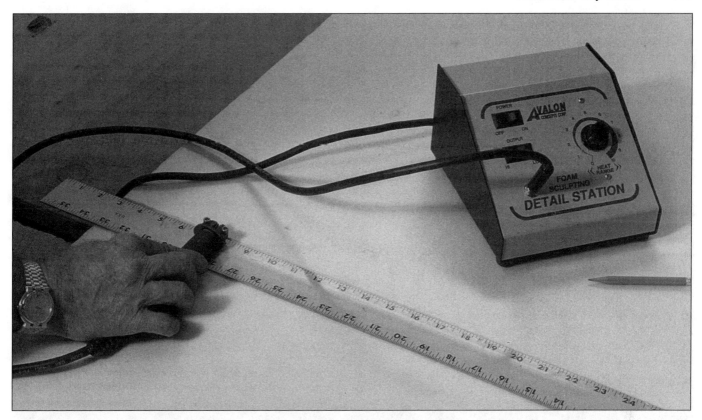

Fig. 9-7. Use a steel ruler to guide the hot wire in the Detail Wand to make a perfectly straight cut through the Styrofoam.

you'd like. Do not use the urethane insulation boards because they are more difficult to cut than Styrofoam and any saw cuts produce more dust. Use carpenter's glue, ChemRex's PL300 Foam Board Adhesive or Liquid Nails for Craft Projects. Other cements and glues may attack the Styrofoam.

Start the construction of the Styrofoam layout with a base to support the legs. 1/8-inch plywood is thick enough if you reinforce the areas where the legs attach to the plywood or use sawhorses for legs. The Styrofoam will provide the strength to keep the thin plywood from flexing (Figure 9-4). I would recommend you attach two of the two-inch-thick layers of blue Styrofoam to the plywood to provide enough thickness so you can carve into the Styrofoam to make valleys, for streams, lakes or rivers, below the level of the tracks. Mark the line you wish to cut with a steel straight edge and pencil.

You can cut the Styrofoam with a hacksaw blade held in a gloved hand. Use a steel ruler to help guide the hacksaw blade (Figure 9-5). The saw produces a lightweight dust that is extremely difficult to control. If you opt for the hacksaw blade, keep a vacuum handy to remove the dust as you cut.

An alternate method is to use a hot wire cutter like that made by Avalon Concepts. These tools are relatively expensive but they make the work easy and clean. The Avalon Concepts Detail Station kit includes a cable with a handle called a Detail Wand that is used as the hot-wire cutter. The Detail Wand includes 12-inch pieces of wire that can be bent to create cutting "blade" shapes. I'd suggest you bend two cutters, one a simple U-shaped loop with 6-inch legs to use as a knife, and the second U-shaped wire about 4-inches long to use for cutting right angles in the Styrofoam boards.

Bend the second U-shaped piece so it will cut at a right angle (90-degrees) when the handle is rested on the top of the Styrofoam sheet (Figure 9-6). Use a steel straight edge to guide the cutter and it will make perfect right-angel cuts (Figure 9-7). Practice on some of the Styrofoam that you know will become scrap.

The Styrofoam panels are sold in 2 x 8-foot sheets. Butt two of the sheets together and cut them to match the length of the 4 x 6-1/2-foot plywood base (Figure 9-8). I would suggest using two-inch thick sheets. If you really do want to cut rivers or streams below the level of the tracks,

Fig. 9-8. Cement the two two-inch thick slabs of blue Styrofoam to the plywood to complete the lightweight tabletop.

Fig. 9-9. These steel sawhorses are used to support the lightweight tabletop.

Fig. 9-10. The sawhorses fold into themselves like the one on the floor and the lightweight tabletop can be stood on edge so the layout can be stored in a minimum amount of space.

add another layer or even two layers of two-inch thick blue Styrofoam insulation boards.

The extra thickness will provide the space needed to cut those channels for rivers, streams, lakes or roads that pass beneath the tracks. There's an extensive layout in HO scale using this method described in the *HO Model Railroading Handbook*. Those techniques will work just as well for toy trains as for HO scale trains.

You have a wide choice of legs for this table-top. You can simply place it on a bed or on top of a picnic table. A card table is not really strong enough for this purpose, however. Sawhorses are, perhaps, the sturdiest "legs" for this type of layout (Figure 9-9). I bought two all-steel saw-horses that have folding legs for compact storage so I can store the 4 x 6-1/2-foot layout upright against a wall and fold-up the saw-horses (Figure 9-10). None of the conventional folding legs are really sturdy enough for this use. You can, of course, use 2 x 4-foot legs and brace them with 1 x 3 boards but it will be far more difficult to remove those legs.

If you cannot store the layout beneath a bed, you can likely find a place to store it on edge. Just be sure the track, ballast and scenery is cemented-down solidly. Do not cement any buildings in place, however, so they can be removed if you want to stand the layout on edge.

I would suggest that you avoid permanent scenery and use the "portable" felt method shown in Chapter 10. With this method, you will need to remove all the track and scenery before you can store this layout on edge, but remov-able scenery provides the options of changing the track layout. As you can see in Chapter 5, there is a wide choice of possible track plans even for this small space. You can certainly build a full 4 x 8-foot layout with this method but it will be a bit heavier and more difficult to store. You can also build two, three, four or more 4 x 6-1/2 (or 4 x 8-foot) tabletops like this, each with its own set of legs, and join them to make a 4 x 13-foot layout, or connect three of them in a U-shape to build a 10-1/2 x 10-1/2-foot layout with a 4 x 4-1/2-foot access aisle in the center.

Remember, these portable layout boards are not sturdy enough to walk on, so you must be able to reach across the tabletop from both sides of the 4-foot width for access.

Upgrades for Over-and-Under Layouts

Upgrades were a construction and an operation nightmare for real railroad builders. For a toy train layout, however, an upgrade, especially one that allows one train to pass over another, is an exciting variation on the typical oval track layout. You can assemble what toy train operators sometimes call an "over-and-under" layout.

Toy train locomotives are powerful, but there is a limit to how steep a grade they will climb. If you are building a really large layout, with 54-inch or 72-inch radius curves, then you have the space for long trains and the uphill grades can be a relatively gentle 2-percent.

If you are building a more compact layout, perhaps as small as 4 x 6-1/2-feet, you have only enough space for relatively short trains, so a steeper 4-percent grade is suitable. A 2 percent grade means the track rises 2 inches in 100-inches and a 4-percent grade elevates the track 4-inches in 100-inches.

The toy trains must climb to about 5-inches if you want one train to pass over another train. To raise the track 5-inches, with a 4-percent grade you'll need 120-inches of track, or about 10-feet. That's about the length of 10 standard toy train track sections. Lionel's number 110 Graduated Trestle Set includes 11 pairs of plastic piers that elevate the track 4-3/4-inches.

These piers have adapters and mounting holes so you can screw the piers to the ties and to the tabletop. If you do screw the piers to the ties, it is possible to use this system on the floor or with a portable model railroad. The piers are not particularly realistic because a bridge should support the track between each pier. A full set of these piers is needed for the inverted figure 8 layout in Figure 4-24 of Chapter 4 (Figure 9-11). The loop-to-loop layout in Figure 8-22 of Chapter 8 uses only a half-set of the 110 Graduated Trestle Set piers

Fig. 9-11. The individual piers in the Lionel 110 Graduated Trestle Set can be attached to the track with screws. For a tabletop layout, the piers can also be attached to the table with screws.

Fig. 9-12. Half of a set of Lionel's 110 Graduated Trestle Set piers were used to bring the track from the lower level reverse loop to the upper level reverse loop.

(Figure 9-12). The toy train track is strong enough to be self-supporting so the system does work.

It is far more realistic to bury the track-support system beneath a sheet of felt (for a portable lay-out), or beneath plaster (for a permanent model railroad). For a permanent layout, you can use the system that HO scale model railroaders have used for 70-years and build an open-grid-style bench-work without a solid tabletop. Cut 1/2-inch of ply-wood for support just beneath the tracks. This plywood roadbed support can then be pushed upward with vertical pieces of 1 x 4 lumber screwed to the benchwork to create uphill grades.

Easy Upgrade Roadbed Construction

Woodland Scenics makes a system of white expanded-polystyrene strips, panels and blocks called the SubTerrain system to construct the forms for scenery shaped with plaster. The system is designed to be constructed on a flat tabletop. The basis of the system are two-inch wide flexible supports to elevate the track above a flat tabletop called "Risers." The Risers are available in 1-inch and 2-inch heights so they can be stacked to raise toy train track far enough above the tabletop to allow one train to pass above another on a bridge.

The SubTerrain system also includes match-ing 2-inch wide track supports that are sloped to produce upgrades called "Inclines" (Figure 9-13). The Inclines are available in 2-percent or 4-percent grades. The Inclines, then, guarantee a steady upgrade, all the way from zero to 5-inches, even through curves.

Both the 2-percent and the 4-percent Incline sets include flexible Inclines in 2-foot sections, so it takes five pieces (10-feet of track)from the 4-percent Incline set to gain 5-inches and ten pieces (20-feet of track) from the of the 2-per-cent Incline set to gain the same 5-inches. You will also need four 2-inch thick Woodland Sce-nics Risers and two 2-inch thick Risers to sup-port the Inclines. To build an upgrade with a 2-percent climb, you will need 10-pieces of the 2-

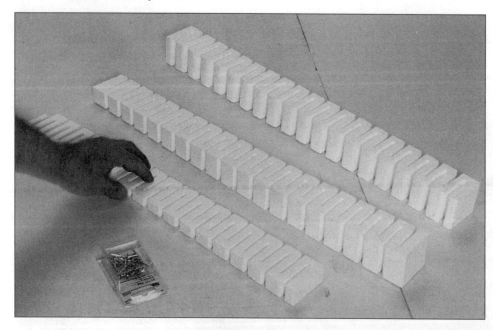

Fig. 9-13. The Woodland Scenics 4-percent "Inclines" to elevate the track from zero to one-inch (bottom), from one-inch to two-inches (center) and the two-inch "Riser" (top).

Fig. 9-14. Mark the edges of the tracks on the tabletop, then remove the tracks.

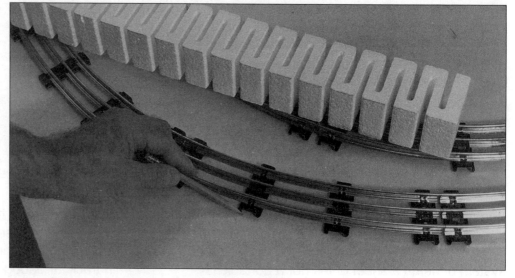

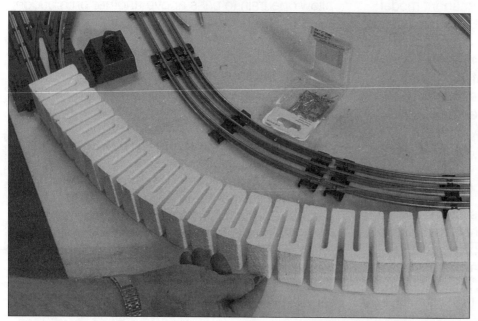

Fig. 9-15. Use T-pins to attach the Risers and Inclines to the table-top so the Styrofoam components can be removed and reused on other layouts. The Riesers and Inclines can be glued to the table top and to each other for a permanent layout.

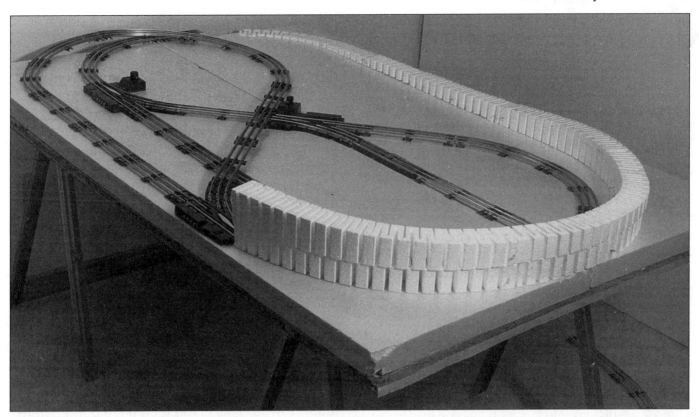

Fig. 9-16. Five two-foot lengths of Woodland Scenics Inclines and Risers are needed to elevate the track five-inches on the point-to-point layout in Chapter 5.

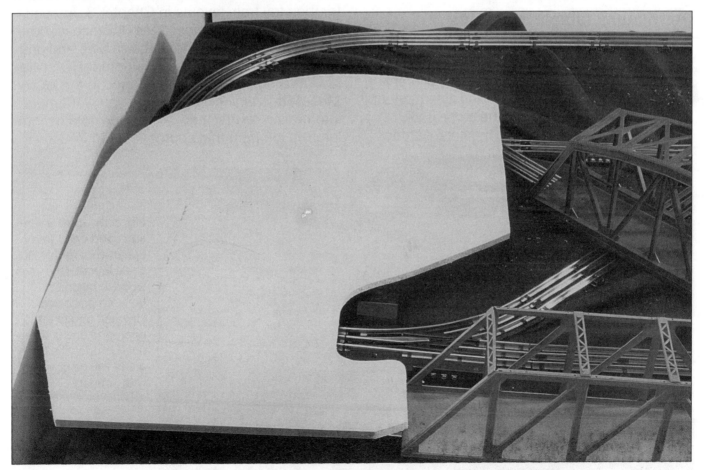

Fig. 9-17. Use 1/4-inch Foamcore board for a lightweight support for the upper level tracks.

percent Inclines to elevate the tracks 5 inches and you'll also need five-1/2-inch Risers, four 1-inch Risers and four 2-inch Risers.

To use the "Inclines" mark the edges of the track on the tabletop with a pencil (Figure 9-14). I used this system for the 4 x 6-1/2-foot loop-to-loop layout in Chapter 5. Remove the track and install the "Inclines" and "Risers" with the T-pins used by dressmakers. The pins are sold by shops that sell cloth for dressmaking and upholstery. If the tabletop is blue Styrofoam, the pins will push in easily (Figure 9-15).

If you are using a plywood tabletop, you may need pliers to push the pins in place. You can use the same pins to attach the "Inclines" to the tops of the "Risers." Five lengths of 4-percent grade "Inclines" with matching "Risers" are enough to elevate the track five-inches to allow the trains to pass over one another (Figure 9-16). Cut a piece of 1/4-inch thick Foamcore or plywood to support the upper level reverse loop (Figure 9-17) as shown in Figures 5-13 and 5-14 in Chapter 5. Cut some 2 x 6 boards into five-inch lengths to support the bridges and the elevated sections of the layout.

Permanent Tabletop Layouts

I would strongly suggest that you operate your trains for at least a year, changing the track layout and design frequently to try out different forms of operations, before building a permanent tabletop layout. You can use the same basic framing techniques shown for the 4 x 6-1/2-foot portable layout to build a portable 20 x 60-foot layout. Use 1 x 3 or 1 x 4 lumber to frame the tables and 2 x 4s for the legs, also braced with diagonal 1 x 3 boards. Build the framework and legs first, then cut 1/2-inch thick plywood to fit.

Essentially, you are building a deck, so place the 1 x 3 or 1 x 4 boards no further than two-feet apart and add 1 x 3 or 1 x 4 lumber every 2 feet so you have an eggcrate-style grid of two-foot square boxes. Model railroads call this "open grid" because it looks like a grid.

Open Grid Benchwork

You may need all those supports that are the result the open grid-style benchwork to attach 1 x 4 risers to elevate the tracks from upgrades. Some modelers do not attach a solid plywood tabletop, they cut the plywood to match the track and place it only beneath the track, using solid sheets of plywood for yard areas, industrial sections and for the sites of future towns. This is the technique John Swanson used for his HO scale layout (Figure 9-18) and by Bruce Pemberton and Ralph Johnson for their toy train layouts in Chapter 3. Attach the tabletop with number 8 x 1-1/2-inch wood screws so you can remove the screws and part or all of the tabletop. There's another HO scale layout using this open-grid method in the *HO Model Railroading Handbook* if you want more information on that method you can obtain more information from that source.

Fig. 9-18. John Swanson used open-grid benchwork for his HO scale layout. Plywood is placed beneath the tracks, elevated above the open grid on 1 x 4 vertical boards. The open areas will be covered with scenery.

Chapter 10

Scenery

Scenery is supposed to provide a backdrop for toy trains. Most toy train operators prefer to have the train, rather than the scenery, dominate the scene. This is, of course, just the opposite of the real world where the mountains and rivers dwarf the largest and longest trains. There's a logic to this approach because it would take some really massive mountains to dwarf O scale trains. If you really want scenery to dominate the scene, choose the N scale trains that are about a fourth the size of the toy trains in this book.

Portable or Permanent?

One of the joys of O scale toy trains is that they are sturdy enough to operate on the floor.

In fact, the track is strong enough to walk on if it's supported well enough.

It is possible to have mountains, rivers, streams, and even cliffs and tunnels on a toy train layout built on the floor. You can use the portable scenery techniques from this chapter for a layout built on a tabletop, as well (Figure 10-1).

I would suggest that you wait at least a year before building a permanent layout. Give yourself some time to rearrange the track and add or alter train routes with new track. This is really one of the joys of toy trains, being able to rearrange the tracks so easily. When you opt for a permanent layout, you loose that advantage.

It is, of course, possible to have both portable and permanent on the same layout. That's what

Fig. 10-1. All of this scenery, including the rock cliffs, can be removed and reused to build other layouts.

Fig. 10-3. Position the wadded-up newspapers or the Life-Like Styrofoam tunnel where you want the mountain, then cover it with the felt and install the track.

Dick Bruning did on his layout shown in Chapter 5 and on the cover. He built a permanent mountain on corner of his layout and permanent lake on the other and left about three-fourths of the 8 x 16-foot table open so he could rearrange the track whenever he wished. He could, then have a country scene with a farm and orchard one week and tear it out the next to have a city scene or tear that out to have a 10-track railroad yard with a roundhouse and turntable for the locomotives.

I define "portable" scenery as that which has no loose materials like ballast for the track or green ground foam or flocking to simulate weeds and grasses. These techniques are fine for layouts with permanent scenery, but the loose materials must be glued-down or they will be attracted to the grease-covered gears of the locomotives to cause damage to the mechanism. The loose materials can also cause permanent damage to turnouts. Another rule: never, ever, have loose ballast, ground foam, dyed sawdust or any other "scatter" material on a toy train layout. If you cannot glue the loose material down firmly, do not use it.

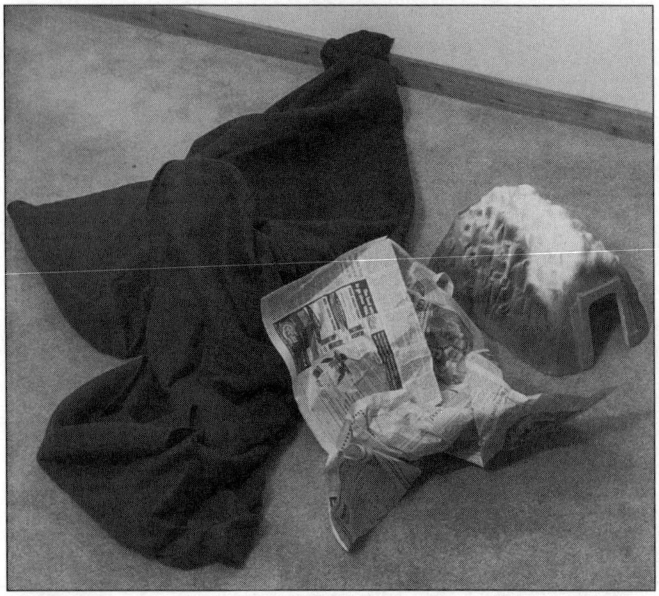

Portable Scenery

Life-Like, Heiki, Noch and others make lightweight mountains with tunnels that can be placed over the tracks to provide a type of "scenery." You can also add Life-Like's trees with bases and clumps of lichen moss bushes to a bare tabletop painted green or even on a layout built on the floor. The effect will be more pleasing, however, if you place common felt on the floor or over the layout table before you add the track.

You can crumple-up some newspapers and stuff them under the felt to push the felt up for mountains or use one of the Life-Like tunnel portals (Figure 10-2). Do not attach the felt in any way so you can reach beneath the felt to tuck-in a mountain or to move that mountain. Rest the track on top of the felt (Figure 10-3). Use the felt to cover the Woodland Scenics "Risers" and "Inclines" if you used them to make

Fig. 10-2. The basic materials for portable scenery include a 5 x 8-foot piece of green felt and wadded-up newspapers or an old Life-Like Styrofoam tunnel.

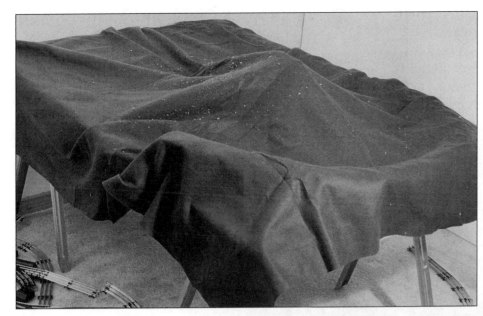

Fig. 10-4. The portable scenery system works just as well on a tabletop layout. This is a view of Figure 9-16 in Chapter 9 after the Woodland Scenics "Risers" and "Inclines" (and a wadded-up pile of newspapers to create the mountain) have been covered with green felt.

Fig. 10-5. The lower level reverse loop and the mainline oval of the point-to-point layout in Chapter 8 are in place, ready for the installation of the upper level reverse loop.

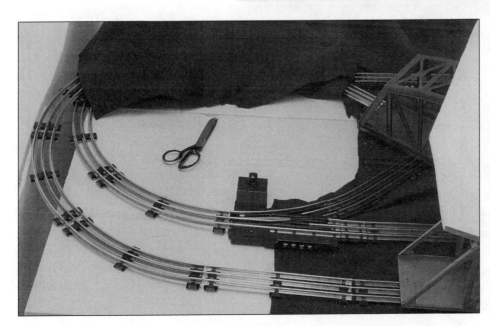

Fig. 10-6. It is not necessary to have felt buried beneath the upper level, so mark the location of the edges of the upper level and cut the felt with scissors.

uphill grades as shown in Figures 9-15, 9-16 and 9-17 in Chapter 9 (Figure 10-4).

If you are using tunnels or have built an upper level, place the elevated track support board over the felt to see where to cut the felt (Figure 10-5). Test-fit the 1/4-inch thick foam core or plywood board, then cut the felt to cover the elevated area (Figure 10-6). This layout is the loop-to-loop layout from Chapter 8. For a winter scene, use white felt like the layouts in the color section. For a fall scene, use beige felt. The felt is available in most sewing supply or cloth stores. I prefer the felt because it effectively simulated loose grass without the need for any loose material.

Portable Rock Cliffs and Tunnels

The Life-Like mountains can be used beneath the felt to form a mountain, or simply use crumpled-up newspaper to provide a hill. It would be possible, too, to drape the felt over a Life-Like mountain to provide a better texture. The felt can be cut to fit the molded-in Life-Like tunnel portals. Mountains-in-Minutes has a variety of expanded polyfoam rock walls and tunnel portals. They also have a very clever "Flex-Rock" in a choice of three different textures to simulate four different types of rock. The "Flex-Rock" can be cut with heavy scissors (Figure 10-7). The rock detail is molded onto flexible foam rubber so you can bend the rocks around

Fig. 10-7. The upper reverse loop Foamcore support is covered with felt. Now the Mountains-in-Minutes "Flex-Rock" can be cut into five-inch widths with scissors to create rock cliffs around the upper level plateau.

Fig. 10-8. Bend the "Flex-Rock" to match the contours of the edges of he Foamcore board that supports the upper level trackage. You can use the T-pins to hold the Flex-Rock to the tabletop and to the Foamcore upper level support board.

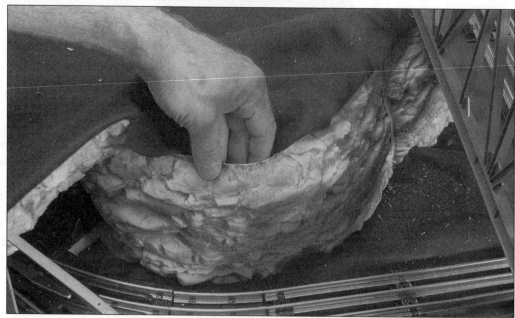

Fig.10-9. Cut one-inch wide strips of Flex-Rock to fit across the tops of the "tunnel portals." Tuck the felt around the Flex-Rock to make a smooth transition from felt to rock.

Fig. 10-10. A one-inch strip of Flex-Rock provides the "roof" of the tunnel on one end of the lower reverse loop on the loop-to-loop layout, with a five-inch high piece of Flex-Rock for the side of the tunnel.

Fig. 10-11. The rock cliffs increases the realism of the scenery on the loop-to-loop lay-out and they leave the maximum amount of space for the river and tracks on the lower level.

corners to fit around the inside or outside of curves (Figure 10-8). The Flex-Rock can be attached to the tabletop or the elevated upper level foamcore or plywood support board with dressmaker's T-pins.

Tuck-in the felt over the tops of the rocks to disguise their edges (Figure 10-9). A few pieces of lichen can be used to further disguise the transition from green felt "grass" to rock cliffs. The rocks are prepainted and ready to use right out of the package. You can attach them to any of the tunnel portals made by Lionel, MTH, Mountains-In-Minutes, or Chooch with rubber cement so the two can be separated if you want to use them elsewhere. To make a Flex-Rock tunnel portal, I cut one-inch strips of the Flex-Rock to make the top of the two tunnel portals and used five-inch tall pieces of Flex-Rock for the vertical sides of the portals on the "Point-To-Point" portable layout in Chapter 8 (Figure 10-10). The ends of the bridges near the Flex-Rock cliffs are actually supported by 5-inch pieces of 2 x 6 lumber hidden behind the rocks (Figure 10-11).

Clearance is Critical

There is a major danger when building scenery for a toy train layout: the scenery must be far enough from tracks so the longer locomotives, freight cars and passenger cars will not sideswipe the cliffs, tunnel portals, bridge abutments and other scenery features to cause fre-

quent derailments. Always test run the longest cars or locomotives through any new sections of scenery before you attach the scenery permanently to the layout.

Portable Rivers and Lakes

It is easy to simulate rivers or lakes on a portable model railroad. You can use crumpled-up aluminum foil that has been flattened, or crumpled-up and flattened plastic wrap. There are also some clear plastic sheets with waves and ripples molded-in available through hobby dealers (Figure 10-12). I used the Kibri 4126 clear

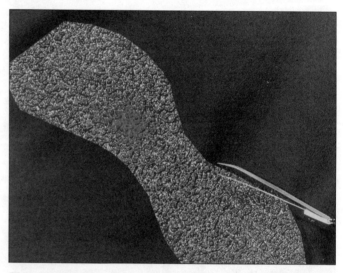

Fig. 10-13. Use scissors to cut the wrinkled Kibri plastic to the meandering shapes of the shores of a river or lake.

Fig. 10-12. The 4 x 7-foot layout in Chapter 5 was finished with portable scenery including this pair of bridges and a Noch plastic stream.

Fig. 10-14. Longer rivers and streams can be made in several sections with the joints hidden beneath the bridges.

Fig. 10-15. Cover all of the edges of the plastic "water" with lichen to disguise the transition from plastic to felt.

plastic water and the Noch 60851 is a similar product. Use scissors to cut the material to the shape of the river or lake you desire, lay it on top of the felt, and slide it beneath the bridges (Figure 10-14). Disguise the edges of the water with clumps of lichen around all the edges of the plastic (Figure 10-15).

Portable Roads

Cut roads from either brown felt or dark grey felt to simulate dirt or paved surfaces. Some craft stores sell a dense foam plastic material that makes excellent roads, This material is smooth enough so you can apply white or yellow strips from a paint pen. Testors has these paint pens available in hobby stores. Use a ruler to make straight highway divider stripes or the stripes that indicate parking spaces. For curves, use a large dinner plate or trash can lid to guide the paint pen. Lionel makes a 117 Grade Crossing (Figure 12-5 in Chapter 12) that will fit beneath most toy train track or you can use 1/4-inch square strips of balsa wood, dyed a light grey/brown to simulate creosoted and weathered wood for a highway crossing.

Portable Trees and Bushes

There are dozens of ready-built trees that are tall enough to be used for portable or permanent toy train layouts. Life-Like, Heiki, Noch and others have large coniferous trees (Figure 10-16). Similar trees are available in a variety of shapes and shades of green, as well as bright orange and yellow fall colors, to simulate deciduous trees (Figure 10-17). The Life-Like trees have molded-in bases so they are free-standing. Some of the other brands do not have bases to be free-standing, but you can use a jigsaw to cut a three-inch diameter disc from a clear plastic box. Use clear or brown silicone bath tub caulking compound to cement the disc to the base of the tree to make the tree free-standing. Or, you can drill a hole in the base of the tree trunk, cut the head off a nail, and push the nail into the trunk. The tree can then be pushed into the scenery.

Hobby shops sell a treated natural moss material called lichen that is used for the limbs and branches on some of these trees. Life-Like, Heiki, Noch, Woodland Scenics and others package the lichen and offer it in a variety of colors including green, brown and bright autumn colors. The lichen can be used as-is for bushes, especially along the shores of clear plastic lakes, streams or rivers (Figure 10-18).

Permanent Scenery

The traditional method of making scenery for model railroads is to shape the hills with door screen then slop-on a few hundred pounds of plaster. There are much easier methods. The modern method of using plaster for scenery is to soak paper towels in Hydrocal plaster or to use plaster-impregnated gauze like Woodland Scenics Plaster Cloth. The Hydrocal plaster is strong enough to be self-supporting, especially when reinforced with gauze. Since no wire

Fig. 10-16. Life-Like makes some medium-size coniferous trees (far left) and Noch and Heiki offer these large trees that make excellent scenery for an O scale toy train layout.

Fig. 10-17. Life-Like has some O scale deciduous trees with lichen leaves (far left) and Noch and Heiki offer larger trees with ground foam leaves.

Fig. 10-18. The Loop-to-Loop layout in Chapter 5 has portable or reusable scenery including trees, lichen bushes and a Noch plastic river.

screen is needed, the mountain shapes can be made with simple crumpled-up piles of wadded-up newspapers. This method starts with either a flat tabletop or an open-grid benchwork so the valleys can dip below the level of the tracks.

The alternate method of building scenery utilizes extruded polystyrene insulation board like the blue-colored Styrofoam made by Dow Corning suggested for lightweight tabletops in Chapter 9. There are other brands in other colors, but the most useful boards for building a toy train layout are extruded polystyrene. The white insulation boards (sometimes called "bead boards") are usually expanded polystyrene and, although are lighter than the extruded polystyrene, they are really not strong enough for rugged toy train scenery. With this layout construction and scenery method, at least one layer of two-inch thick blue Styrofoam is placed between the tabletop and the track. Two layers are even better. The thickness allows space for rivers and streams and even roads to be below the level of the tracks. Lay the tracks on top of the Styrofoam, even rearrange them for a year or so until you have the layout you know works best. Then carve the valleys into the Styrofoam "earth" using either a hacksaw blade or one of the electrically-heated "hot wire" cutting tools like the Avalon Concepts' Detail Wand.

Carving Styrofoam Valleys

I would suggest you make a model of the scenery you wish to carve using child's modeling clay. It's far easier to see how step a slope must be by working in clay than trying to guess what will happen when you carve the Styrofoam. The blue Styrofoam can be carved with a hacksaw blade held in a gloved hand or you can mount the blade in one of the handles that grip just one end of the blade. The sawing will produce a fine sawdust that clings to everything. You can minimize the mess by having a flexible vacuum hose near the cutting area with the vacuum turned on to collect the sawdust as you create it.

If you are going to carve much scenery, you might consider investing in one of the hot wire cutters. Woodland Scenics makes a couple of cutters with handles shaped like jigsaws. These can be used for cutting loose boards, but they cannot dig down into the surface. For that, you need either a hacksaw blade or a heated wire cutter like the Detail Wand in Avalon Concepts' Foam Sculpting Detail Station. This tool consists of an insulated handle with a heavy electrical wire running from the handle to a control box that regulates the amount of electricity that flows into the handle. The electrical current heats a wire that is clamped to the Detail Wand handle and the wire melts its way through the Styrofoam. The handle has two clamps to grip the opposite ends of a 12-inch long piece of wire. You can bend the wire into a 6-inch long U-shaped loops to make what is effectively a "hot knife" with a six-inch blade. That will allow

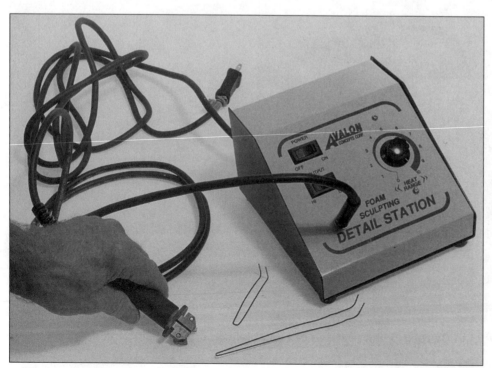

Fig. 10-19. The Avalon Concepts "Detail Station" includes the "Detail Wand" handle. Bend the wires for the Detail Wand into 4-inch and 6-inch long U-shapes and clamp them into the handle.

you to carve down from the surface of the blue Styrofoam to make those valleys.

The U-shaped blade can also be bent at a right angle to produce a tool for cutting straight edges to cut the Styrofoam boards to size as shown in Chapter 9 (Figures 9-6 and 9-7). Bend the wire so it makes a perfect 90-degree cut with the handle resting on the surface of the Styrofoam. Use a ruler to guide the wire so the cut is straight. The heated wire produces fumes, as it cuts through the Styrofoam, and those fumes can be toxic so always work outdoors or provide forced fresh air ventilation (Figure 10-19).

The wire can become as hot as an electric stove and the melted plastic that can drip-off the wire is hotter than melted candle wax, so burns are possible. Wear cloth gloves and long sleeves so no skin is exposed. Caution: Do not try to use a hot wire cutter with the urethane foam insulation boards or with Mountains-in-Minutes or other brands of molded urethane rocks, tunnel portals and retaining walls because the fumes produced can be toxic.

Most real railroad cuts through the earth and earthen fills or embankments have slopes that are no steeper than about 30-degrees. Use the hacksaw blade or the Avalon Concepts' Detail Wand hot wire cutter when making those cuts. The hot wire is only long enough to make a cut a 30-degree cut through a single 2-inch layer of blue Styrofoam. If you are making shallower cuts, use the hot wire to cut as deeply as possible, then use the cutter vertically to remove the just-cut material and make a second pass. When the cut is complete, remove the first layer of blue Styrofoam (Figure 10-20) and resume cutting the slope through the second layer. You can replace portions of the Styrofoam material as well as remove it. If, for example, you discover that you have made any portion of the valley too deep, find the chunk of blue Styrofoam you removed and slice-off the bottom of it to fill-in the bottom of the valley.

The blue extruded-polystyrene like Dow Corning's Styrofoam or the lighter and softer white expanded Styrofoam can be glued with latex cement like ChemRex's PL300, Liquid Nails' Foamboard cement or latex caulking. Woodland Scenics' Foam Tack Glue becomes sticky soon after application to speed-up installing the various Styrofoam components. Wood-

Fig. 10-20. Use the hot wire in the Detail Wand to melt through the blue Styrofoam to make hillside slopes or to cut into the Styrofoam to make valleys.

land Scenics has a new low-temperature Low Temp, Foam Gun with matching glue sticks that can be used for faster bonds

Preparing for Bridges

This scenery construction system allows you to make decisions about bridges and tunnels after you see that there would be a need for such features. Remember that the embankments beneath the bridge should be no steeper than 30-degrees, and make the cuts through the embankment with the hacksaw blade or hot wire. The embankment can then be removed from beneath the track. The shapes of the valley sides and floor can be sculpted by trimming-off potato-chip-size pieces of the blue Styrofoam with either a hot wire or a hacksaw blade.

Carving Styrofoam Mountains and Tunnels

The Styrofoam hills are carved with a process that is opposite of that used for carving valleys. Leftover pieces of blue Styrofoam cut from the valleys can be turned upside down and used for small hills. To make larger hills, begin by laying a piece of the 2-inch thick blue extruded-Styrofoam over the layout where you will want the hill. Cut into the Styrofoam with a hacksaw blade (Figure 10-21) or use a hot wire cutter to carve the slopes of the hillsides. When the hillsides are completely cut, notice if there is still a flat top. If so, you can pin another piece of two-inch thick blue Styrofoam to the cut piece using 4-inch long concrete nails.

Use the slopes from the original piece as a guide for the hacksaw blade or hot wire to cut into the new piece to complete the top of the hill. When the cuts are completed, hold the hills to the table-top with 4-inch long concrete nails. If the hill or mountain is large enough, repeat the process with a third piece of two-inch thick Styrofoam if a taller mountain is needed. If you find that that three layers of carved Styrofoam still allow a flat top, you may have a place where a tunnel can be used. Repeat the process used for carving the hills to carve the top of the tunnel.

Woodland Scenics SubTerrain System

Woodland Scenics is producing a layout-construction system they call "SubTerrain." The system is based on a flexible white expanded-Styrofoam subroadbed to support the track as described in Chapter 9. The scenery itself can be constructed from Hydrocal-soaked paper towels or Woodland Scenic's own plaster-soaked gauze they call "Plaster Cloth." Woodland Scenics also makes a Hot Wire Foam Cutter, that can be used to cut any of this material. Plastruct offers a battery-powered hot wire cutter as well as a table saw-style hot wire cutter. Avalon Concepts' Foam Sculpting Detail Station jigsaw-shaped handle or the Detail Wand described earlier can also be used for cutting white Styrofoam. If you use any of these hot wire cutters, I recommend that you work outdoors so the slight fumes produced by the cutting will not be as likely affect any allergies you may have.

Fig. 10-21. A hacksaw blade can be used to cut the blue Styrofoam but it produces a nearly weightless dust that must be vacuumed away immediately.

The Sub Terrain system is designed to be used with a flat tabletop. That tabletop can be a sheet of 1/4-inch plywood or a sheet of 1/4-inch chipboard or particle board (braced every 12-square-inches with a 1 x 3 or 1 x 4 benchwork grid to avoid sag). You can also use blue expanded-Styrofoam insulation boards supported by an open-grid system. The track is to be supported on 2-inch thick or higher "Risers" and upgrades constructed using the "Inclines" shown in Figures 9-14, 9-15, 9-16 and 9-17 in Chapter 9.

The SubTerrain system also includes ribbed Profile Boards that interlock for extra length and to form corners. These Profile Boards are meant to surround the edges of the layout. Begin scenery construction by surrounding the edges of the layout with the Profile Boards, then begin wadding-up newspapers as you would for the standard paper towel-soaked plaster system. Tape the newspaper wads down and, if necessary, spray them with water to reduce the springiness. To get a better feel for the actual shapes, drape the newspapers with damp industrial-grade brown paper towels.

When the scenery shapes are finalized, surround the layout with Woodland Scenics Profile Boards and cut the shape of the edges of the scenery into the Profile Boards. The final hard shell can be either industrial-grade paper towels dipped in Hydrocal or the shapes can be draped with Woodland Scenics' Plaster Cloth Hydrocal-impregnated gauze that is similar to that used to make casts for broken arms or legs (Figure 10-22).

Fig. 10-22. Make permanent scenery by covering mountains made from wadded-up newspaper with Woodland Scenics Plaster Cloth or with paper towels dipped in wet Hydrocal plaster.

Fig. 10-23. Smooth the wet Plaster Cloth to work the plaster into the gauze. Use two layers so the scenery will be self-supporting.

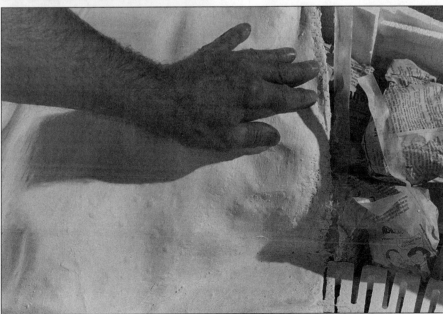

Woodland Scenics suggests that you use the track to precisely position the Risers and Inclines, but that you remove the track while you apply the Plaster Cloth so you can drape the Plaster Cloth right over the subroadbed to bond the entire layout surface to the Profile Boards at the edges in a sturdy Hydrocal plaster shell (Figure 10-23). When the Plaster Cloth has set, use a sanding block to smooth the subroadbed surface. It's important to sand within a minute after the plaster sets because it gets almost rock hard in hours.

If you brace the Profile boards with cut-off scraps of Styrofoam glued to the tabletop and to the Profile Boards, the system should be strong enough so you can leave the track in place and merely bring the Plaster Cloth (or Hydrocal-soaked paper towels) up to the edges of the roadbed as you would with conventional construction (Figure 10-25). There's just enough room on the tops of the Risers and Inclines to provide a mounting perch for the Plaster Cloth. For insurance, you can stick Woodland Scenics' Foam Nails T-pins into the still-wet Plaster Cloth or Hydrocal. Similar T-pins are also available at fabric stores.

It is certainly possible to use either Woodland Scenic's system or the traditional model railroad scenery of industrial paper towels dipped in Hydrocal plaster to shape the mountains (Figure 10-25). The system is illustrated in my *HO Model Railroading Handbook*, also published by Krause, if you need more information.

Rock Cliffs, Walls and Tunnel Portals

Mountains-In-Minutes makes rock cliffs, retaining walls and tunnel portals from stiff urethane foam as well as the flexible foam "Flex Rocks" described earlier. Chooch has similar products cast in resin. All of these detail items are prepainted and they can be cut with a hacksaw, then attached with either plaster or silicone caulking compound.

Earth, Grass and Weeds

You can finish the surface of permanent scenery with a thick layer of latex wall paint and sifted-on fine ground foam rubber. Or, you can cover the foam with green or beige felt to simulate grass and weeds. For permanent scenery, the felt can be glued-down with contact cement and the felt applied while the cement is still wet. Sift real dirt through a tea strainer to cover some of the felt where bare ground might appear (Figure 10-26). Use a stiff wire brush to work the dirt into the felt so at least half of the visible surface is dirt. I call this the "Grass-That-Grows" system because the individual strands or fibers of the felt really do stick up through the sifted-on dirt as though they were growing. Fix the dirt to the felt by spraying it with a mixture of one-part Artist's Matte Medium to four-parts water plus a drop or two of dish washing detergent to act as a wetting agent. Use one of the hand-pump spray bottles like those used for spraying hair or for misting plants to spray the

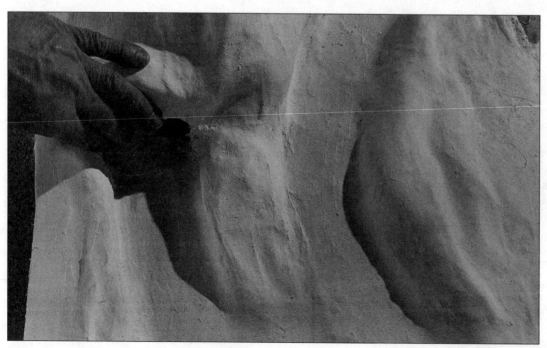

Fig 10-24. Woodland Scenics recommends that you remove the track to spread the Plaster Cloth over the roadbed when using their SubTerrain system.

Fig 10-25. The traditional method of building a model railroad utilizes open-grid benchwork with mountains made of wire screen covered with plaster.

Fig. 10-26. Use a tea strainer to sift real dirt onto the scenery, then cement the dirt in place by spraying it with a mixture of Artist's Matte Medium and water.

water and Matte Medium mixture. If you cover the surface with plaster, paper towels dipped in plaster or Plaster Cloth, you will be adding unnecessary weight to the layout. I would recommend that you use this Grass-That-Grows system of treated felt for as much of the surface as possible because it adds only ounces of weight.

Ballast for Toy Train Track

I do not recommend using loose ballast with toy trains because the particles can cause damage to locomotive mechanism, action accessories and turnouts. If you insist on using loose ballast, it can be applied to the track directly from the bag (Figure 10-27). Use a paint brush to shape the ballast and to brush it from the tops of the ties. Wood-

land Scenics, Life-Like and Rick Johnson all offer packaged ballast suitable for toy trains. When applying the ballast, be sure to brush any particles away from the rails before flooding the area with the mixture of one-part Artist's Matte Medium to four-parts water plus a drop of two of dish washing detergent to act as a wetting agent. The Matte Medium looks like white glue but it dries with much more flexibility and no gloss. Keep any loose ballast away from any turnouts. If you must have ballast, do not allow it to bounce anywhere near the turnouts, paint the turnout area gray, and daub-on a darker gray or beige to blend it into the ballasted track. Loose ballast is bad for the working parts of a turnout, but loose ballast cemented solidly into the working parts of a turnout can ruin the turnout.

Fig. 10-27. Pour the ballast right from the bag and use a paint brush to remove the ballast from the ties and to shape the edges.

Chapter 11

Buildings & Structures

Your toy train layout will seem much more realistic if you provide a setting for the trains so they roll past something that looks like the real world. You can build hills, valleys and mountains, and install trees and bushes as described in Chapter 10 to provide a natural environment. For most of us, however, the sights we want to duplicate on our layouts are those of trains running past stations picking up freight, or where locomotives are serviced. Specific buildings help us to identify each of these sites.

Selecting the Best Buildings

There are dozens of buildings available for toy trains. Usually, these are plastic kits marked "O Scale" like the Walthers 3307 Fairfield Station (Figure 11-1). Atlas, Bachmann, Plasticville, IHC,

Lionel, MTH, K-Line, Model Power and Walthers all make plastic kits suitable for toy train layouts. Model Power offers a variety of ready-built versions of their kits. Korber and Downtown Deco have cast resin or plaster kits that require a bit more skill to assemble and paint than plastic kits. There's no reason why you cannot use the assembled ceramic or cast resin "collector village" buildings from company's like Department 56 on your toy train layout.

Try to find buildings that are small enough to fit your layout. An O scale building can be a rather large model and you'll probably not have the room for all the buildings you want. You can reduce the size of some buildings by cutting-off portions of them as described later in this chapter.

You're the only one who must be satisfied with your layout and the buildings that occupy

Fig. 11-1. Walthers 3307 Fairfield Station with Preiser people and boxes for extra details.

its real estate. Some modelers prefer railroad-oriented buildings like stations, coaling towers, freight stations or industries served by the railroad like warehouses, lumber yards, oil depots, cattle pens and the like. Still others want to model a small town or a city. You won't likely have space for all of these options, so make your choices carefully.

Assembling Plastic Building Kits

It is possible to assemble a plastic building kit with just cement and a hobby knife. There are a number of tools that can make the assembly easier and that can make it possible for you to custom-modify any plastic structure kit. I would suggest an X-Acto razor saw blade and handle, quality scissors, pointed tweezers, a steel ruler with O scale feet and inches marked on the side, a cabinet maker's file, needlenose pliers, regular pliers, flush-cut diagonal cutters or sprue cutters, a regular screwdriver, a small Phillips head screwdriver, a small screwdriver and a jeweler's screwdriver (Figure 11-2).

The plastic building kits are molded on runners or sprues. Never break the parts from these sprues. Use a hobby knife, flush-cut diagonal cutters, or the special Testor's Sprue Cutters to remove the walls, doors, windows, roof, and detail parts from the sprues (Figure 11-3). Before you remove the parts, however, read the instructions and do a "dry run" assembly of the building so you know where each part fits. Often, the numbers of the parts are molded onto the sprue beside the part and, sometimes, there are very similar parts.

Check the fit of all the parts, especially the larger pieces like walls and roofs. You may need to use a flat file to smooth some of the joints for perfect fit. I suggest that you try to locate a cabinet maker's or countertop-installer's file (Figure 11-4). These files are about a foot long with all four sides perfectly parallel. One wide side and one narrow side have medium-cut teeth and one wide side has coarse-cut teeth. One narrow side is smooth. The files make it much easier to keep the

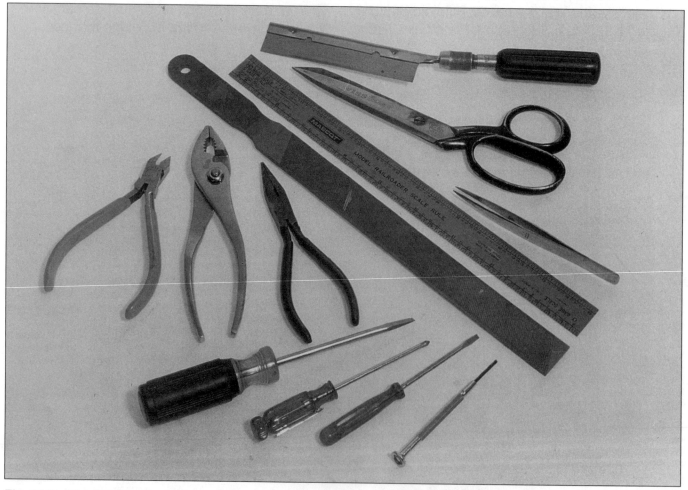

Fig. 11-2. A basic assortment of tools to assemble or custom-modify plastic structure kits.

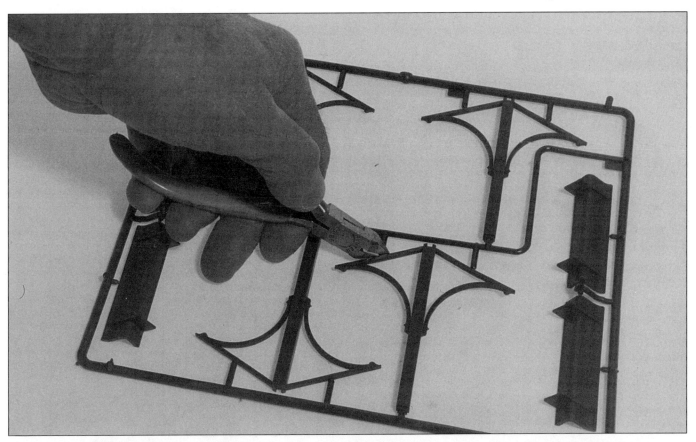

Fig. 11-3. Use diagonal cutters (shown) or Testors' Sprue Cutters to remove the plastic parts from the molding.

Fig. 11-4. Use a cabinet maker's file to smooth joining edges of the plastic parts.

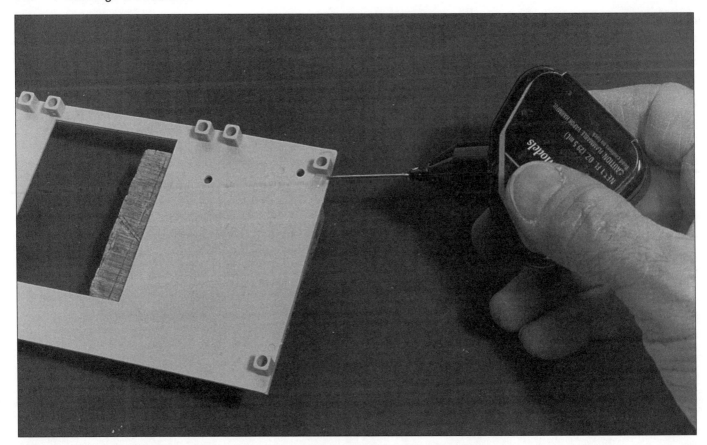

Fig. 11-5. Spread a bead of plastic cement along both surfaces to be joined.

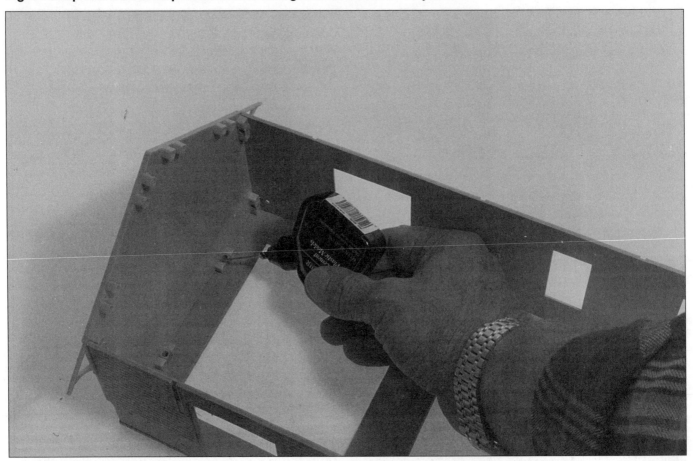

Fig. 11-6. Apply additional cement to the locking tabs or areas that are not joined tightly.

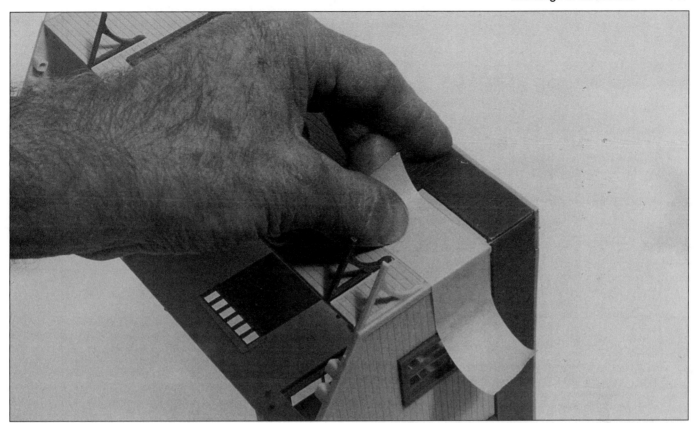

Fig. 11-7. If the joints do not fit tightly, use masking tape to hold them together until the cement dries overnight.

assembly joint straight, particularly if you are cutting the plastic to modify the building as described later in this chapter.

Use the thicker cements in applicator bottles like Testors' Model Master Cement For Plastic Models to assemble these kits (Figure 11-5). You can use the tube-type plastic cements, but it is a bit too easy to get excess cement. If you do apply too much cement wipe it off immediately with a paper towel. The needle-type applicator on the Testors' Model Master Liquid Cement For Plastic Models makes it easy to control the amount of cement.

Apply a thin bead of the cement on both of the surfaces to be joined and, if necessary, add a drop to the assembled joint (Figure 11-6). When you press the joints together, move them very slightly to scrub the cement into the plastic. The cement acts to dissolve the plastic so the plastic itself forms much of the strength of the joint. If the building is especially large, you may want to hold the joints together with masking tape until the cement dries overnight (Figure 11-7).

If you paint the model, you must scrape away the paint to use any plastic cement. It's easier to use one of the cyanoacrylate cements, such as Aron-Alpha, Hot Stuff, Zap or Super

Glue, or five-minute epoxy to install painted parts. The plastic cements (either tube-type or liquid) will etch or craze the clear plastic windows, so use Testors Clear Parts Cement or white glue to install the windows.

Painting Plastic Buildings

Most of the plastic building kits are molded in three or more colors so there is no apparent reason to paint them. The plastic is slightly translucent and a bit too shiny, however, so it will look like plastic unless you paint it. You can simply spray the model with Testor's clear, flat-finish DullCote to produce a painted look. Apply the DullCote before cementing any clear windows in place because the clear paint can etch or frost the windows.

If you want to change the color, the model will be much more realistic if you use a flat finish paint rather than a glossy paint. Floquil's Polly-Scale paint is good for plastics but it not available in spray cans, so you must apply it with a brush or purchase an airbrush and air supply so you can spray paint your models. Testors' Model Master series of paints are available in both bottles and spray cans in colors that are typical of those used on structures. Hobby

Fig. 11-8. Double-over masking tape to provide a sticky surface to hold small parts while you paint them.

Fig. 11-9. Scrape paint from the joining surfaces of windows and walls before applying the plastic cement.

Fig. 11-10. Use sepia-color drafting ink or India ink to accent the molded-in detail on station platforms like this Atlas 6902 Station Platform.

Fig. 11-11. Use a damp rag to wipe the ink from the surface before the ink has a chance to dry.

Fig. 11-12. The Atlas 6902 Station Platform with the telephone booth from the Atlas 6901 Suburban Station.

shops sell a variety of flat-finish spray paints from Testors and some hardware stores have flat finish enamel or acrylic spray paints. If you can only find the color you want in a gloss, use it, then spray the model with Testors' Dullcote.

Paint the windows and doors before cementing them to the model. Paint the walls after they are assembled. Paint the roof as individual pieces, and touch-up any seams after the roof is assembled. A scrap of wood can be used to hold the windows and doors for painting. Tear off a foot-long loop of masking tape and fold it back over itself so the sticky side is out. Press the tape onto a scrap of 1 x 2 wood or lath so it provides a sticky surface to hold the windows and doors. Use the wood as a handle while you spray the windows and doors your choice of color (Figure 11-8). Use plastic cement to install the windows and doors if the backsides, parts and walls are unpainted (Figure 11-9). If the parts are painted, it's best to use the thickened hobby-type cyanoacrylate cements.

To simulate concrete, paint the surface a medium beige/grey. If there are no molded-in cracks, simulate them by slicing lightly through the paint with the tip of hobby knife. When the paint is dry, brush-on some sepia-colored drafting or India ink (Figure 11-10) from an artist's supply store. The ink will collect in the cracks to accent them and when lit they will highlight the concrete texture (Figure 11-11). When the ink dries, complete the assembly. The platform for this Atlas 6902 Station Platform was painted using these techniques (Figure 11-12).

Assembling and Painting Resin and Plaster Buildings

The cast resin or cast plaster kits can be assembled with Walthers Goo cement (available from most hobby shops) or Goodyear Pliobond cement (available for most hardware stores). Glue a piece of fine sandpaper to a foot-long piece of straight 1 x 4 wood to use a sanding block. Carefully rub each of the wall's assembly joints over the sandpaper and test-fit each joint to be sure it fits perfectly before gluing the parts in place. Some of these buildings have the windows molded-in, so they must be painted in place. The easy way to do that is to spray paint the entire wall the color you want for the windows, then paint the walls with a paint brush.

Applying Decal Signs

Many of these structure kits include decals for signs. Most hobby shops carry Microscale's

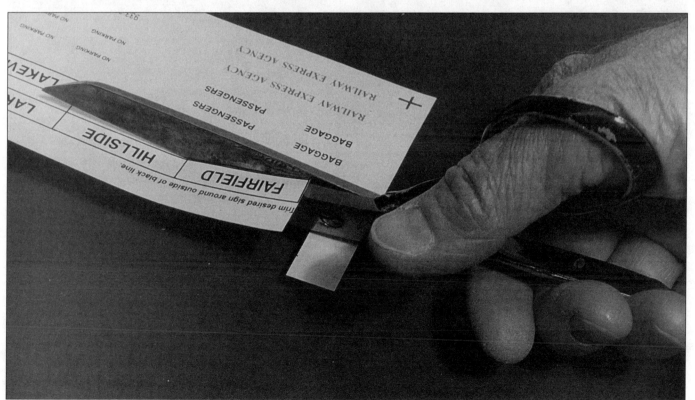

Fig. 11-13. Cut the decals from the paper with scissors.

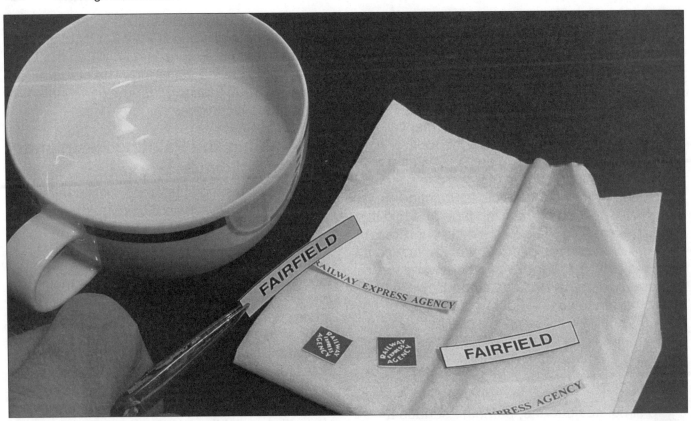

Fig. 11-14. Dip the decal in warm water and rest it on a paper towel while the water soaks through the decal's paper backing.

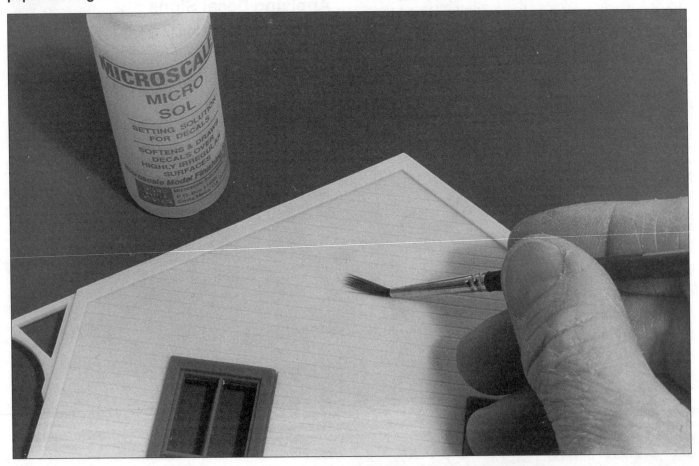

Fig. 11-15. Coat the area that will be covered by the decal with decal softening fluid.

Fig. 11-16. Hold the decal in position with a wet paint brush while you slide the paper backing from beneath the decal with tweezers.

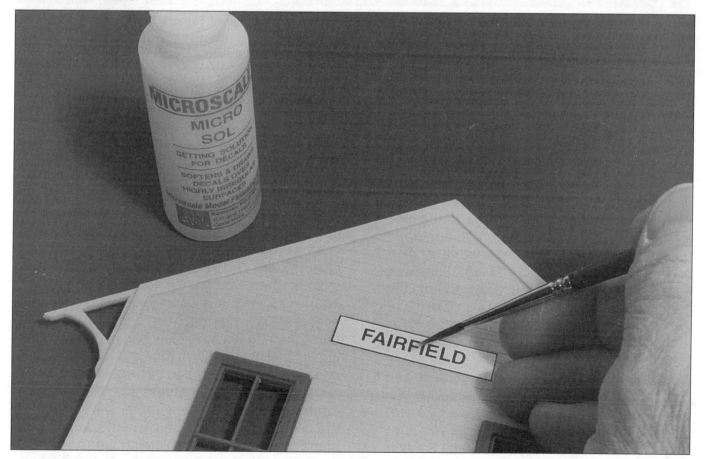

Fig 11-17. Coat the decal with decal softening fluid.

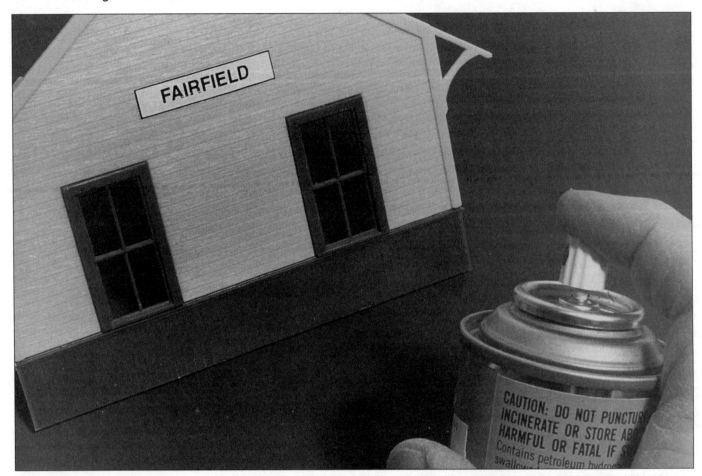

Fig. 11-18. When the decal has dried overnight, seal and protect it with a coat of Testors' DullCote.

decals that include a wide selection of O scale signs for city businesses, industries and railroad-related structures. Signs add a touch of humanity to a building that can make it much more realistic.

To apply decals, purchase one of the decal-softening fluids like Walthers' Solvaset, Champ's Decalset or Microscale's Microsol. These fluids soften the decal, after it is applied, so it clings to the surface of the model as tightly as paint. Use scissors to cut the decal from the paper sheet as near the colored portion as possible (Figure 11-13). Use tweezers to hold the individual decals and dip them into a cup of warm water for a count of 20 (Figure 11-14). Place the decal on a paper towel and allow it to sit for about 3 minutes while the water works its way through the paper to dissolve the glue. You can test the decal to see if it will move without moving the paper by pushing the decal with the point of a hobby knife.

Support the building so the area you are about to decal is perfectly horizontal. Apply a coat of decal-softening fluid to the area where you want to place the decal (Figure 11-15). When the decal is ready to move, pick it up with tweezers and hold both the decal and its paper backing in the place where you want the decal. Hold the decal lightly with the tip of a hobby knife or a paint brush dipped in water while you pull the paper backing from beneath it with tweezers (Figure 11-16). The decal should be floating slightly in a thin layer of decal-softening fluid so you can move the decal into the exact position with the tip of the hobby knife. Apply another coat of decal softening fluid to the decal itself (Figure 11-17). When you have the decal exactly where you want it, leave it alone for an hour or so while the water and softening fluid evaporate. Do not touch the decal until the softening fluid dries completely because the softening fluid will have made the decal about the consistency of paint. You can apply all of the decals you need on that one wall. Repeat the process to apply decals to other walls. When the decal areas are dry, protect the decals and blend them into the surrounding areas by spraying them with Testor's DullCote (Figure 11-18).

Custom Buildings

Some modelers prefer to modify every building they build. It's rare to see an identical building in more than one town out there in the real world, but many model railroads often have the same building. You can "customize" your buildings somewhat by painting them in colors that are different for those on the box. You can also cut the walls, roof and floors of any kit before the kit is assembled to make a smaller or different-shaped structure. The Walthers 3307 Fairfield Station is a fairly large structure. I wanted it to be about the size of the Atlas 6901 Suburban Station, so I decided to shorten it by removing a portion of the passenger waiting room (right) end.

Use masking tape to mark the line you want to cut. The parts in many of the plastic kits snap together, so you can test-fit the walls and roof to determine exactly where you want to cut, then disassemble the building to cut the parts. If the parts do not snap together, use masking tape to temporarily assemble the building to see where you might want to modify it. The two side walls

of the Walthers' station were cut to remove 3-3/4-inches (Figure 11-20). The roof overhang seemed excessive when I test-fitted the parts, so I removed 4 inches from the roof (Figure 11-19). Use an X-Acto razor saw (available in hobby shops) to make the cuts.

Smooth the cuts and match any joint angles using a cabinet maker's file described earlier in this chapter. Use flush-cut diagonal cutters to remove any of the tabs that interfere with the construction (Figure 11-21). Some of the lower wainscoting trim pieces must also be cut to fit the shortened walls. Cut and fit the base to match the modified structure by first marking where to cut the base (Figure 11-22).

Similar shortening steps can be used on many kits or a two-story building can be cut-down to a single story. Paint the walls and roof if you wish, then paint the windows, doors and trim. Apply the decals before assembling the walls. Assemble the building following the kit instructions (Figure 11-23). Install the roof, trim and chimney to complete the modified station (Figure 11-24).

Fig. 11-19. Use masking tape to mark where to cut the panels to custom-modify structure kits.

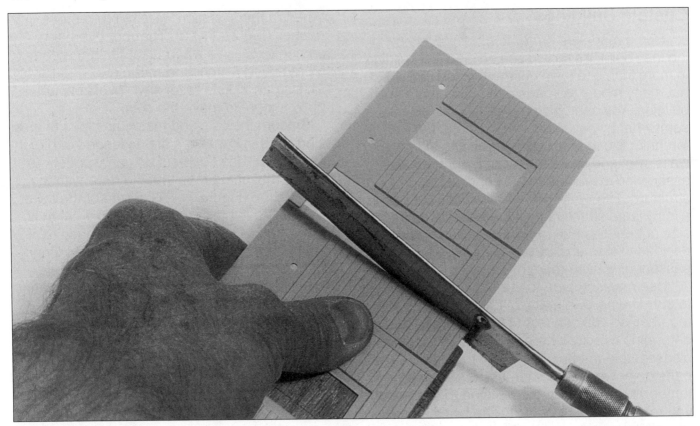

Fig. 11-20. Use a razor saw to cut the panels. The masking tape used to mark the cut line is on the backside of this wall.

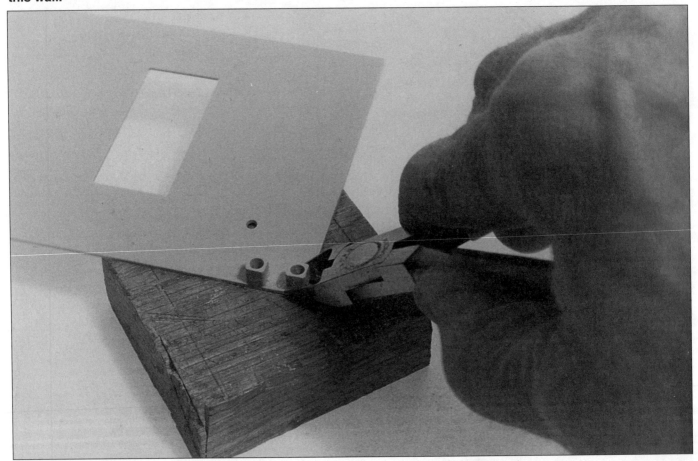

Fig. 11-21. Remove any extra interlocking tabs with flush-cut diagonal cutters.

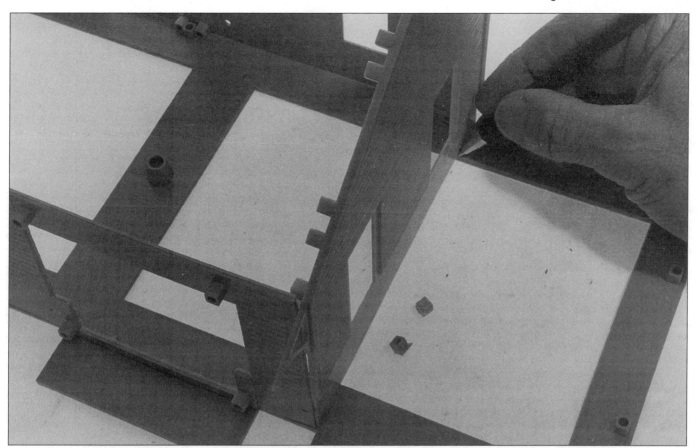

Fig. 11-22. Mark the places to cut the base for the shortened station.

Fig. 11-23. Install the clear plastic window glazing before cementing the roof in place.

Fig 11-24. The shortened Walthers 3307 Fairfield Station.

Build a Coal Mine

The coal mine was assembled by adding 3/16 x 3/16 inch balsa wood legs and 1/16 x 3/16-inch balsa wood diagonal braces to a Lionel 824K Freight Platform (Figure 11-25). Assemble the building but do not install the platform or the roof. Cut the roof to remove the overhang over the open platform. Use a hobby knife to cut the wood braces. It's easier to add them to the model before the roof is in place because you can rest the model on its side. Lay the model on flat surface covered with wax paper while you apply the braces. I would suggest cutting all the wood parts to fit, then staining them with india ink or drafting ink. Use thickened hobby-type cyanoacrylate cement to assemble the parts. The work will go faster if you also spray-on some "accelerator" for the cyanoacrylate cement to make an instant bond. The mine provides a spot to simulate coal-loading on a compact layout. If you want to load real coal, Lionel makes a 32921 Electric Coaling Station that could fit in this layout in place of the Lionel 164 Log Loader visible in the upper left (Figure 11-26).

Interior Lighting

Some of the Lionel and MTH accessory buildings include interior lighting. A few of the plastic building kits, like the Walthers 3307 Fairfield Station kit also include interior lighting (Figure 11-27). The wires must, however, be connected to a transformer to provide lighting. It is difficult to route the wires on a portable layout, so you might want to skip interior lighting for all the buildings. If you have just one or two buildings, you might consider modifying a flashlight to provide battery-power interior lighting. Life-Like offers a bracket to hold light bulbs if you want to add lighting to other kit-built buildings. It is dangerous to use lighting inside plastic buildings if the light bulbs are turned-on to their full intensity. I would suggest you use one of the inexpensive toy train transformers exclusively for lighting so you will be able to turn-down the voltage so the lights glow at about half-power. The lower voltage will prolong the life of the lights and minimize the chance of their overheating inside the building which could cause it to warp or catch fire.

11-26 Lionel offers a variety of remote-controlled accessories to load or unload cars. The Lionel 164 Log Loader is visible in the upper left. The modified Lionel 824K Freight Platform provides a source of imaginary loads of coal.

Fig 11-25. Shorten the roof of the Lionel 824K Freight Platform and add some balsa wood legs to created a coal mine. For a run-down look, break one or more of the legs or braces.

An American Models' GP35 heads a freight on Ken Zieska's 20 x 40-foot S scale layout. The freight cars were built from American Models plastic kits. This layout utilizes accurate-scale Scenery Unlimited track and turnouts with code 125 rail so the locomotive and rolling stock have wheels with smaller flanges than the usual American Flyer trains. The couplers are all scale-size Kadee products. The trees are made from sage brush branches, hedge clippings and weeds with Woodland Scenics mesh and ground foam for the leaves. The river is bare plywood painted dark blue/green, with white rapids, coated with clear urethane.

The 19 x 72-foot layout at the Carnegie Science Center in Pittsburgh, Pennsylvania includes dozens of industrial scenes like this coal mine. The buildings were built from sheets and strips of bass wood.

The hobo jungle scene on the Carnegie Science Center's layout includes a fire that twinkles as a hidden light bulb is turned on and off automatically with a hand-made electronic circuit. The trees on this gigantic layout are painted Yarrow and Queen of the Meadow weeds.

Bruce Pemberton has three ovals of GarGraves three-rail — scale track running around on 2-1/2-foot wide shelves along the four walls of his 20 x 20-foot layout room. Three mpre ovals of two-rail American Flyer track run around the layout closest to the walls. He operates the smaller Lionel 0-27 locomotives and cars on the three-rail tracks and American Flyer equipment on the two-rail tracks.

Bob Yeakel has three large ovals of three-rail GarGraves track to operate Lionel trains on his layout and three even-larger ovals of two-rail track to operate the slightly larger O scale trains. Here, three Lionel trains occupy the three Mainline tracks while a fourth Lionel train waits on a siding.

Lionel has made dozens of variations on their popular New York Central 4-6-4 Hudson steam locomotive. Number 646 is Bob Yeakel's model from the late forties. The F3A and F3B diesels in the background are also Lionel as are all of the freight and passenger cars.

The O scale trains on Bob Yeakel's 13 x 24-foot layout operate on two-rail track. These trains are exact 1/48 scale, with smaller wheel flanges and smaller couplers than the Lionel toy trains he operates on the three inner ovals.

The three loops of O scale two-rail track wrap around the outer edges of the 13 x 24-foot tabletop on Bob Yeakel's layout. The oil depot in the foreground was made from baking powder cans with wire to simulate the pipes. The three-rail Lionel layout is just visible in the far upper right above the two Plasticville houses.

Bruce Pemberton buys well-worn used Lionel 0-27 locomotives at swap meets and cuts them apart to make custom models. The Pennsylvania tender is a combination of two Lionel tenders to match the "long haul" tenders used on the prototype railroad. He combines the smaller Lionel 0-27 locomotives and rolling stock with American Flyer S scale models like the blue and silver Alco diesel in the background. He is even converting many of his 0-27 models to operate on a two-rail American Flyer track with used American Flyer mechanisms beneath Lionel bodies. He also replaces the Lionel trucks and couplers with American Flyer parts.

The mining area on Bruce Pemberton's layout occupies one corner of a peninsula that protrudes from one of the room's walls. Bruce built the tables, then placed the tracks where he thought they looked best, and could provide three separate loops with passing sidings and holding tracks. He never bothered to draw a track plan.

Bruce Pemberton displays the Lionel and American Flyer toy trains that are too valuable as collector's items to be painted and modified on shelves behind his layout. The three top shelves hold Lionel 0-27 locomotives and rolling stock and the bottom three shelves hold American Flyer S scale locomotives and rolling stock.

The Lionel operating Milk Car has been one of their most popular accessories since it was introduced in 1946. Here are four highly-collectible examples including a car from the first 3462-series produced in 1947 and 1948 with unpainted metal doors, a 3472-series car from the 1949-1953 period, a larger car from the 3662-series produced from 1966 to 1960 and again from 1964 to 1966, and a more modern 9220-series car from the 1983-1986 period. The Dairyman's car visible in some of the photographs of 4 x 6-1/2-foot layouts is similar to the 9220, but it was produced in 1994.

John DiCrisci has a floor-level oval beneath his layout table that houses his operating collection of Lionel military trains including the 175 Rocket Launcher, 470 Missile Launcher, a matching 44 Missile Launch locomotive, a variety of military cars and accessories.

John DiCrisci operates most of his collection of Lionel equipment. Strings of nearly-identical box cars and tank cars include collectible variations of a similar car. He also has many of Lionel's action accessories, including the 282 Gantry Crane, 356 Station, 321 Trestle Bridge, 362 Barrel Loader, 455 oil Derrick, 464 Lumber Mill and others.

John DiCrisci has two pairs of Lionel F3 diesels in operation on his layout, a Santa Fe silver and red "Warbonnet" pair of F3A units and a red and white Katy "Texas Special" F3A and F3B set visible in the upper right.

Bob Yeakel operates all of his collectible Lionel locomotives and cars. Most of these toy trains were produced during the late forties and fifties. The maroon locomotive is Lionel's first replica of the Pennsylvania Railroad's GG-1 electric locomotive. The green passenger cars were Lionel's first post-World War II streamlined passenger cars. During this period, most of Lionel's trains were the relatively small 0-27 miniatures.

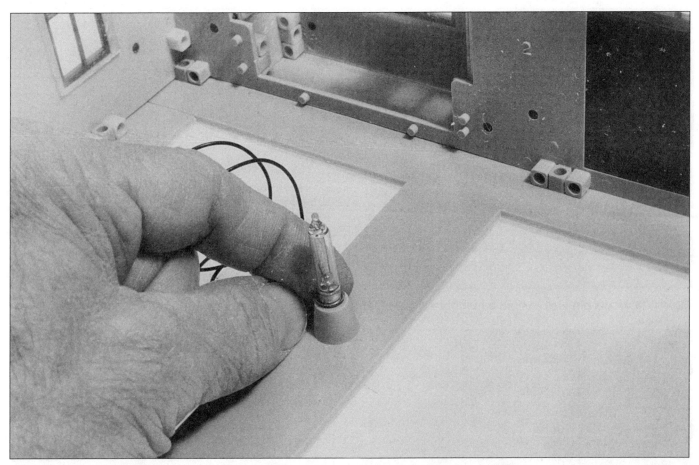

Fig. 11-27. Some structures include interior lighting or you can buy bulbs and brackets at your hobby dealer to illuminate any building.

People for Your Empire

Painted people figures are available from Life-Like, Model Power and Preiser from O scale and from Preiser in S scale. Preiser also offers painted horses, cows, sheep and assorted barnyard animals. Many of the smaller Lionel plastic building kits are furnished with at least one unpainted figure, including the 822K Watchman Shanty, 826K Barrel Loader Building, 828 K Log Loading Station, 832K Lumber Shed and 834K Barrel Shed. K-Line also has a series of plastic building kits that include unpainted figures and Preiser and Plastruct also have unpainted figures available for both O scale and S scale.

The Life-Like, Model Power and Preiser figures have small clear plastic bases so they are self-standing. Most of the Lionel and K-Line figures have no provision to keep them standing. You can cut a small disc of clear plastic from a notebook and attach the figures to the discs with rubber cement. If you want the figures to have no clear plastic bases, simply slice-of the bases with a hobby knife. Use a pin vise (available in hobby stores) to hold a number 72 drill bit and drill a hole about 1/4-inch into the shoe of the figure (Figure 11-28). Use diagonal cutters to cut the head from a pin. Use needlenose pliers to press the blunt end of the pin into the hole in the shoe (Figure 11-29).

The pin can be pushed into Styrofoam scenery and it will even work as-is on some carpet and on felt. If you want the figure to stand on a plywood tabletop, on a plastic platform, or on a plaster surface, you will have to use the pin vise and the number 72 drill bit to drill a hole for the pin in the plywood, plastic or plaster.

Use any of the hobby paints and a number 00-size paint brush to paint the figures. You can leave the faces a solid skin color and use a "wash" to highlight the eyes and mouth. Mix a "wash" of about equal parts water and dark brown acrylic paint. Brush this wash over the figure and the color will automatically collect in the crevices and hollows to accent the eyes, the mouth, hair and any folds or creases in the simulated cloth (Figure 11-30).

Fig. 11-28. Use a pin vise to hold a number 72 drill bit and drill a 1/4-inch deep hole through the shoe of the figure.

Fig. 11-29. Use needlenose pliers to push the straight pin into the hole in the shoe.

Fig. 11-30. Accent the details on faces and clothing with a thin wash of dark brown acrylic paint and water.

Fig. 11-31. Toy stores and toy departments carry an ever-changing variety of vehicles in 1/64 to /143 scale that are usable with toy train layouts.

Cars and Trucks for Your Railroad

There are very few trucks or automobiles available in exact 1/48 scale. 1/43 scale is, however, the most common size for die-cast model cars and trucks and, although the automobiles and trucks are a bit oversize, the effect is worthwhile, especially considering the almost limitless selection. If you search, you can find a number of 1/64 scale vehicles at both toy stores and hobby shops and, for most toy trains, these are probably closer to the scale of the models than 1/43 scale vehicles. Some hobby shops carry relatively costly 1/43 scale cast metal kits and some carry assembled cast-metal models.

The toy store chains and the discount stores' toy departments are some of the best sources for relatively inexpensive die-cast metal automobiles and trucks.

The exact models and paint schemes change frequently so you may not be able to buy precisely what you see here but you will find others. These four include a Maisto 1998 Ford-F-Series (marked 1/46 scale), a 1948 Ford Pickup (marked 1/36 scale), a Road Champs 1953 Chevrolet pickup and a Road Champs 1998 Chrysler Grand Cherokee (Figure 11-31). None of these companies offer catalogs or sell direct to consumers, so you must search for the products in toy stores, toy departments and hobby stores.

Chapter 12

Action Accessories

One of the joys of toy trains is watching animation, in addition to the movement of trains. The most exciting accessories are those that actually move automatically or by remote control. The classic automatic gateman, for example, opens the door to his building and moves onto the platform every time a train passes. The industrial accessories load coal, logs, barrels, oil drums and boxes or unload logs, coal or milk cans. Some action accessories simulate locomotive repairs or sawmills. Action cars unload coal, logs, boxes, barrels, mail bags, or milk cans. There is also a variety of sound-producing buildings available for toy trains. The lighted signals, crossing gates and signs, streetlights, floodlights, and illuminated structures also add the "life" effect that comes from illumination.

Operating Accessories

The uncoupling ramps described in Chapter 7 are also used to activate most of the Lionel operating cars. A small steel disc (similar to the discs that actuate automatic couplers) is suspended beneath the car, this time near the center of the car. This disc connects to the linkage on the dump cars or the levers on the operating box cars (where the worker pushes a barrel or box out the door). When the electromagnet on

The Lionel magnetic crane, operating milk car and log loader provide real freight loads on this 4 x 6-1/2-foot double-track layout.

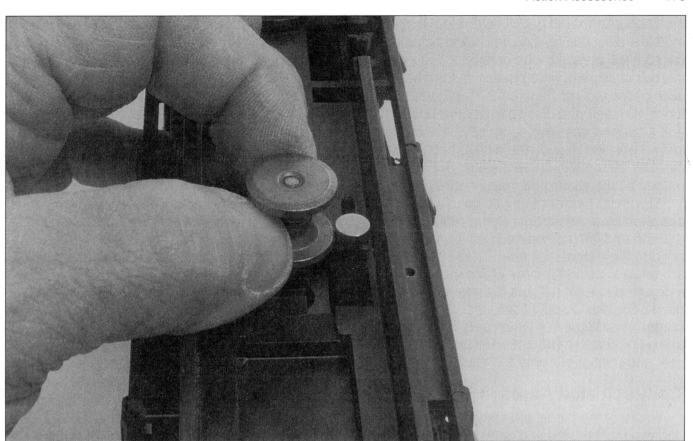

Fig. 12-2. The electromagnet in the remote uncouplertrack attracts this large metal disc (on the bottom of many of the coal-dump, log-dump and load-ejecting box cars) to dump the car's loads.

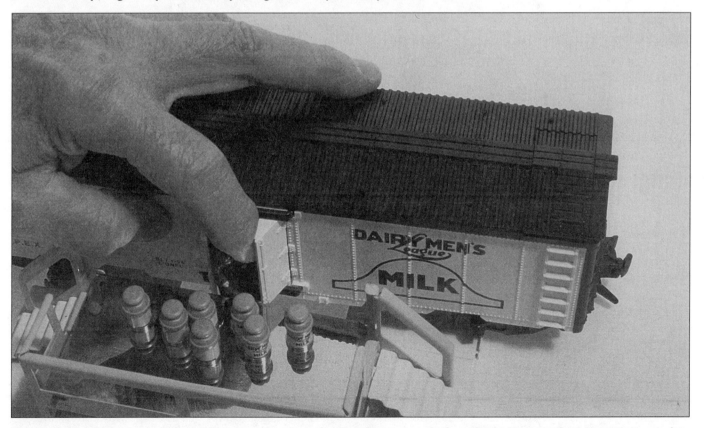

Fig 12-3. The Lionel operating milk car unloads a single milk can each time the button on the remote uncoupler track is pushed.

the uncoupling ramp track is activated, it attracts the steel disc, pulling it downward to actuate the car so it will dump its load of logs or coal or so the box or barrel will be pushed-out the box car door by the worker (Figure 12-2). When the button is released, the disc springs back upward and a spring forces the dump bay back into its locked position or pulls the worker back into the car. The button should be pressed and released quickly so the electromagnet is not overheated.

The older Lionel magnetic couplers were operated by an electronic signal picked-up from a fourth and fifth rail located between the center rail and the outer track rails. These same rails are used to activate some of the more expensive Lionel operating cars like the milk car (Figure 12-3). The O scale track section activates a magnet inside the car which sets the milk unloading worker into action to pickup a can of milk and push it out onto the platform.

Train-Actuated Accessories

Some of the Lionel train sets include semaphore signals or crossing gates that are actuated by the weight of the train passing over the track. The weight of the locomotive actuates a series of levers to move the signal arm on this semaphore signal (Figure 12-4). This Lionel crossing gate is also activated by the weight of a passing train. It is shown, here, with the Lionel 117 Grade Crossing to provide a ramp to allow roads to cross the track (Figure 12-5). Lionel offers a similar accessory that is lighted and actuated by an electronic contact. Lionel offers far more complex and reliable train-actuated action accessories where the accessory is activated electronically when the train closes or opens an electrical contact.

The Lionel operating gateman, some signals, and other devices include one of the Lionel 145C, 153C or 154C Contactors (Figure 12-6). Attach one of these devices to the rail and it will be actuated by the weight of the locomotive passing over the device's metal lever which, in turn, closes an electrical switch to send current to actuate the accessory (or a remote-control turnout) electronically. The 153C Contactor only provides the electrical power to actuate the accessory, the accessory also needs a separate

Fig. 12-5. This Lionel crossing gate is lowered by the weight of a passing locomotive.

Fig. 12-4. This Lionel semaphore signal was included in many O-27 train sets. It is activated by the weight of the passing locomotive.

Fig 12-6. The Lionel 145 Automatic Gateman can be powered from the track through the Lockon (right) or connected directly to the transformer. It is activated by the train closing the electrical circuit on the "Contactor that is attached below the rails."

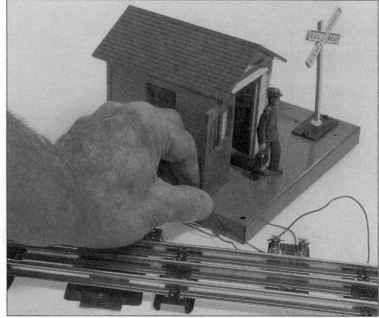

Fig.12-7. When the train closes the circuit on the Contactor (beneath my palm), the door opens and the gateman moves outside.

Fig. 12-8. Pry upward on the three tabs that hold the inside of the rails to the straight track section and remove the rail.

source of power. You can use the power from the track by connecting the accessory to the track with a Lockon. This method should, however, only be used for temporary layouts where you don't wish to run two wires all the way to a separate power pack (Figure 12-7). It is always best to have a separate power pack for accessories and to connect the two power wires from the accessory to that power pack.

Some of the Lionel signals include an electronic unit that will automatically throw a switch to pre-select the train's route. The passing train actuates the signal and the route selection automatically when the signal is wired following the diagram included with the signal. Other signals are simply changed from red to green as the train passes.

A 145C, 153C or 154C Contactor can also be used to activate Lionel's O scale remote-control turnouts. These remote-control turnouts have a non-derailing feature for trains entering the turnout from the alternate routes. This function is activated simply by installing the turnout with an insulated track pin in place of a steel track-connecting pin in the two inside rails nearest the frog or crossing area of the turnout. If you want to have a train automatically throw the turnout's moving points when the train is entering from the single-track side of the turnout, you can use the contactor to provide the electrical signal. The turnouts are furnished with wiring diagrams to show the proper connections.

Build an Automatic Track Section

A more reliable method to actuate these accessories, or to provide train-actuated automatic routes through turnouts, is to modify a track section to include a second insulated rail. The center rail is already insulated on all three-rail track. To insulate one outside rail, pry-open the tabs holding the base of the rail and wiggle the rail free (Figure 12-8). Pry the rail-mounting tabs on the ties back far enough so the rail can be easily slipped into place (Figure 12-9). Cut some pieces of thick insulating tape. Do not use regular plastic insulation tape because it can be easily cut by the tabs. I've found two layers of the filament-style package-sealing tape (the tape that is nearly clear but has visible fiber threads woven into it) to be strong enough not be pierced by the rail-holding tabs. You can also use black duct tape.

Cut the tape into 1/2-inch squares and place it over the bottom of the rail at the points where the rail will be gripped by the tabs on the ties (Figure 12-10). Bend the tape over the web of the rail. Carefully insert the rail into the tabs. Be careful not to move the pieces of tape aside.

Look at the center insulated rail to see how that black fiber is used to insulate the rail from the tabs—that's the effect you're trying to duplicate with the filament tape. When the rail is in place, Gently push the tabs back down to firmly clamp the rail (Figure 12-11). Remove the track connecting pins from the non-insulated rail and replace

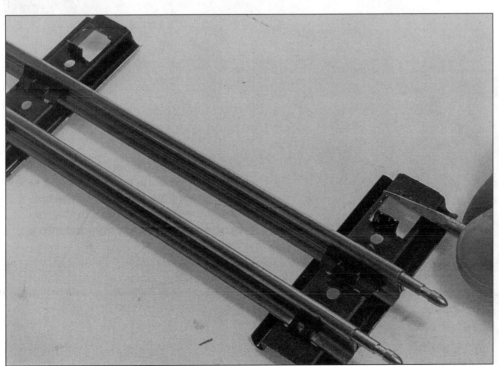

Fig. 12-9. Pry the tabs up far enough so the rail with the extra insulation strips can slip easily beneath the tabs.

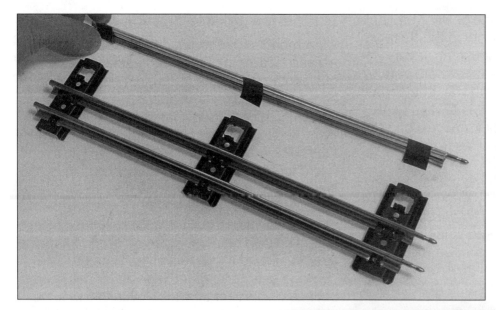

Fig. 12-10. Wrap 1/2-inch squares of filament-style packaging tape or thick black duct tape over the base of the rail at each tie location.

Fig. 12-11. Use a screwdriver to force the tabs back over the base of the rail to grip the now-electrically-insulated rail firmly.

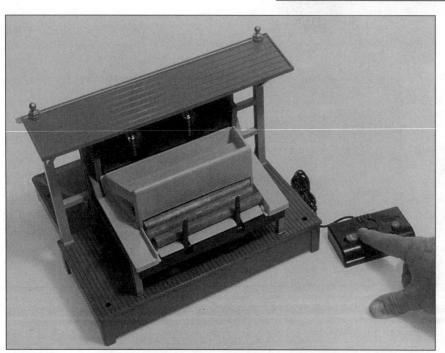

Fig. 12-12. The Lionel 164 Log Loader carries logs dumped on the back side up a chain link conveyor to the bin. When the remote control button is pushed, the logs are dumped into a waiting car.

them with plastic or fiber insulating pins. Note that the trains will still receive power through this track section through the other outside rail.

Connect the accessory to the track using a Lockon clipped to the insulated rail. Follow the wiring instructions furnished with the accessory.

Car-Loading and Unloading Accessories

Lionel has produced nearly a dozen freight car loading and unloading accessories since the forties. Many of the original accessories have been reproduced by Lionel themselves in China. Often, the reproduction version will have different colors, lettering or even materials, but it usually operates just as well as the original. The 282 Triple Action Crane, the operating milk car, and the 164 Log Loader (Figure 12-12) are shown in use on some of the layouts in this book.

The 464 Animated Sawmill, 22997 Oil Drum Loader (originally offered by American Flyer), 32921 Electric Coaling Station and 22918 Locomotive Backshop are some of the more exciting Lionel operating industries. These accessories are driven by motors.

The accessories should be wired so they receive their power from a separate transformer so the operation of the trains does not affect the operation of the accessory (Figure 12-13). Usually, the operating accesories require only minimal maintenance, other than frequent cleaning and occasional lubrication following the instructions furnished with the accessory.

Most power packs have a second pair of electrical-connection terminals with a fixed AC output. These connections are for operating accessories like signals, lighted stations or signals and powered accessories. Most action accessories require about 25 watts. If you plan on operating these accessories with the same power pack as the trains, you will have to include the total number of watts needed for the accessories in the total number you'll want for the power pack. For most toy train layouts, it is best to purchase a separate transformer to power the accessories, leaving the separate power packs for the locomotives.

If you connect the accessory to track power, the locomotive will slow down or perhaps even stop whenever the accessory is actuated. It's not very realistic, for example, for a diesel to slow down in concert with the time you are depressing the horn button to sound the horn.

Fig. 12-13. The action accessories can be wired directly to a separate transformer so their operation does not affect the speed of the trains.

Chapter 13

Steam & Diesel Locomotives

The image most of us see when we dream about toy trains is a locomotive. The rolling stock, the accessories, the track, the bridges and tunnels are all background to the locomotive. The power that makes a train run is housed inside that giant piece of machinery. The real railroads have operated an incredible variety of locomotives, from small 4-4-0 steam locomotives that would fit inside one of today's highway trailers, to steam locomotives nearly the length of a football field, to true electric locomotives, to diesels. There are accurate toy replicas of all the most significant steam, electric and diesel locomotives.

Electric Locomotives, Real and Toy

The diesel locomotives that pull nearly all of the freight and passenger trains today develop their power with diesel engines or, as rail fans

Fig. 13-1. Ralph Johnson's huge Lionel layout includes storage tracks for dozens of locomotives.

call them, "prime movers." These huge engines produce as much as 6,000 horsepower. It is not, however, the diesel engine itself that actually moves the train. The diesel engine drives a type of generator to produce electric power for the electric motors that actually move the locomotive and the train. The electric motors are wrapped around the axles, but with some gear reduction to provide more control. All of the locomotives in the yard on Ralph Johnson's layout are Lionel diesels, including four F3A diesels, five GP9 diesels and a 44-ton switchers (Figure 13-1).

That's about how a toy train locomotive is designed. Electric motors, sometimes mounted in the trucks that support the wheels, provide the power very much like a real locomotive. Most real locomotive motors are DC, but some of the more modern diesels use AC motors, again similar to your toy trains.

There are also some toy trains that are replicas of the real locomotives that have no power-generating diesel, but that receive electrical power from overhead wires. Lionel's replica of the famous Pennsylvania Railroad GG-1 is one of the classics and this same prototype locomotive has also been made by MTH, Weaver and Williams. The General Motors EP-5 electric locomotive is another Lionel classic locomotive from the fifties-era that has also been recreated by MTH and Williams. Atlas offers O scale toy train replicas of the modern-era Amtrak AEM-7 electric.

Toy Train Locomotives

Toy train locomotives are available to duplicate just about any prototype locomotive. Some of these miniature locomotives are only made for a limited period of time and in relatively small numbers. Certainly, these models become collectors items, but they are available for sale at various toy train collector meets. If you are searching for some out-of-production model, you might want to join the Toy Train Collectors of America (TCA), P. O. Box 248, Strassburg, PA17579-0248, or visit their web site at toytrain@ptdprolog.net or http.//www.traincollectors.org and attend some of their swap meets.

Lionel, MTH, Weaver, Williams and Third Rail have offered dozens of different steam, diesel and electric locomotives that are not currently in production. These limited-run models usually sell in the $400 to $1000 price range.

Specific Locomotives for Specific Chores

The manufacturers of real railroad locomotives designed their locomotives to be best-suited to specific duties. In the steam era, for example, locomotives without the small pilot wheels in front of the larger driving wheels or drivers, and no small trailing wheels behind the drivers, were designed as switchers to work in yards and heavy industrial areas.

Steam locomotives are designated by numbers, so a 0-6-0 would be a switcher with no pilot wheels, six large drivers and no trailing wheels. An 0-4-0 would be a switcher with four drivers and a 0-8-0 would be a switcher with eight drivers. Larger steam locomotives were designated by both numbers and by names. Locomotives that had a single pair of pilot wheels, like a 2-6-0 Mogul, a 2-6-2 Prairie, a 2-8-0 Consolidation, a 2-8-2 Mikado, or a 2-8-4 Berkshire, were usually used for freight service. Locomotives with four leading wheels, like a 4-6-2 Pacific, 4-6-4 Hudson, 4-8-2 Mountain, or 4-8-4 Northern were usually used for passenger service.

The most common toy train locomotives are replicas of the New York Central Railroad's 4-6-4 Hudson. Lionel made the locomotive famous when they produced an O scale replica in the forties and they have offered many variations. K-Line and MTH have similar replicas of the NYC Hudson.

In the forties, real diesel locomotives intended for use on the mainline were called road switchers, but that term was dropped when heavier diesels began to haul the nation's freight trains. Generally, road switchers had a long hood on one end of the cab and a short hood on the other. Most railroads ran these locomotives with the short hood forward for better visibility, yet some roads, like the Southern and Norfolk Southern, ran the long hood forward for increased protection of the engineer and crew. Usually, yard switchers had no short hood and were equipped with four-axles. There was no design rule with the number of wheels beneath a diesel. Some four-axle diesels were used only for freight on one railroad, while another might use four-axle diesels for both freight and passenger service.

The first diesels to be sold in quantity for freight, mainline freight, and passenger service had full-width bodies like the EMD F3 or the Alco FA1. These diesels were designed to be run alone or in sets, with the second or third diesel controlled from the cab of the first locomotive, so only the first locomotive had a cab and windows. The locomotives that have cabs are called "A units" and the locomotives without cabs are called "B units." The F3A diesel has the cab and front windows while the F3B diesel has no cab and only the small windows on the sides. Sometimes, a second A unit was coupled, back-to-back, with the first A unit (with, perhaps one, two, or three B units in between), so the set of locomotives could be operated in either direction and did not have to be turned at the end of its run.

The real railroads operated diesels in sets of two or more whenever more power was needed. The real railroads also did that with steam locomotives. They would double-head two locomotives for long trains or to climb especially steep grades. In the thirties, forties and fifties, the real railroads usually ran the wide hood-style diesels, like the F3A and F3B, together and grouped the narrow-hood "cab" diesels, like the GP7 and GP9, together. By the sixties, however, it was not unusual to see mixed sets of hood and cab diesels. Most of the hood diesels had been scrapped by the seventies except those in passenger service.

Recreating a Specific Time Period

There are enough toy train freight and passenger cars and locomotives available so you can focus your purchases on equipment that was common to a specific era in time. The buildings have not changed all that much, so you can change eras on your toy train layout by merely changing trains. If you have more trains than places to hold them on the layout, dividing your roster of locomotives and rolling stock by era is a fine way of providing authentic real railroad variety in miniature.

You can, for example, recreate the turn-of-the century with 4-4-0 steam locomotives from Lionel (Figure 13-3) and MTH. Steam locomotives that are replicas of prototypes built during the thirties and forties are available from all the major toy train makers in O-27, O and S scales.

Most of the major examples of prototype diesels from the fifties and sixties, like the replicas of the Alco FA1, PA1 and RS3; replicas of the Baldwin Locomotive Works' "Shark" four-axle freight diesels; replicas of EMD's [Electro-Motive Division (of General Motors)] GP7, GP9, E8, F3, F7, SW8 and SW9; replicas of Fairbanks-Morse' H12-44 switchers and "Trainmaster" freight diesels; and replicas of General Electric's U25B and U33C have all been available from one or more of the toy train manufacturers in various paint schemes.

Modern era diesels are available to duplicate General Electric's "Dash-9" heavy freight diesels and Amtrak "Genesis" and to duplicate Electro-Motive Division's GP38-2, GP60M, MP15, SD40 and SD45. You may have to search swap meets and train collector shows to find the exact locomotive you want, or you may need to repaint an existing locomotive, but the models have been produced.

Fig. 13-3. Lionel has offered this 1865-era 4-4-0 steam locomotive in dozens of different paint and lettering schemes.

Locomotive Maintenance

A frequent cause of problems with locomotives is lint. The cure is to establish a regular maintenance schedule for your trains, say once a month, or every tenth time you operate the layout. Lint can usually be removed from the gears with a toothpick, followed by a gentle scrub with toothbrush or pipe cleaner (Figure 13-4).

Wheels and the small roller that picks up electricity from the third rail can become dirty and pitted. The pickup roller on this K-Line F3A diesel (Figure 13-5) extends from the end of the truck toward the fuel tank (which houses the speaker for he sound system). The pickup rollers on this K-Line MP15 diesel rest just below the wheels (Figure 13-6). Clean them with one of the toy train track cleaning fluids, using a pipe cleaner or piece of cloth (Figure 13-7). Inspect the wheels to see if the rubber traction tires (if fitted) are not cracked or broken (Figure 13-8). Replace any broken traction tires.

Replacements are available direct from the manufacturer. Polish the wheels (Figure 13-9) and the rollers (Figure 13-10) so they are per-

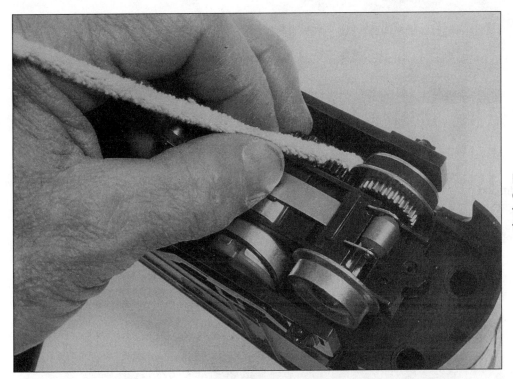

Fig. 13-4. Use a pipe cleaner dipped in track cleaning fluid to remove dirt from around the exposed gears.

Fig. 13-5. The electrical pickup rollers extended inward from the trucks on K-Line's F3A diesel.

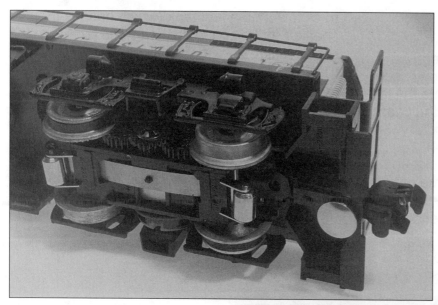

Fig. 13-6. The electrical pickup rollers are nearly beneath the wheels on K-Line's MP15 (shown) and FA1 diesels.

Fig. 13-7. Use a pipe cleaner dipped in track cleaner to remove any grit or fibers from the ends and bearing surfaces of the electrical pickup rollers.

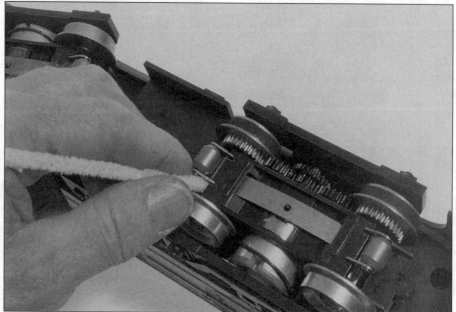

Fig. 13-8. Inspect the black plastic traction tires to be sure they are not cracked or twisted.

Fig. 13-9. Use a track cleaning eraser to scrub any grit from the wheels of the locomotives.

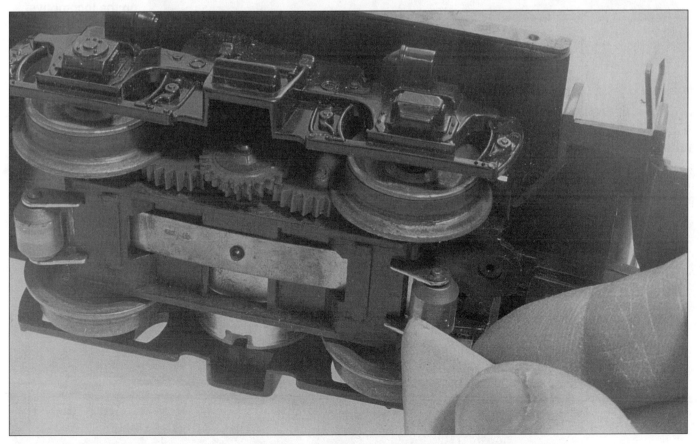

Fig. 13-10. The track cleaning eraser can also be used to polish the electrical pickup rollers.

fectly clean with a track cleaning eraser like those sold by Lionel, Atlas and Life-Like. Use that same eraser to clean the pickup rollers.

It is as important to clean the gears, wheels and axles of locomotives and cars as it is apply lubrication. Also, excess lubrication can cause more harm than help because it can attract grit and lint. Always clean the gears thoroughly with pipe cleaner dipped in track cleaning fluid before applying more grease. Clean around the wheel, axle and driver bearings too. When you apply grease, use just enough to fill the bottoms of each of the teeth on the gear with no excess

grease on the sides of the gears or the gear teeth (Figure 13-11). When you apply oil, a single drop is enough (Figure 13-12). Again, wipe away any visible excess. Usually, the motor is accessible from beneath the locomotive.

To replace burned-out lights, remove the locomotive's body. The bodies are usually retained by two or more fairly obvious screws like those on the ends of this Lionel GP7 (Figure 13-13). If you have doubts about what the screws are really holding, loosen them—but do not remove—them to see if you are actually loosening the body's attachment to the chassis

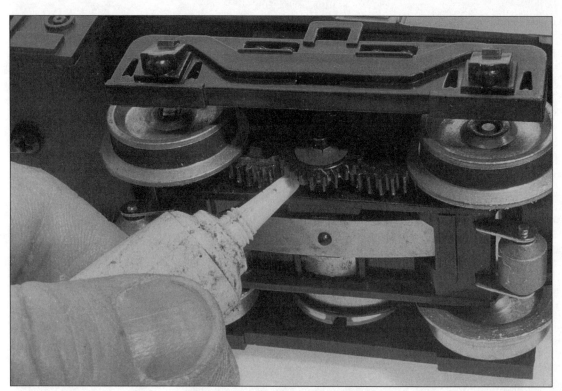

Fig. 13-11. Use just a trace of plastic-compatible grease to lubricate the gears on the locomotive.

Fig. 13-12. Apply a drop of light electrical-conductive oil to the bearings on the pickup wheels.

Fig 13-13. A single screw on each end of the body holds the Lionel GP7 and GP9 body to the chassis.

Fig. 13-14. The screws that retain the body on larger Lionel locomotives, like this Lionel "Phantom," can be reached by inserting the screwdriver through the access holes in the trucks.

Fig. 13-15. Use only a few drops of the smoke fluid recommended by the locomotive manufacturer.

or just loosening some internal part. The screws that attach the body on this Lionel "Phantom" are reached through rectangular access holes in the trucks (Figure 13-14). Your hobby dealer can order replacement bulbs or you can obtain direct from the toy train manufacturer.

Many toy train steam locomotives include smoke units to produce puffs of smoke as he locomotive runs down the track. Usually, the smoke fluid is replenished by adding a few drops through the top of the stack (Figure 13-15). Use the fluid recommended by the locomotive's manufacturer to avoid damaging the smoke mechanism.

Lionel Locomotives

Lionel has used a variety of different mechanisms for their toy train locomotives. The lower-cost O-27 diesels usually have the motors built into the trucks. The medium-priced steam locomotives, like this 4-4-0, have a motor that drives the wheels or drivers through a series of gears (Figure 13-16). The more expensive O scale diesel and steam locomotives have a separate motor or motors mounted inside the body. The top-of-the-line Lionel steam and diesel locomotives are the TrainMaster™ series that include digital con-

trol to allow up to 99 locomotives to operate on the same track and couplers that can be activated anywhere on the track with a hand-held throttle. There's more information on Lionel's TrainMaster system in chapters 7 and 8. Most of the Lionel locomotives are made in America.

MTH Locomotives

MTH has two series of locomotives: the lower-priced "Rail King" line that includes some smaller than scale O-27 steam and diesel locomotives and the "Premier" series locomotives which are usually full O scale models. The drive mechanisms are similar in all the diesels, but the Premier diesels and steam locomotives are more powerful and have built-in sound systems and smoke generators. The Rail King locomotives can be fitted with plug-in sound modules. Most MTH locomotives are made in Korea.

K-Line Locomotives

K-Line has a small O-27 scale Alco FA diesel about the size of Lionel's, a near-scale MP15 and an O-27 scale 4-6-2 steam locomotive. The newer K-Line locomotives are the larger O scale models,

Fig. 13-16. A horizontal motor drives the wheels (called "drivers") on Lionel's 4-4-0 steam locomotive.

Fig. 13-17. Two vertical motors, each with a flywheel, drive the trucks on K-Line's GP38-2 diesel.

including the GP38-2 and a new series of large 4-6-2 and 4-6-4 steam locomotives. The Alco and MP15 diesels have motors built into the trucks. The GP38-2 has two vertical motors with flywheels (Figure 13-17). They are made in Korea.

Weaver Locomotives

All of the Weaver locomotives are full O scale and are available with either "hi-rail" wheels and couplers for toy train operation or smaller O scale wheels and couplers for operation on two-rail track (Figure 13-18). The Weaver diesels are powered by a horizontal motor that drives all the wheels through a chain drive to one truck (Figure 13-19) and a shaft from that truck to the opposite truck. These diesel locomotives are made in America.

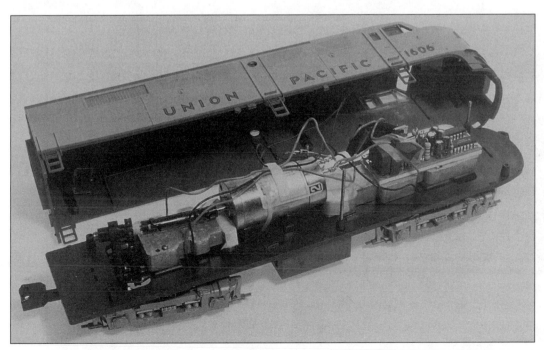

Fig. 13-18. A single horizontal motor drives one truck on the Weaver locomotives and a drive shaft carries that power to the second truck.

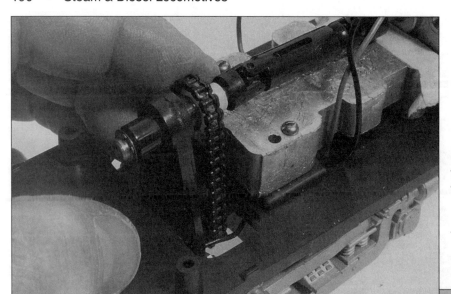

Fig. 13-19. A plastic drive chain carries the power from the motor shaft down to the truck on the Weaver diesels.

Fig.13-20. The single motor in the Atlas diesels has a flywheel on each end and a drive shaft to each truck. Each drive shaft turns a worm gear and a series of spur gears inside each truck.

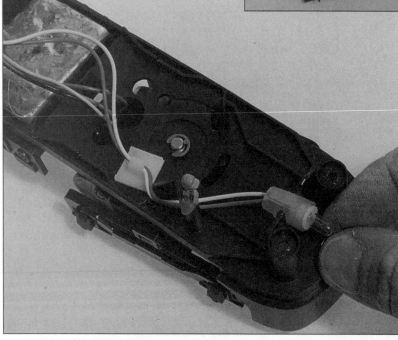

Fig. 13-21. The light bulbs inside toy train diesels can be replaced by removing the body and the bracket that holds the bulb.

Atlas Locomotives

The Atlas diesels are O scale with a horizontal motor that drives all the wheels through a series of gears (Figure 13-20). These locomotives are available with either "hi-rail" wheels and couplers for toy train operation or with the smaller wheel flanges and couplers for operation on two-rail track. They are made in China.

Headlight and Fan Belt Replacement

The bulbs that illuminate the headlights, interiors and number lights of toy train locomotives can be replaced. The body of the locomotive must be removed, however, for access to the bulb. Usually, the bulb is held in a socket which is attached with a simple clip like that in this K-Line FA1 diesel (Figure 13-21).

The more expensive diesels sometimes have separate motors to drive the simulated cooling fans beneath the hood. This K-Line GP38-2 has a small motor mounted inside the hood with a belt drive to the fans (Figure 13-22). MTH and Lionel have similar fan drives. Check the belts to be sure they are in their proper places on the pulleys. Apply a single small drop of oil to the motor shaft and wipe away any excess oil.

Locomotive Troubleshooting

The most frequent cause of problems with locomotives is actually track, rather than the loco-motives themselves. The track joints can work loose from the rocking action of passing trains to cause an interruption in the flow of electricity or an actual derailment. If your locomotive does not run or derails, try it on different part of the layout before you blame the locomotive. Also, check the troubleshooting tips in Chapter 6 to find short circuits on the track and in Chapter 7 on wiring.

If the locomotive fails to operate, remove it from the track, then remove the two wires leading from the power pack to the Lockon. Turn the throttle to about 1/3 speed, then touch one of the wires to one of the locomotive's wheels and the second wire to one of the pickup rollers. If the locomotive runs, the problem probably lies in the track or the electrical connections to the track. It may be that the locomotive has dirty wheels or a dirty third rail roller, so clean them. Also, check to be certain that each of the rollers has enough spring tension to push itself below the wheel level so it will maintain contact with the center rail.

If the locomotive still does not operate, try turning the power on and off several times and increasing or decreasing the throttle setting. If the locomotive runs, it may just need a thorough cleaning. If the locomotive still fails to operate, remove the body and check the attachment points of all the wires to be certain none have worked loose. If this still does not solve the problem, perform the troubleshooting checks listed in Chapter 6 on track and Chapter 7 on electrical wiring. If that too fails to solve the

Fig. 13-22. This K-Line GP38-2 has a third motor to drive the simulated cooling fans beneath the radiators in the long hood.

Fig.13-23. Lionel did not make this number 1908 GP7 in Burlington Northern green and black, but you can paint and decal your diesels to match almost any prototype paint scheme.

Fig 13-24. Use decal softening fluid to force the decals to nestle down around the louvers and panel lines.

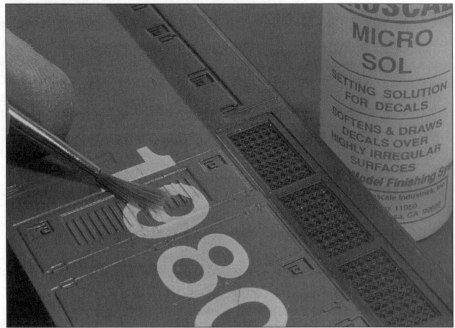

Fig. 13-25. Protect the decals and blend them into the paint with a thin coat of Testors' DullCote clear flat

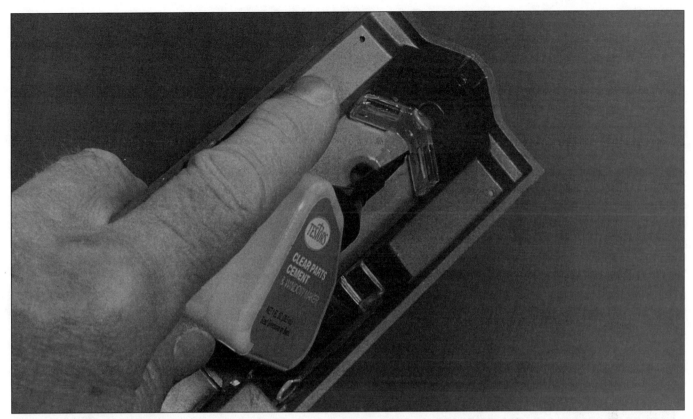

Fig. 13-26. If the windows or headlight and number board plastic pieces are loose, cement them in place with Testors' Clear Parts Cement or plain white glue.

problem, contact the manufacturer to locate the nearest repair shop or look under "Hobbies" in the telephone book's yellow pages to see if a toy train repair department is available in any local hobby shop.

Painting and Lettering Locomotives

If you can buy the locomotive you want, but it lacks the paint scheme you prefer, consider the option of painting and lettering the model yourself. The Lionel Burlington Northern GP7 in some of the photographs was painted with Floquil Burlington Northern Green and Engine Black and lettered with Microscale decals because, at the time I wanted one, Lionel did not make a Burlington Northern GP7 (Figure 13-23). This is not something you would want to do with a rare collector's item because you will destroy its collector value. If possible, buy a

second replacement body through your dealer and paint and letter the replacement. If the locomotive costs less than $200, however, it is not likely to become a collector's piece and it might be worth much more to you painted and lettered the way you want it.

The steps used to paint and letter buildings in Chapter 11 can be used to paint and letter any toy locomotive. Use decal-softening fluid (Figure 13-24) to be sure the decals hug the louvers and other details as well as if they were printed-on at the factory. Protect the finished paint and decal work with a thin spray of Testors' DullCote. (Figure 13-25). Remove the windows or mask them before spraying with DullCote because the flat, clear paint can etch or craze the clear plastic. Cement the windows in place with white glue or Testors' Clear Parts Cement (Figure 13-26).

Chapter 14

Freight And Passenger Cars

Yes, your toy trains really can carry freight and, if you cannot actually carry miniature passengers, the passenger trains can operate on schedules to duplicate the movements of real passenger trains. With toy trains, you have the option of actually loading and unloading your freight cars or just pretending they are loaded. The reliable operations that these trains provide also makes it fun to create challenging timetables for passenger trains to reach each station at their "advertised" time.

There's never enough space for a toy train layout. Even if you have 20 x 70-feet of space, you still only have a fraction of the distance a real railroad will travel. Carrying vast quantities of freight and passengers vast distances is, after all, the main reason why real railroads exist. We can add to the distance our train travels by specifying that it takes, say, ten-laps of an oval of track to reach the next station. The next station may be the same one we just departed, but that's where your imagination steps in. You certainly do not have to use your imagination, however, to recreate the specific types of freight cars and passenger cars that appear on the real railroads, they're nearly all available as toy trains.

Hauling the Freight

Each real railroad car is designed to haul a specific type of commodity (Figure 14-1). The cars are usually designated in terms that describe them by what they contain or how they look. A box car, for example, is shaped like a box and it usually is loaded with boxes. A tank car is shaped like a round tank. A stock or cattle car is designed to carry animals, a flat car is just that, it's flat; it's designed to carry large or bulky loads. A gondola uses the word to describe its dish-like shape so it can carry bulky but loose materials like scrap steel, bulk produce like sugar beets, or logs or lumber. A reefer is a slang word for refrigerator, cars that have built-in cooling either by ice in bun-

kers or by mechanical refrigeration. A hopper has bins or hoppers in the bottom of the car that are opened to dump the load. A covered hopper is like a regular hopper, but with a roof and hatches; it's likely used for bulky dry commodities like wheat, cement, carbon black, or dry chemicals.

The intermodal cars are gradually replacing both the box cars and the reefers on real railroads. These cars carry either highway trailers or containers. Both trailers and containers are sometimes fitted with refrigeration equipment. An intermodal car is designed to haul those containers or trailers. The term intermodal means that the trailers or containers are moved by several modes of transport including trucks, railroad cars and ocean-going ships. Often, there are solid trains of intermodal cars. In fact, a single train may transport most of the containers from a single ship that may have traveled from Japan to San Francisco. The railroad will then haul the containers to a second port, perhaps New York, to be loaded on another ship. This type of intermodal transport is sometimes called a "land bridge."

Freight Trains

A freight train on a real railroad is certainly not a random assortment of cars. Usually, there are groups of cars originating from one customer in one city, That group of cars may consist of just two boxcars or it may be a dozen covered hopper cars full of grain. We don't have the space for the 100-car freight trains, so we must condense the makeup of our trains. Still, it's more realistic two have a freight train with two or more cars that are similar if not identical except for the numbers on the sides of the cars. When you've collected enough freight cars to make up those assorted-style freights, consider buying three or four or more identical cars so you can have a solid train of say, hoppers. Real railroads call such a train a "drag" and it's an exciting sight on a toy train layout.

Fig. 14-1. If the freight car existed on a real railroad, you can probably buy it as a toy recreation. (Union Pacific Railroad photo)

Real Freight for Your Freight Cars

One of the joys of toy trains is operating freight cars that can be loaded with coal, logs, milk cans, boxes and barrels or steel scrap from remote control loading accessories, then dumped or unloaded, all by remote control.

The real railroads hauled cans of milk in insulated milk cars from about 1900 to 1960 (Figure 14-2). Lionel has reproduced the milk car and its unloading operations for over 50 years. An assortment of the older Lionel operating milk cars is shown in the color section. The milk car offered in 1994 was lettered for Dairyman's League (Figure 14-3). When the car is spotted on a remote uncoupling track and the button to the track is pressed, the workman pushes a can of milk onto the platform. A new

can is unloaded each time you press the button. Lionel has similar cars that unload barrels, boxes and mail bags (Figure 14-4).

Lionel has produced a long series of operating coal dump cars (Figure 14-5) and similar log-dump cars. I find that the coal-dump cars are easier to load and unload with logs than the log-dump cars. A simple mechanical latch and spring assembly dumps the load when the small steel disc below the car is attracted by the electromagnet on the remote uncoupling track. The cars are especially useful when used to load and unload the Lionel 164 Log Loader or 32921 Electric Coaling Station. Toy train operators never tire of repeating the remote-control cycle of dumping logs (or coal) into the receiving side of the operating log loader or coal loader to be reloaded on the opposite side.

Fig. 14-2. The railroads really did haul milk in milk cars during the 1900-1960 period, much like Lionel's operating milk car. (Association of American Railroads photo)

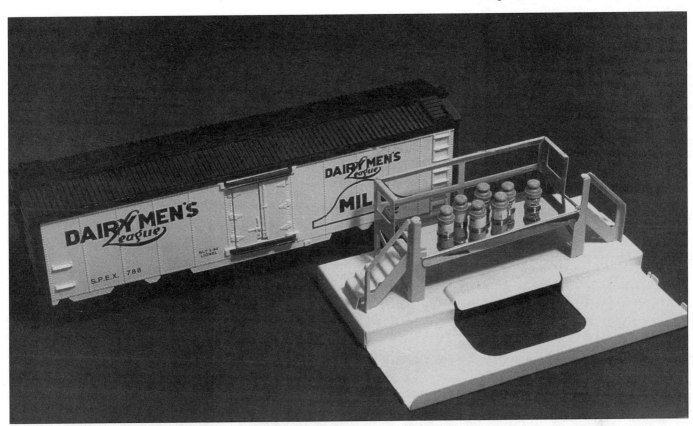

Fig. 14-3. Lionel's operating milk car and the platform to receive the metal milk cans.

Fig. 14-4. The workmen inside many of Lionel's operating box cars are actuated when the metal disc on the bottom of the car is attracted by the electromagnet on the remote uncoupling track.

Fig. 14-5. The Lionel operating coal-dump and log-dump cars are also actuated by the electromagnet on the remote uncoupling track.

Passenger Trains

The real railroads have operated a variety of passenger cars, from turn-of-the-century wood cars, to heavy steel cars during the twenties and thirties, to streamlined and stainless steel cars in the forties and fifties, to the modern "Hi-Level" cars of the Amtrak era. You can buy examples of all of these as toy trains. For example, Lionel, MTH and Weaver have offered replicas of the Southern Pacific's Alco PA1 diesels and red and orange passenger cars in O scale and American Flyer and American Models has offered them in S scale (Figure 14-6).

The simplest form of passenger trains are the commuter trains that bring workers from the suburbs to the city and home again. These trains are solid strings of coaches (cars with seats). When passengers are traveling across larger distances, however, the makeup of the train may change dramatically.

There may still be some coaches, and also some sleeping cars (often referred to as "Pullman" cars) that have sleeping accommodations as well as showers in addition to sinks and toilets. Longer trains will usually have a dining car and, perhaps, a lounge car that may be the observation or last car in the train. Often, a baggage car may be added for the passengers and to carry smaller freight shipments. In the first sixty years of the century, the railroads also carried most of the mail for the post office so there might be a postal car as part of the passenger train. The postal car was really a traveling post office where postal workers worked through the night sorting mail for, say, towns in New York state as the train speeds eastward from Chicago. Yes, there were solid trains of baggage cars and solid trains of postal cars with a few baggage cars mixed-in to store unsorted mail.

Fig. 14-6. The Southern Pacific Alco PA diesels in red and orange with matching streamlined passenger cars have been offered by Lionel, K-Line and MTH. (Photo courtesy Southern Pacific)

Mixed Trains

The real railroads operated "mixed" trains including both freight and passenger cars from the turn-of-the-century through the seventies. Often, these trains were operated on short branchlines from the main line where there was not enough passenger traffic to warrant a full passenger train. A passenger coach or combine (a car with space for both baggage and passengers) were just tacked onto the end of the local freight. Sometimes, passengers and small items of freight were carried in the cabooses of these mixed trains.

Era-Specific Freight Trains

Locomotives are available to recreate trains from any era including the turn-of-the-century, the steam era, the early diesel era and the most modern era. Freight cars are available to match the locomotives. Both Lionel and K-line have turn-of-the-century stock cars, flat cars and box cars. All the toy train makers offer replicas of the forties and fifties-era cars. Steam era wood cabooses and diesel era steel cabooses are offered by Lionel and MTH.

The most visible modern era freight cars are the Intermodal cars that carry single containers or trailers or even double-stacks of containers. Replicas of these real railroad cars are available from Lionel. MTH and K-Line in O scale and American Models in S scale.

Era-Specific Passenger Trains

Replicas of wood-side passenger cars that were common in the 1860-1900 era, with truss-rod-braced underframes, are available from Lionel and MTH. At the opposite end of the time spectrum, Amtrak's latest Hi-Level passenger cars and "Genesis" diesels are available from MTH. The heavyweight era of steel passenger cars is epitomized by Lionel's classic "Irving" series that has been replicated by MTH, K-Line and Williams. Streamlined passenger cars are also available.

Fig. 14-7. The Lionel smooth-side O-27 streamlined cars were first offered in the forties and reproductions are still available.

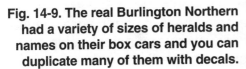

Fig. 14-8. Use decal softening fluid to force the decals to fit snugly around the rivets and ribs on the side of the car.

Fig. 14-9. The real Burlington Northern had a variety of sizes of heralds and names on their box cars and you can duplicate many of them with decals.

Lionel made the first production runs of these O-27 smooth-side streamlined cars in the late forties (Figure 14-7). They have been reproduced several times in the intervening years. MTH and K-Line also offer smooth-side streamlined cars and MTH and Lionel have corrugated-side passenger cars.

Painting and Lettering Freight Cars

There are times when you cannot buy a freight car in the paint and lettering scheme you desire. You do have the option of buying the least-expensive version of the car you desire and painting and lettering it. You probably don't want to do that with one of he rare collector item cars, but the less-expensive O-27 or O scale cars are

suitable subjects. Microscale has a selection of decals for cars, locomotives and structures in both O and S scales that can be used to letter a repainted model. Champ also makes a selection of O scale decals for O scale cars and locomotives. I purchased a K-Line car and painted it with Floquil Burlington Northern Green and Engine Black and lettered it with Microscale decals. The decal-softening fluid was used to help the decals fit tightly around the rivets on the side of the car (Figure 14-8). I wanted an O scale Burlington Northern box car about the size of K-Line's but I could not locate one, so painting and decaling provided the car I could not buy (Figure 14-9). The techniques for painting and lettering with decals are shown in Chapter 11.

Chapter 15

Operating A Model Railroad

Real railroad trains spend most of their time rolling along the mainline. At least, that's the hope, if the railroad expects to make a profit. That's good news for toy train operators, because we like to see trains rolling around our layouts. The real railroads, however, have a definite purpose in keeping those trains rolling. We can simulate much of that purpose, at least in our imaginations, when we operate our trains.

The real railroads have operated trains in just about every conceivable combination of locomotive and cars, they simply have a different purpose than you do when you operate your toy trains. It's great fun to operate random assortments of cars and run them around the layout and through the turnouts just to please yourself. You may, however, have even more fun if you duplicate the operations of the real railroads. Every move those real railroad locomotives make is expensive, so the railroad engineers have developed specific moves to pickup, set out, and rearrange cars as efficiently as possible.

On a real railroad, the freight cars are brought to a yard where a switch engine assembles them into trains for other cities. Usually the cars are routed to interchange yards with a second railroad and that railroad may forward the car to the customer. Sometimes, a car will travel through four or five interchange yards before reaching its destination. When the train reaches its destination, another switch engine breaks-down the train so another train can be made-up to take the car or cars on to the customer.

The trains that actually deliver the cars to the customers are generally referred to as "local" freights or peddler freights because they may stop at several industries to spot (drop off) or pull (pick up) a single car or 50 cars. You can increase the enjoyment of your toy train layout by providing industries that actually ship and receive freight cars, like these warehouses and factories on the Carnegie Science Center layout from Chapter 3 (Figure 15-1).

Fig. 15-1. A warehouse and factory occupy this siding on the Carnegie Institute's gigantic toy train layout.

Switching Moves

When you understand how to perform switching moves, you'll discover why those freight trains seem to go back and forth so many times. And once you know the reasons for those moves, you'll realize that it can be an important part of your model railroad operations. When you've learned how to perform switching moves, you may find you like that kind of action far more than just running trains. When you learn how to operate the "Waybill" switching system (discussed in Chapter 16), you may want to spend most of the time at any operating session just switching cars in and out of trains. Even without the "Waybill" system, though, you'll want to learn the basic switching moves. Then you can make-up trains and break them down, using a locomotive, rather than your hands, as a switch engine.

Track Planning for Operation

There are really only three basic switching moves, the "trailing-point" move, the "facing point" or "run-around" move, and the "reverse" move (which reverses a train through a track arrangement called a reverse loop or a track arrangement called a wye). There are examples of track plans with a reverse loop and a track plan with a wye in Chapter 4. These are the ways to move railroad cars on railroad track by pushing or pulling them with locomotives.

You may want to create a different track plan, or select one from this book, that includes the track arrangements necessary to allow your trains to perform all the possible switching moves. For the trailing point move, you need just a single turnout to create a stub-ended siding. For the facing point move, you will need a pair of turnouts to create a passing or double-ended siding and a third turnout to create a stub-ended siding.

The track plans in Chapter 4 include examples of layouts that include reverse loops and wyes as well as plans with stub-ended sidings and passing sidings. You can, of course, combine features from two or more track plans to obtain the operating features you want for your toy train layout; there are endless combinations.

Fig. 15-2. The freight train will pick up that unloaded coal dump car by the log loader on its next trip to town.

Picking Up a Car with Trailing-Point Moves

The "trailing point" simply describes the direction of the turnout's moving points relative to the direction of the train on the main line. If the siding (and the turnout's points) trails off behind the train as it passes, it is considered a trailing-point siding. The direction of the train determines the type of maneuver; if the train was traveling in the opposite direction (counter-clockwise in the illustrations), the siding and the turnout points would be facing the train. This would become a "facing-point" turnout. However, the moves necessary to get a car in or out

of a siding that is a facing point are much more complicated than the moves needed to switch a car in or out of a trailing-point siding.

Figures 15-2 through 15-7, on the 4 x 6-1/2-foot double-track layout in Chapter 5, illustrate where the train is uncoupled and switched to pickup the empty coal dump car from behind the log loader (Figure 15-2) and add it to the train.

The locomotive pulls its train forward so it can uncouple from however much of the train is behind the car that is to go onto the trailing-point siding (Figure 15-3). The locomotive then pulls forward with the box car.

Why include the box car? Because it is going to be left on the siding in the next series

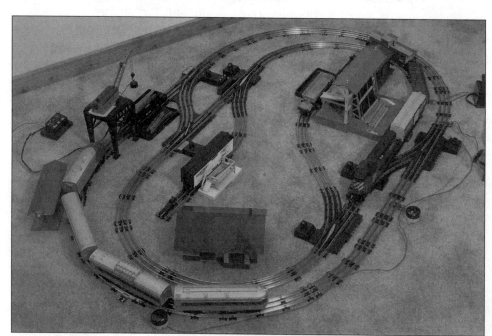

Fig. 15-3. The siding trails-off behind the train, so this will be a "trailing point" switching move.

Fig. 15-4. The locomotive and box car uncouple from the train and pull forward to clear the siding to the turnout.

of moves (Figures 15-8 through 15-12). The locomotive pulls forward until the box car clears the moving switch points at the turnout leading to the siding. The locomotive stops while the brakeman throws the switch. The locomotive then backs up to push the box car into the siding until it couples with the empty coal-dump car (Figure 15-5). The locomotive then pulls back forward until the empty coal-dump car clears the moving switch points at the turnout (Figure 15-6). Finally, the locomotive backs up to couple the empty coal-dump car into the train. The train can then proceed unless another car is to be switched into the siding.

Spotting a Car with Trailing-Point Moves

Most of the sequence for putting the car into the siding (called "spotting" the car) would, of course, be reversed if a car was in the train waiting to be dropped-off or "spotted" at the customer (Figures 15-8 through 15-12). In this case, the box car immediately behind the locomotive is to be spotted at the freight house just visible above the log loader. The car happens to be just behind the locomotive (Figure 15-8), but there could just as well be two or more cars between the locomotive and the car that is to be switched or "spotted" on the siding.

Fig. 15-5. The locomotive backs up to couple onto the unloaded coal dump car.

Fig. 15-6. The locomotive now pulls the box car and the unloaded coal dump car out onto the mainline.

Fig. 15-7. The locomotive backs the box car and empty coal dump car to couple onto the train, then heads on to the next town.

Fig. 15-8. It's now time to spot the box car at the freight station just behind the log loader.

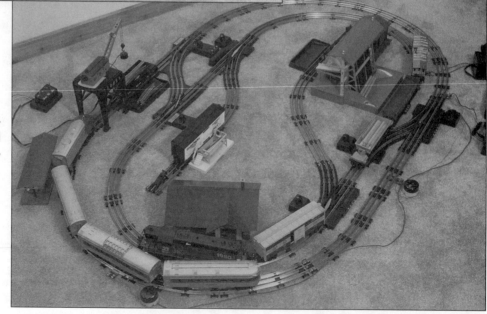

Fig. 15-9. The box car is uncoupled from the train and pulled forward until it clears the turnout leading back to the siding.

The locomotive moves forward with the car to be spotted on the siding until the wheels of the car clear the points of the turnout (Figure 15-9). The locomotive stops while the brakeman throws the turnout from the main line to the siding. The locomotive then reverses to shove the car into the siding and stops while the car is uncoupled (Figure 15-10). The locomotive pulls forward again until it (or the last car) clears the turnout points, where it will stop, while the brakeman moves the turnout from the siding position to the main-line alignment (Figure 15-11).

The locomotive reverses until it gently couples back to the remainder of the train (Figure 15-12). Then it stops while the brakeman sets the couplers and connects the air hoses. The train then moves forward to its next destination. Each time the train starts and stops is counted as a "move"; the fewer moves, in a complex switching situation, the quicker the time.

Run-Around or Facing-Point Moves

The switching moves are more complex when the siding is facing the direction in which the train is traveling. In the old days, the train crews would make such a move with a "flying switch." This means running the locomotive forward past the switch, throwing the switch just as the locomotive

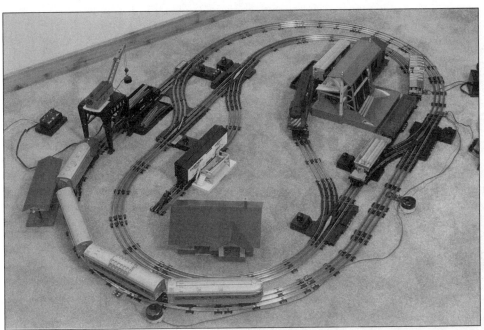

Fig. 15-10. The locomotive now backs up to push the box car on into the siding and in front of the freight station.

Fig. 15-11. The locomotive uncouples from the box car and pulls back onto the main line, backs up, and couples onto the train.

clears it (but while the train is still moving), and uncoupling the car so it will roll on into the siding.

That's no longer "legal" on real railroads, and it's impossible to do on a model railroad because there's no way to uncouple while the train is still in motion. The only way to get that car into or out of a "facing-point siding" is to "run around" the car at the nearest passing siding. A passing siding is generally considered to be a siding that has a switch at both ends, although a train can back into a stub-ended siding (and they often do) to wait while another train passes by. The siding with a switch at both ends is needed so the locomotive can literally run around its train to couple onto the back of it.

The sequence of the "run-around" moves in Figures 15-13 through 15-21, again on the 4 x 6-1/2-foot double-track layout, show the essential moves that are used to pick up the loaded coal-dump car, now loaded with logs, and to place it in the train. The illustrations skip one or two of the obvious start-stop moves. You can understand, from studying these moves and from trying them on a section of your own railroad, how complicated even this basic switching situation can be. Now, the train is traveling around the layout in a counterclockwise direction (Figure 15-13).

It would be possible to complete these moves by using the lower half of the oval, but we are going to consider the area in front of the

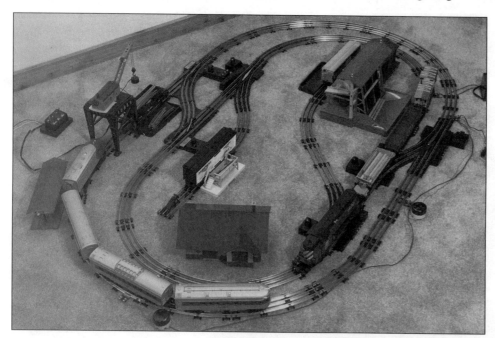

Fig. 15-12. The train now proceeds down the mainline for the next town where that load of logs may be delivered.

Fig. 15-13. The coal dump car loaded with logs is ready to be picked up but the train is traveling in the wrong direction to be able to simply back into the siding to pickup the car. The locomotive must stop, uncouple part of the train, runaround the train on the outer oval, then push the remainder of the train into the siding to pick up the load of logs.

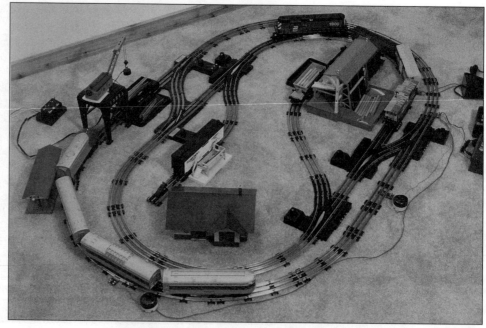

passenger station, on both the inner and outer ovals, to be disconnected portions of the railroad, perhaps a hundred miles away from the log loader and freight station siding. The passenger train is parked there to help remind you that that portion of the layout is not usable for this switching move, and because real railroads don't operate on endless ovals of track.

First, the train stops with the caboose just clear of the pair of turnouts that name the first crossover to the siding. Next, the train is uncoupled just ahead of the box car. In this case, a single gondola is left behind the locomotive. The locomotive then proceeds forward

until the gondola just clears the switch points leading to the second crossover to the passing siding (Figure 15-14).

The two crossovers on the layout form the entry and exit to a double-ended passing siding. The locomotive now backs up with the gondola to run backwards around the passing siding (the outer oval) (Figure 15-15). The locomotive will back past its train and on through the second crossover (Figure 15-16). It then will continue until the gondola has cleared the switch points of the crossover and stop while the brakeman throws the switch points on the crossover. The locomotive will

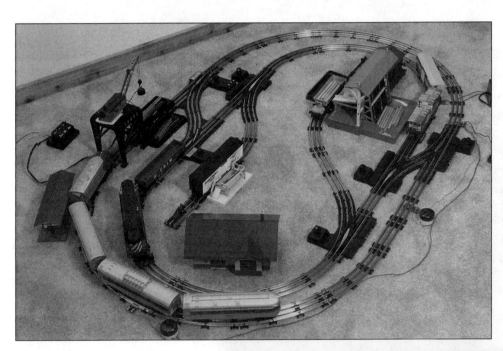

Fig. 15-14. The locomotive uncouples from the last two cars and heads counterclockwise down the mainline to stop when the gondola clears the crossover turnout.

Fig. 15-15. The locomotive now backs up through the crossover to run around the remainder of the train on the passing siding (the outer oval).

Fig. 15-16. The locomotive and gondola continue to back up through the crossover to complete running around the train.

Fig 15-17. The locomotive and gondola proceed forward to couple onto the caboose and box car.

Figure 15-18. The locomotive, now in the middle of the train, backs up until the box car clears the turnout leading to the siding.

the proceed forward to couple onto the end of the train's caboose (Figure 15-17).

Next, the train will back up until the box car clears the points of the turnout to the siding (Figure 15-18). The train will then pull forward to shove the box car into the siding until it couples onto the coal-dump car loaded with logs (Figure 15-19). The train will then back up until the log car clears the switch points at the turnout (Figure 15-20). The train will then push the caboose, the box car, and the loaded coal-dump car forward until the caboose clears the points of the right cross- over's turnout (Figure 15-21). The train will then back up to clear the points of the cross-over, the brakeman will throw the points of the

crossover turnouts, and the locomotive will proceed around the outer oval in the reverse direction of Figure 15-15 and 15-16 (to "run around" its train a second time) until it clears the crossover on the left. The train will then back up through the inner oval to couple the gondola onto the loaded coal-dump car. When the cars are coupled, the train will proceed on its route still traveling counterclockwise.

The "facing-point" or "run-around" sequence can be completed in a total of eleven "moves" if done in the manner shown in the illustrations. It would also be possible to use one of several alternate methods, such as leaving the remainder of the train back on the main line behind the bridge.

Fig. 15-19. The train proceeds forward into the siding to couple onto the coal dump car loaded with logs.

Fig. 15-20. The train backs up to "pull" the loaded car onto the mainline.

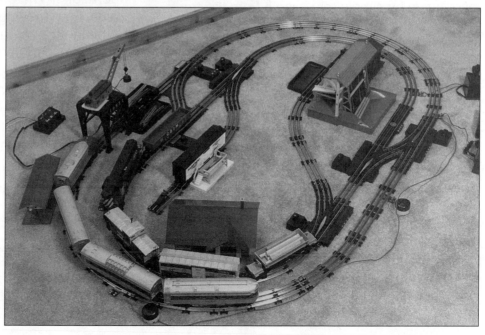

Fig. 15-21. The train now pushes the caboose, box car, and loaded coal dump car down the mainline until the caboose clears the crossover. The locomotive and gondola will then reverse the series of moves shown in Figures 15-13, 15-14, 15-15 and 15-16 to couple the gondola onto the loaded coal dump car and the train will proceed around the inner oval mainline in a counterclockwise direction.

The moves shown are typical of those used by the real railroads' switch crews, who must leave the main line clear for as long as possible.

Reversing Operations

You can, of course, reverse the direction of a locomotive by simply removing it from the track and replacing it heading in the opposite direction. It's more fun, and much more like real railroading, to arrange the track so you can reverse at least a single locomotive and, perhaps, an entire train. Reverse loops and wyes are usually used to reverse entire trains. Wyes and turntables are usually used to reverse just a single locomotive.

If you have just a single reverse loop, you can only reverse a train going in one direction. To re-reverse that train you must back the entire train through the reverse loop. An alternate method of re-reversing the train is to arrange the track so there is a second reverse loop. The plans in Chapter 4 include one with a single reverse loop and one with two overlapping reverse loops. Examples of plans with overlapping reverse loops are shown in Chapter 4 and with one reverse loop

stacked 5-inches above the first loop on a second level are shown in Chapter 5.

The 4 x 6-1/2-foot double-track layout with a reverse loop in Chapter 8 (Figures 8-8 and 8-9) includes most of the basic elements of track arrangements needed to duplicate real railroad operations. The sequence for running two trains, then moving one train from the outer oval to the inner oval, and the second train from the inner oval to the outer oval, is shown in Chapter 8. The sequence for reversing both trains, using a single reverse loop on the inner oval, is also shown in Chapter 8.

Reversing with a Wye

A wye track arrangement can be used to reverse an entire train. The wye is an arrangement of track shaped like a triangle with a turnout at each corner. To turn an entire train, each corner of the wye must have enough track to hold a full train. On real railroads, the wye is often used to turn just a single car and locomotive, so one of the three stub ends is fairly short. The wye is often seen in the tight trackage in

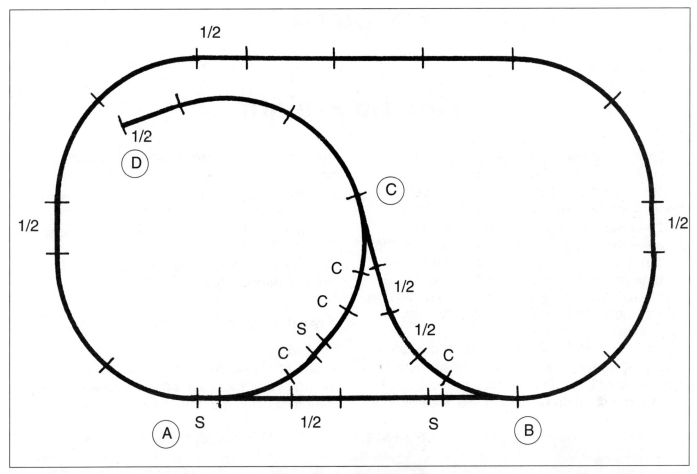

Fig. 15-22. To reverse a train traveling counterclockwise (from A to B), the train must move past B, back up through C to D, then pull forward through C until the entire train clears turnout A.

older industrial areas and yards on the real railroads, so the problems are as real as any you'll duplicate on your model railroad.

The reversing sequence for turning trains (or just for turning locomotives or cabooses, when the stub end of the wye is short) is simple enough. Start with a train moving counterclockwise from A to B in Figure 15-22. The train moves forward along the "main-line" leg of the wye until the caboose clears the turnout at B. The train then backs up through turnout C and the first curved

leg of the wye to the stub end of the wye at D and so the locomotive is clear of turnout C. Note that the maximum length of train that can be reversed is the distance from the moving points of turnout C to the bumper at D. Next, the train heads forward through turnout C but, this time, headed for turnout A. The train continues to head forward out onto the mainline of the oval until the caboose clears the switch points at turnout A. The train is now traveling in the opposite direction (now, clockwise from B to A) from the way it entered the wye.

Chapter 16

Moving Freight

Those real trains are really collections of individual cars from individual shippers on their way to individual customers or, conversely, empties ready to receive loads. The real railroad's primary concern is each individual car because the shipper, whose shipment is in that car, expects it to be delivered to the customer at the time promised by the railroad. Real railroads are, then, really in the business of moving freight, running trains is only the way they accomplish that purpose.

You can add the element of shipping real freight from real shippers to real customers to your toy train operations. There are enough "action" cars that dump scrap steel, logs or coal, that unload milk cans, boxes, barrels and mail bags, so you can see the products being unloaded. There are industries to unload milk cans, freight, logs, and oil at this compact town on the 4 x 6-1/2-foot layout (Figure 16-1) from Chapter 5 and there's information on how to switch cars in and out of the sidings on this layout in Chapter 15.

Freight Train Makeup

Today, most of the shipments on real railroads are large enough to require several cars. When two or more cars are designated to be sent to a single customer the cars are referred

Fig. 16-1. The freight station, log loader and milk platform provide three visible industries in this small town.

to as a "block." You can use a single car, however, on your toy train layout to represent a block of 10 or even 40 cars so you can reduce the length of your trains to a manageable size. Thus, a toy train with as few as six cars can duplicate the operations of a real railroad train that might have 100 cars but grouped in blocks of, say 6 hoppers of coal, 24 box cars of auto parts, 50 gondolas of steel, 20 tank cars of vegetable oil, 10 reefers of fruit and, of course, a caboose. Your toy train would simply have a hopper, a box car, a gondola, a tank car, a reefer and caboose. If your layout is large enough you might use 2 box cars, 5 gondolas, and 2 tank cars to better represent the size of the blocks of cars, so your train would have 10 cars. The number of cars and their type (and imaginary loads) is completely up to you and your imagination.

There are exceptions to the common trains of assorted freight cars, including solid trains of coal-carrying gondolas or hoppers that travel directly from the mine to the power plant or dock for loading onto ships. Other solid trains of specific cars include trains of grain traveling from giant midwest grain elevators to seaside docks, solid trains of intermodal cars or flat cars carrying containers from one port to another, and solid trains of reefers or refrigerator cars carrying fruit or vegetables from California to the east or from Florida to the north or west.

In the first six decades of the century, it was also common for the railroads to operate solid trains of stock cars from the midwest to major packing plants in Omaha, Kansas City, Chicago and similar cities or for solid trains of tank cars filled with oil from refinery or crude oil direct from the oil fields in Pennsylvania (in the early part of the century), Texas, California or Oklahoma to major cities.

Hauling Real Freight

You can buy cars and action accessories to allow your trains to load and unload real logs, coal, barrels, boxes, milk cans, mail bags and other commodities that makeup the freight traffic on a real railroad. The only missing element is the answer to the questions, "Who shipped that freight?" and "Who is that freight consigned to?"

You can imagine that a single log-loader, for example, serves as the railroad's shipping cus-

tomer when the logs are loaded. After the loaded car is picked up and placed in a train it can make several laps around the layout to be spotted at the same log loader to be dumped. When it is being unloaded, however, your imagination steps in and designates the log loader as the receiving customer located hundreds, perhaps thousands, of miles away from the shipping customer.

You can help your imagination along by providing some written materials like small signs, printed on self-sticking labels. Make the signs by hand-lettering or buy some self-adhesive paper and create the signs with a computer. In the example of the log loader, the logs are shipped from one side of the loader and received from the opposite side.

Make a small stick-on label or sign for one side of the log loader that might say, for example, JACOBS LOGGING COMPANY (the shipper, on the log-loading side) and a second sign that might say SMITHWAY LUMBER MILL (on the dumping or receiving side of the log loader).

The Waybill Freight Forwarding System

On a real railroad, that shipment of logs from Jacobs Logging, consigned to Smithway Lumber, would have been identified with a paper "waybill" filled out by the shipping customer with information about the receiving customer or who the carload (of, for example, logs) is consigned to. You can make simulated waybills for your toy train operations, so you can place less strain on your imagination, even when the shipping and receiving customer is the same log loader.

Every shipment made by rail is the result of a variety of paper forms that order the car to be delivered to the customer to load the shipment and to route that loaded car to the customer. Paperwork is seldom enjoyable enough to become a hobby, and we certainly don't need it to operate a toy train layout. But you can use this system to direct the flow of each and every car over your railroad so that your line will have the appearance of really moving goods, not just freight cars (Figure 16-2).

The waybill system will make every car have a definite purpose as it moves empty or loaded with a specific commodity bound for a specific destination. The system requires only a 2 x 3-inch clear plastic envelope for each and every freight car you operate. Apply a self-adhesive

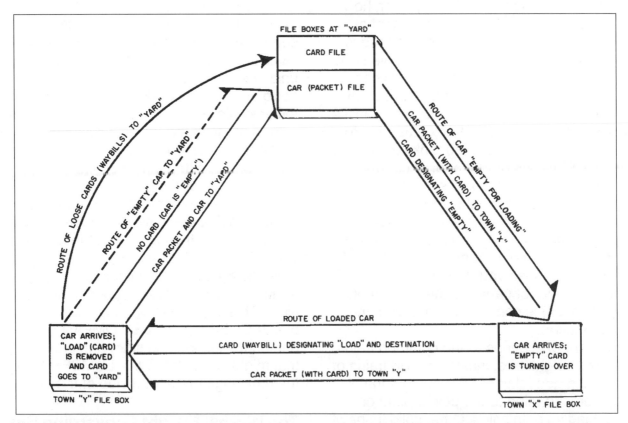

Fig. 16-2. The cycle for each standard type of Waybill. The plastic envelope for each car also follows this pattern.

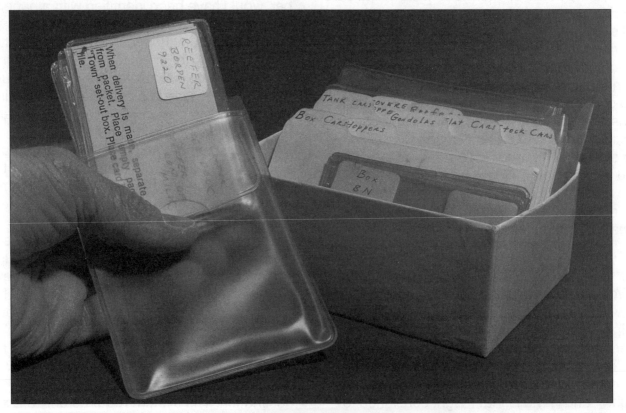

Fig. 16-3. Find or make some boxes to hold the file cards and 2 x 3-inch plastic "car" envelopes. Use a pocket protector envelope (shown) to hold a stack of these car envelopes for each train.

white sticker to the upper-left corner of each of the clear plastic envelopes and shows the car's railroad initials and the car number.

The envelope then "follows" that car wherever it goes on your layout. A small box can be glued to the side of the table near every town to hold the envelopes for any cars that may be sitting in that town. The envelopes for cars in trains are simply carried by the engineer (that's you) along with the walk-around throttle.

Place a larger file box near whatever area you consider to be your main yard to hold the cars stored there. Put some dividers in the box for stock, refrigerator (reefer), tank, flat, box, gondola, hopper, log-dump, coal-dump, intermodal and covered hopper cars to make it easier to find them when you need a specific car and its matching card (Figure 16-3). That main yard may well be the shelf or box where you store the cars that you don't have room for on the layout!

Waybills

The second part of the system is the paper waybills. These are patterned after the waybills the real railroads use with most shipments, but they are somewhat simpler and are much more "powerful" and versatile in directing the railroad crew's actions. Four blank waybills are included in Figure 16-4.

Have photocopies made of that page so you will have about four times as many waybills as you do freight cars. Because waybills are supposed to be folded in half, you need only one-sided copies. You can then cut the waybills apart, apply some rubber cement to the backside, and fold them to give a two-ply piece of paper that is about as stiff as cardboard (Figure 16-5). You might want to spray them with clear paint (the same kind you use on your models after decal applications) so they will last forever without any fingerprint-grease smudges.

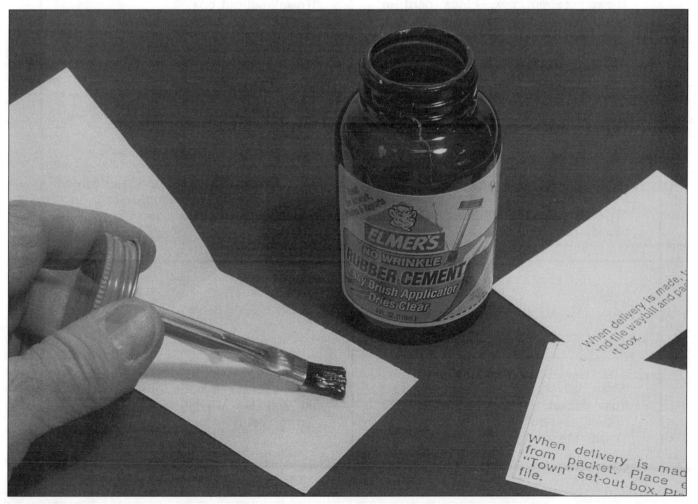

Fig. 16-5. Photocopy the Waybills in Figure 16-4 and cut them apart, then fold them and cement the backs together with rubber cement.

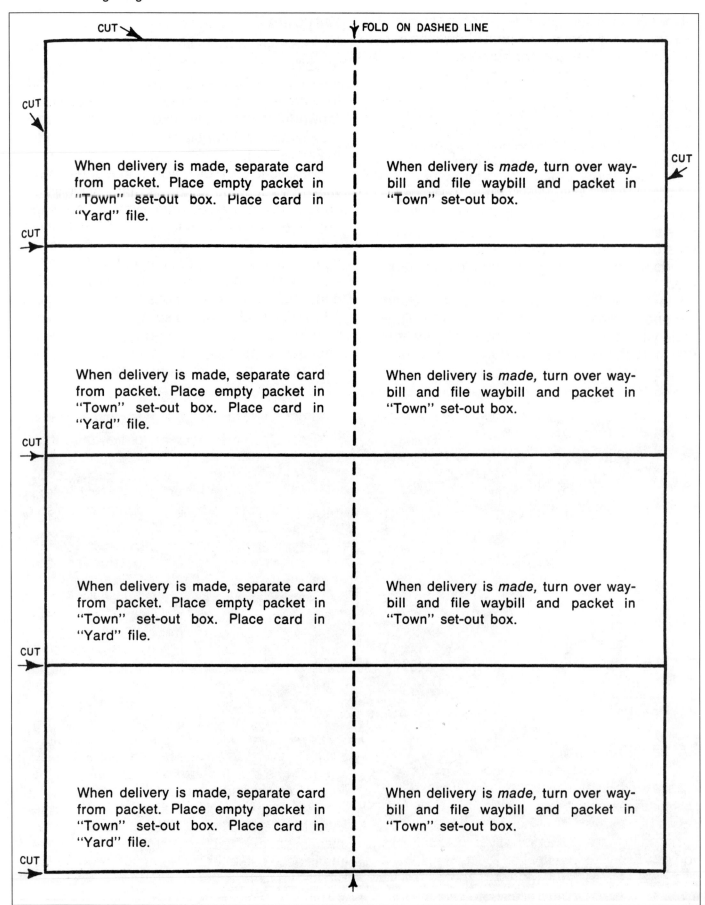

Fig. 16-4. Four Waybills that can be photocopied and cut apart.

Fig. 16-6. Make several Waybills for each car on your layout and place a single Way-bill in each "car" envelope.

Save the clear coat, though, until you've used the waybills for a week or so and you know you don't need to change the information on them. Each of the waybills must be filled out to indicate how its particular commodity should be transported.

Shipping and Receiving

Use the waybills to decide which cars to move and where to move them. The first consideration, when creating the waybills, however, will be the industries and other sources of freight on your own railroad.

On a pad of paper, list each of the industries you plan to locate on the sidings of your layout. The industries don't have to be there yet, but the sidings must be, so you'll have a place to spot that freight car. Many of these future "industries" may be the cutout paper signs of future action accessories like a magnetic crane, log loader, milk platform, coal loader and the like that you intend to purchase. The industries certainly do not need to actually load or unload commodities, you can use your imagination to load logs, barrels, coal, milk cans or whatever. The waybill system will make it much easier to imagine the car is loaded with a commodity because you have the paperwork (the waybill) to "prove" it.

Write down the goods or commodities that might be received by each industry under an "IN" column and the goods or commodities it might ship under an "OUT" column. However, there is no reason why any industry would ship or receive everything by rail.

A power plant, for instance, would receive coal, but it would "ship" electrical power over wires rather than over rails. And some firms, like warehouses, would ship small boxes of manufactured products by truck or, a concrete plant might receive raw materials like coal or ore by barge or conveyor. You'll need to do this paperwork only once; when it and the waybills are completed, operations will only involve placing cards in the clear plastic "car" envelopes (Figure 16-6). You can also add additional goods or commodities to the list to make more waybills after you have used the system for a few months and you are more familiar with the kind of freight traffic your railroad needs.

Add two more columns beside each of those industries for "TO" and "FROM." List all of the places that each industry might ship those commodities to in the "TO" column and the places where it might get the stuff from in the "FROM" column. Those places can be other industries on your own railroad. A fuel dealer for instance, might receive its coal "FROM" the coal mine on your layout. About half of the places should be "off" your layout because that's a bit more like real life; few railroads are lucky enough to have both the shipper and the receiver.

Interchanges

It is most common for a shipment to be loaded on one railroad and transferred (railroads use the word "interchanged") with three or four or more other railroads before it reaches its final destination. For our purposes, the "offline" places can be marked simply "interchange," and one end of a stub-end siding can be designated as the "industry interchange."

I suggest that you arrange the track and turnouts so you have one stub-ended siding that leads off the edge of the table to the outer edge of the layout. Use that siding as your "interchange" and you can actually remove cars from the layout to store them on a box or shelf where you store extra cars. That track is designated "interchange" and the shelf itself is the interchange "yard." That way, cars destined for interchange really do travel off the layout.

Filling Out the Waybill

Use your list of industries and their shipments to fill in both sides of the waybills. Begin on the side of each waybill that ends with the sentence "Place card in 'Yard' file." Then, follow these steps:

1. Write "TO:" and list the name of the town where the industry is located, followed by the name of the industry.

2. List the type of car that would be used for the commodity that that industry "receives."

(This is the "FROM" commodity from your list.) Then write "Empty— For Loading."

3. Turn the card over, and write "TO:" and the destination for that industry's products. The destination can be a bit tricky, but it's logical if you think it out: List the name of any city (say, Chicago) as the destination, write "VIA" (meaning "through"), the name of the town on your layout, and the interchange track in that town (write "Interchange").

4. Note the type of car, just as you did on the opposite side of the waybill, but here add the words "Carload" (or "Loaded") and the commodity the car will actually carry.

That completes the standard waybill. A variation would be simply to list the town and industry name for a "receiver" industry that is actually on your layout. Make about four cards, each with a different destination, for each industry on your layout.

You will also want to make some variations on those "standard" cards to suit particular industries and track situations. If the car is a flat car or a gondola, try to list a "load" on both sides of the waybill so there will be no "Empty—For Loading," just two different loads. You can do the same thing for any type of car that might appear on both the "FROM" and "TO" lists for a specific industry.

Operating with the Waybill System

The waybill system of operation begins when you pick some of the waybills at random that match the types of cars in your "yard" area. On a toy train layout, a single stub-ended siding can be designated as "yard" or you may want to build a two or three track yard so you can use a locomotive to pull cars from the sidings to arrange and rearrange trains. The makeup of those trains can be determined by using a Waybill for each car. Pull enough Waybills to makeup a train the length you wish, then use a locomotive to assemble a train (or lift the cars into the train with your hands).

Follow the directions on those cards to switch the now-loaded cars onto the appropriate sidings. From that point on the system is self-perpetuating, as long as you follow the instructions on the waybills. Keep the extra waybills in that "yard" file and return the "used" waybills to the rear of the waybill pack. Draw fresh ones each time you're ready to operate a train. Figure 16-7 shows how the car (and its clear plastic envelope) originates in the "yard" where the waybill is inserted. The waybill is then turned over (according to its own printed instructions), and that car is ready to be picked up by the next train through town. In some cases, the car may go directly back to the yard. If you want the car to sit on the siding for awhile, add another "hold" card with a note stating it is to be picked up after one or more passes ("days" or "weeks") by the freight trains through town.

Timetable Operations

You can establish a timetable just like the real railroads when you establish a point-to-

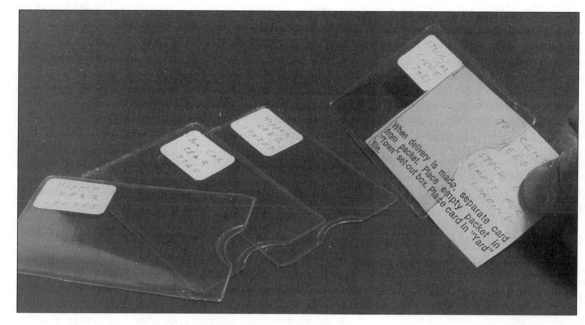

Fig. 16-7. Each car should have a "Waybill" inserted in its envelope at the beginning each operating session.

point run around your layout. You can designate a single station to simulate as many towns as you wish, Just decide that it takes, for example, three laps around the layout to travel from the original "Action" town, to "Benson", then perhaps, four more laps to travel from "Benson to "Carter", another six laps to travel from "Carter" to "Derby", perhaps three more laps to travel from "Derby" to "Eastwind" and so forth.

You can use a stop watch to actually time how long it takes the train to travel those laps around the oval between the towns. You can also decide how many minutes the train should wait in each town. You can then write all those arrival and departure times down and that becomes the "Timetable" for your railroad. If the times seem too short, just multiply them by 60 so the actual seconds become "minutes" in your miniature railroad world.

The timetable is one of the things that helps to keep the real trains from running into each other. If your railroad is large enough to operate two trains, you can use this timetable for a similar purpose.

The "Sequence" Timetable

If you have as many as four trains waiting on the holding tracks or passing sidings, no more than one or two ever need to be running at one time. With that thought in mind, you can stage what I call "sequence" timetable operations. The sequence timetable merely means that you establish an operating pattern for your trains. Write

down which train travels around the layout first, for how long (call each lap and "hour" or fraction of an hour, if you wish), and when it stops. Use that list or sequence to determine which trains to operate and when to operate them. If you have more trains than space on your layout to store them, you can even use a list like this to determine which trains you will take from storage shelves and which trains to replace on those shelves.

From Imaginary to Real

The waybill system, as well as every operating and construction idea on these pages, is based on the actual operations of the prototype. None of this was created for toy trains, it all originated on real railroads and has been adapted by serious scale model railroaders. You can use these systems, however, to have more operating fun with your toy trains.

When you operate with the quick "through freight" system of endless oval operations to simulate cross-country trains, when you make up trains using a switch engine in the yards, when you move every freight car with the waybill system, and when you operate with a sequence timetable, you are running a real railroad in miniature. Combine all these types of operation with, perhaps, one or more of those freight trains that interchanges with another railroad, or a passenger train added to the sequence timetable, and you can plan to keep yourself busy for years before you even think about building another railroad.

Glossary

AAR: The full-size railroad's trade group, the Association of American Railroads, that establishes their standards for equipment and safety.

Articulated: A steam locomotive with two separate sets of drivers, rods, and cylinders beneath a single boiler. Usually one set of drivers, rods, and cylinders is pivoted so it can swing from side-to-side around curves while the boiler remains rigidly attached to the rear set of drivers, rods, and cylinders.

Bad order: The term the real railroads use to describe a malfunctioning part.

Big Hook: The wrecking crane.

Block: A section of track that is electrically isolated from the adjoining sections for multiple-train operation or to prevent short circuits.

Bolster: The portion of a railroad freight or passenger car that runs across the underbody of the car to connect the trucks' pivot points to the body of the car. Sometimes used to describe all the cross members, including the ends, of a car's underframe.

Branch: A portion of a real railroad that branches off from the main line to reach a town or industry or to connect with another railroad.

Bumper: A device placed at the stub end of a track siding so cars or locomotives do not derail.

Caboose: The rolling office and living quarters for the crew of a freight train. Usually identifiable by a small box with windows on the roof (called a cupola) or one on each side (called bay windows) so the crew can see the length of the train from inside. Sometimes called crummy, bobber, or way car.

Catenary: Overhead trolley wires, usually used by prototype interurbans (electric-powered locomotives and self-propelled cars) with diamond-shaped current pick up devices on the roofs called pantographs. The prototypes for Lionel's GG-1 locomotive, for example, operated by collecting their electric current from the overhead catenary.

Coaling station: Any building where coal for steam locomotives is stored and shoveled or dumped through chutes into the locomotives' tenders. When the storage bins are elevated and the coal hoisted by conveyor belts or buckets, the structure is usually called a coaling tower. When the elevated storage bins are reached by a trestle so the coal can be dumped from the cars or shoveled right into the storage bins, the structure is usually called a coaling trestle.

Crossing: When two tracks cross each other, as in the center of a one-level figure-eight-style model railroad.

Crossover: The pair of turnouts that allow trains to travel from one parallel track to the adjacent one on double-track systems.

Cut: When the railroad has to dig or blast through a hill or mountain to maintain a level roadbed. Also, a few cars coupled together.

DCC: Short for Digital Command Control. A system for controlling model locomotives that sends a signal through the track to a decoder in the locomotive to instruct the locomotive to go forward or backward, to change its speed or to stop or go. More expensive systems can control over 200 locomotives as well as activate sound systems and operate turnouts.

D.P.D.T.: An electrical slide or toggle-type switch that is used for reversing the flow of current to the tracks by wiring across the back of the switch. Some types have an "off" position midway in their throw and these "Center-off D.P.D.T." switches are often used for wiring model railroads to allow two-train and two-throttle operation.

Draft gear: The box under the ends of a prototype car or locomotive (and on most models) where the coupler is spring-mounted to center it and to help absorb shocks and bumps.

Fiddle yard: A hidden track or series of tracks used by modelers to make up or break down trains, lifting the equipment by hand.

Fill: When the prototype railroad has to haul dirt to fill in a valley with an embankment to bring the roadbed level up to that of the nearest trackage.

Flange: The portion of any railroad wheel that guides the wheel down the rails. The flange extends around the circumference of each railroad wheel as its largest diameter.

Frog: The point where the track rails actually cross at every turnout and rail/rail crossing.

Gap: A break in the rails to electrically isolate some portion of the track from another to prevent short circuits or to allow for multiple-train operation on the same stretch of track.

Gauge: The spacing of the rails as measured from the inside of one rail head to the next. The "standard gauge" for most American railroads is 4 feet 8-1/2-inches; this distance was also once the standard center-to-center spacing for horse-drawn wagon wheels.

Grade: The angled rise or fall of the track so it can pass over another track or so it can follow the rising or falling contour of the land.

Grab iron: The steel hand rails on the sides, ends, and roofs of rolling stock.

Head-end cars: The cars that are normally coupled to the front of a passenger train, including express refrigerator, express baggage, and mail cars.

Helper: The locomotive that is added to a train to supply extra power that may be needed to surmount a steep grade.

Hi-Rail: The term used to describe O scale toy trains that operate on three-rail track with oversize rails and wheel flanges. The rails are about three-times the size they would be if reduced to 1/48 the size of the prototype and, hence, the rails are higher. The hi-rail cars and locomotives are usually exact O scale except for the wheel flanges and, sometimes, the couplers are also oversize to match Lionel and other brands of toy trains. The term is also used to describe American Flyer equipment and other brands of S scale equipment with oversize wheel flanges and couplers that can operate on American Flyer track.

Hostler: Men who service and sometimes move locomotives from one servicing facility to another to prepare the locomotive for the engineer.

Hotbox: A bearing that has become overheated from lack of lubrication.

Interchange: A section of track or several tracks where one railroad connects with another so trains or individual cars can move from one railroad to the next.

Interlocking: A system of mechanical or electrical controls so only one train at a time can move through a junction of two or more tracks like a crossing or yard throat.

Intermodal: The transportation concept of using railroads, trucks and/or ships to carry the same container or trailer from its shipper to its destination without having to unload and reload along the way. If the railroads are carrying just trailers, some refer to it as "piggyback" service.

Interurban: Prototype railroads and railroad cars that were self-propelled with electrical power pick-up from an overhead wire, catenary, or from a third rail suspended alongside the track. The cars ran from city-to-city as well as inside the city limits and hence the name. (See also trolley and traction.)

Journal: The bearing that supports the load on the end of a railroad car or locomotive axle.

Kingpin: The pivot point for a freight or passenger car truck where it connects to the bolster.

Kit-bash: To combine parts from two or more kits to produce a model different from both. Sometimes called cross-kitting, customizing, or converting. The process is also a kit-conversion.

LCL: Less-than-carload lot; freight shipments that are too small to require an entire car.

Lockon: The metal and fiber clip that snaps onto the bottom of three rail track to allow wires from the transformer or on-off toggle switches to be connected to the track.

Main line: The most heavily trafficked routes of the railroad.

Maintenance-of-way: The rolling stock or structures that are directly associated with maintaining the railroad or with repairing and righting wrecked trains.

Narrow gauge: Railroads that were built with their rails spaced closer than the 4-feet 8-1/2-inch standard gauge. Two-foot and three-foot spacings between the rail heads were the most common in this country, particularly in the 1880-1900 period.

Pedlar freight: A freight train that switches cars at most towns along its route from terminal to terminal. Also called a way freight.

Piggyback: The modern railroads' special flatcar service to transport highway trailers. Sometimes called TOFC. Also see "intermodal."

Points: The portions of a turnout that move to change the track's route from the main line to a siding. The point where the rails actually cross is called the "frog" part of the switch.

Prototype: The term used to describe the full-size version that any model is supposed to duplicate.

Pullman: The passenger cars that were owned and operated by the Pullman company, usually sleeping cars, diners, or parlor cars. Sometimes used to describe any sleeping car.

Rail joiner: The pieces of metal that join two lengths of rail together. They slide onto the ends of the rail on a model railroad; they are bolted to the rails on the prototype.

Reefer: The insulated cars, cooled by either ice in bunkers fed through hatches on the roof or, in modern times, by mechanical refrigeration units.

Right of way: The property and the track owned by the railroad.

r-t-r: Abbreviation for ready-to-run that also includes the simple snap-together and glue-together plastic kits.

Siding: A length of track connected to the mainline by one or more turnouts. A siding may be stub-ended or it may be a "through" siding, with a turnout to connect it to the mainline on both ends. The through siding is sometimes called a "passing siding" because it can be used for one train to pass another.

Snowshed: The protective buildings that cover the track, usually in mountain areas, so deep snow and drifts won't cover the tracks themselves.

Spot: The switching maneuver whereby a freight or passenger car is moved to the desired position on the track, usually beside some industry's loading platform.

Superelevation: Banking the tracks in a curve so the trains can travel at some designated speed with a minimum of load on the outer wheels and rails and with a minimum of sway.

Switch: Usually used to refer to the portion of the railroad track that allows the trains to change routes, but also used for electrical switches on model railroads, such as D.P.D.T. or S.P.S.T. switches. Track switches are often called "turnouts" to avoid this confusion.

Switch machine: The electrical solenoid-type devices that move the track switch from one route to another to allow remote-controlled operation of trains over diverging trackage.

Switch points: The moving portion of a turnout that changes the route. Also called turnout points.

Talgo: Model railroad trucks with the couplers mounted to them so the couplers swivel with the trucks to allow operation of longer cars on tighter radius curves. Talgo trucks can, however, cause derailments when pushing or backing a long train.

Tangent: Straight sections of trackage.

Tank engine: A steam locomotive without a tender where the coal or fuel oil is carried in a bunker behind the cab and the water in a tank over the top of the boiler. Often used for switching on the prototype and on model railroads.

Tender: The car just behind most steam locomotives that carries the water and coal, wood, or fuel oil.

Throat: The point where the yard trackage begins to diverge into the multiple tracks for storage and switching.

Timetable: A schedule, usually printed, to tell railroad employees and customers when trains are scheduled to be at certain stations or points on the railroad.

Traction: The term used to describe all prototype locomotives and self-powered cars like trolleys and interurbans that operate by electrical power.

Transistor throttle: An electrical speed control for model railroad layouts that is used in place of the older wire-wound rheostat to provide infinitely better and smoother slow speed and starting control for locomotives.

Transition curve: A length of track where any curve joins a tangent with gradually diminishing radius to ease the sudden transition of straight-to-curve for smoother operation and to help prevent derailments of extra-length cars that are caused by coupler bind in such areas of trackage. Also called an easement.

Turnout: Where two diverging tracks join; also called a switch. The moving parts that divert the trains from the straight to the curved-path are called "turnout points" or "switch points."

Trolley: Self-propelled, electric-powered cars that ran almost exclusively in city streets as opposed to the interurbans that ran through the country between cities and towns.

Truck: The sprung frame and four (or more) wheels under each end of most railroad freight and passenger cars.

Turntable: A rotating steel or wooden bridge to turn locomotives or cars and/or to position them to align with the tracks in the engine house or round house.

Vestibule: The enclosed area, usually in both ends of a passenger car, where patrons enter the car from the station platform and where they walk to move from one car to the next.

Way freight: See Pedlar freight.

Wye: A track switch where both diverging routes curve away in opposite directions from the single straight track. Also, the triangular-shaped track (in plain view) where trains can be reversed.

SOURCES OF SUPPLY

The majority of the manufacturers of toy trains and accessories sell only through hobby dealers. The best use for this list, then, is to provide your hobby dealer with an address to contact to order the items you need. Some of the manufacturers and importers offer catalogs but there is usually a charge. If you do contact any of these importers or manufacturers, always include a stamped, self-addressed envelope if you expect a reply. You can ask for the price and availability of catalogs or price sheets.

American Flyer (see Lionel)

American Models
1007 Colonial Industrial Dr.
So. Lyon, MI 48178

Atlas O
603 Sweetland Ave.
Hillside, NJ07205

Avalon Concepts
1055 Leiszs Bridge Rd.
Leesport, PA19533

Bachmann Industries
1400 E. Erie Ave.
Philadelphia, PA 19124

Centralia Car Shops
1468 Lee St.
Des Plaines, IL 60018

Champ Decals
Division Champion Decal Co.
P.O. Box 1178
Minot, ND 58702

Chooch Enterprises
Box 217
Redmond, WA 98052

Crown Model Products
(see Port Line Hobby Supply)

Dallee Electronics
246 W. Main St.
Leola, PA17540

Department 56
P.O. Box 44456
Eden Prairie, MN 55344

Digitrax, Inc.
450 Cemetery St., #206
Norcross, GA 30071

Downtown Deco
4319 Rainbow Dr.
Missoula, MT 59803

E-R Model Importers, Inc.
1000 So. Main St.
Newark, NY 14513

F&H Enterprises
2562 Silver State parkway
Building C, Suite 3
Minden, NV 89423

GarGraves Trackage Corporation
8967 Blue Ridge Rd.
North Rose, NY 14516-9793

Heiki (see E-R Models, Portman, or Walthers)

IHC (International Hobby Corp.)
413 E. Allegheny Ave.
Philadelphia, PA19134-2322

Industrial Rail
Division United Model Distributors
301 Holbrook Dr., Box O
Wheeling, IL 60090-5868

InterMountain Railway
Box 839
Longmont, CO 80501

Rick Johnson Rubber Roadbed
19333 Sturgess Dr.
Torrance, CA90503

K-Line Electric Trains
Box 2831
Chapel Hill, NC 27515

Kadee Quality Products
673 Avenue C
White City, OR 97503-1078

Kibri (see E-R Models, Portman, or Walthers)

Korber Models
2 Tidswell Ave.
Medford, NJ 08055

Life-Like Products
1600 Union Ave.
Baltimore, MD 21211-1998

Lionel LLC
50625 Richard W. Blvd.
Chesterfield, MI48051-2493

MRC (Model Rectifier Corp.)
80 Newfield, Ave., Box 6312
Edison, NJ 08818-6312

MTH Electric Trains
7020 Columbia Gateway Dr.
Columbia, MD 21046

Marx Trains
209 E. Butterfield Rd., Suite 228
Elmhurst, IL 60126

Microscale Industries
18435 Bandilier Cr.
Fountain Valley, CA 92708

Model Power
180 Smith St.
Farmingdale, NY 11735

Mountains-In-Minutes
I.S.L.E. Laboratories
Box 663
Sylvania, OH 43560

NJ International
230 W. Old Country Rd.
Hicksville, NY 11801

Noch (see E-R Models, Portman, or Walthers)

Pacific Rail Shops
P.O. Box 867
Coos Bay, OR 97420

Peco (see F&H or Walthers)

Plasticville (see Bachmann)

Plastruct
1020 So. Wallace Dr.
City of Industry, CA 91748

Port Line Hobby Supply
6 Storeybrook Dr.
Newburyport, MA01950

Portman Hobby Distributors
851 Washington St., Box 2551
Peeksill, NY10566

Preiser (see E-RModels or Walthers)

QSI (Q. S. Industries)
3800 S.W.Cedar Hills Blvd., Suite 224
Beaverton, OR97005

Red Caboose
Box 250
Mead, CO 80542

Roco (see E-RModels or Walthers)

S Helper Services
2 Roberts Rd.
New Brunswick, NJ08901-1621

Scenery Unlimited
7236 W. Madison St.
Forest Park, IL 60130

Third Rail
Division of Sunset Models, Inc.
37 S. Fourth St.
Campbell, CA95008

Wm. K. Walthers, Inc.
5601 W. Florist Ave.
Milwaukee, WI53201-0770

Weaver Models
Division of Quality Craft
Box 231
Northumberland, PA17857

Williams Electric Trains
8835 Columbia 100 Pkwy.
Columbia, MD 21045

Woodland Scenics
101 E. Valley Dr., Box 98
Linn Creek, MO65052